Beginning Joomla!® Web Site Development

D1377320

Beginning
Joomla!® Web Site Development

Beginning
Joomla!® Web Site Development

Cory Webb

WILEY

Wiley Publishing, Inc.

Beginning Joomla!® Web Site Development

Published by
Wiley Publishing, Inc.
10475 Crosspoint Boulevard
Indianapolis, IN 46256
www.wiley.com

Published simultaneously in Canada

ISBN: 978-0-470-43853-4

Manufactured in the United States of America

10 9 8 7 6 5 4 3 2 1

Library of Congress Cataloging-in-Publication Data

Webb, Cory, 1979-
    Beginning Joomla web site development / Cory Webb.
        p. cm.
    Includes index.
    ISBN 978-0-470-43853-4 (paper/website)
  1.   Web sites — Authoring programs. 2.   Web site development. 3.   Joomla!
(Computer file) I. Title.
  TK5105.8883.W47 2009
  006.7'8 — dc22

                                                    2009007403

I would like to dedicate this book to my wife, Carly.
Without her love, support, and patience, none of this would be possible.

About the Authors

Cory Webb is a web designer and developer and the owner of Cory Webb Media, LLC, where he specializes in building web sites with the premier content management system (CMS), Joomla!. He is perhaps best known for his instructional site, HowToJoomla.net, where he shares his insights and experiences through tips and tricks for beginning Joomla! users. Since the inception of HowToJoomla.net, he has written dozens of articles that have been well received by the Joomla! community. He has received numerous accolades such as "Sweet Jesus, thank you! I spent a day and a half looking for this bit of code! You've saved my sanity!" and "Thank You! I REALLY needed this solution!" He began working with Joomla!'s predecessor, Mambo, in 2003 when he was given the task of building a web site for his employer. After an exhaustive search for the right CMS, he found Mambo and never looked back. In May 2006, Cory started working part-time as a freelance developer for JoomlaShack.com. In February 2008, he parlayed that freelance work into a full-time career as the founder of Cory Webb Media, LLC.

Credits

Acquisitions Editor
Jennifer Watson

Development Editor
Sydney Jones

Technical Editor
Shane Sevo

Production Editor
Kathleen Wisor

Copy Editor
Kim Cofer

Editorial Manager
Mary Beth Wakefield

Production Manager
Tim Tate

Vice President and Executive Group Publisher
Richard Swadley

Vice President and Executive Publisher
Joseph B. Wikert

Associate Publisher
Jim Minatel

Project Coordinator, Cover
Lynsey Stanford

Proofreader
Jen Larsen, Word One

Indexer
Robert Swanson

Acknowledgments

The Joomla! project was founded on the principle that open source matters, and that a truly successful open source project is only successful with a thriving community. I would like to thank the Joomla! core team, working group members, contributors, and countless other volunteers who have worked together to build one of the best open source projects in the world.

I would also like to thank the kind people at Wrox for giving me the opportunity to share my thoughts, insights, and experience with the Joomla! community. This has been a truly humbling and rewarding experience, and I am grateful for every minute of it. Special thanks to Jenny Watson for approaching me about the possibility of writing a book about my favorite CMS. Thank you also to the development editor, Sydney Jones, whose patience and encouragement have helped me get through this process more than she'll ever know. I also want to thank Shane Sevo, the technical editor. His insights and suggestions have been tremendously helpful in making this book the best it can be. Thank you also to the rest of the Wrox team who have worked to bring this book to the Joomla! community.

Finally, and most importantly, I want to thank my wife Carly for supporting me throughout this whole process. She put up with many weeks of long hours, late nights, and a cranky, sleep-deprived husband. From the bottom of my heart, I could not have done this without her.

Contents

Contents

Contents

Contents

Contents

Introduction

Content management systems have been around in one form or another for as long as there has been content. The efficient and effective management and presentation of content is one of the most important tasks facing web designers, web developers, and web site administrators. Some systems of managing and presenting content are more efficient and effective than others.

Ten years ago (and perhaps for some of you, ten minutes ago) web content was managed and presented in a terribly inefficient manner. The system consisted of web directories full of HTML (HyperText Markup Language) files, images, and other media files, and was organized in a directory tree structure much like your computer operating system is organized. Each page of content in a web site represented a single, stand-alone HTML file. Making any sort of changes to your content required a working knowledge of HTML, and the patience to dig through all of the files to find the correct file to change. Changing the overall look and feel of the site was an even more arduous task, because it required changing the HTML of each and every file in the system. What a nightmare!

It didn't take long for many to transition from this system to a slightly more efficient system of server side includes (SSI). This was a method of building one HTML file to serve as the framework for the look and feel of the site, and "including" content from other text files within that HTML file. This was one way to separate the presentation of the content from the actual content itself. You could more easily make a change to the look and feel of the site by changing the main HTML file, but making changes to content still required a working knowledge of HTML.

As server-side scripting languages like PHP (Hypertext Preprocessor), ASP (Active Server Pages), and Macromedia's Cold Fusion, and open source database systems like MySQL and PostgreSQL began to gain traction, newer and more efficient means of managing and presenting content began to emerge. Content could now be easily stored in a database system and retrieved for presentation in a web browser by a server-side language. To the end user, nothing was different because content was still consumed as HTML in a web browser. The major difference was that web administrators could now more easily manage the content that was being displayed.

In 2000, an Australian company called Miro Construct Pty. Ltd. began development on a closed source, proprietary content management system called Mambo. Then, in 2001, apparently recognizing the value of open source development, the company released Mambo under the General Public License (GPL), and an open source project was born. In the years that followed, Mambo began to experience tremendous growth and attract a core team of top-notch developers from all over the world.

By mid 2005, Mambo had become one of the premier content management systems in the world and had gained a huge following among developers and hobbyists alike. In August of 2005, Mambo Foundation, Inc. was formed as a not-for-profit organization to handle legal and financial matters related to Mambo.

Due to concerns over the structure of the foundation and fears that Mambo would depart from the open source principles that got it to where it was, the entire core development team left the project and formed Open Source Matters, Inc. (OSM), which is the not-for-profit organization that handles organizational, legal, and financial matters for the Joomla! project.

The OSM team and the community came up with the name Joomla! to re-brand Mambo, and Joomla! 1.0 was released on September 1, 2005. Since that time, Joomla! has grown to become one of the most popular open source content management systems in the world. As of December 2008, it has been downloaded more than 7.5 million times. The official Joomla! forums have almost 240,000 registered members with nearly 1.5 million posts in close to 320,000 topics. It has one of the most active communities of any open source project in the world.

Joomla! is used by individuals and organizations of all shapes and sizes. Some of the larger organizations using Joomla! include the United Nations, MTV Networks, International House of Pancakes (IHOP), and Harvard University, just to name a few. Besides giving large organizations a platform for building rich, interactive web sites, Joomla! makes it possible for individuals of all levels of experience to build a professional, easily managed site. Joomla! is used by churches, soccer teams, newspapers, families, schools, communities, and so on. The list goes on and on.

This book is an effort to introduce you to Joomla!, and help you get started with one of the most powerful, versatile tools in the world for developing and managing web sites. The goal of this book is to take you through the process of building a web site with Joomla! by teaching you important concepts that every beginner should know, and reinforcing those concepts with real-world examples.

My desire is that by reading this book, you will not only gain an understanding of the language of Joomla!, but also a real-world, nuts-and-bolts understanding of how to get things done within the Joomla! framework. With this book, I hope that you will begin to learn how to harness the power of Joomla! and use it to accomplish the goals you want to achieve with your web site.

For more information, you can visit the following web sites:

❑ http://www.joomlacode.org

❑ http://en.wikipedia.org/wiki/Mambo_(software)#Timeline_of_Mambo_History

❑ http://www.opensourcematters.org/

❑ http://forum.joomla.org/

❑ http://www.joomla.org/about-joomla.html

❑ http://help.joomla.org/content/section/42/278/

Who This Book Is For

Beginning Joomla! is for you. By opening this book and reading this introduction, you have already demonstrated an interest in learning what Joomla! is all about and how it can benefit you in your quest to build the ultimate web site. This book is for anyone interested in getting started with Joomla!, or just brushing up on some Joomla! concepts that you may have forgotten.

Joomla! is a system that anyone can use, so this book was written in such a way that anyone with a basic understanding of the Internet should be able to use it as a resource to get started using Joomla!. However, certain parts of this book require me to make certain assumptions about the reader's level of web design and development understanding.

If you are completely new to Joomla!, regardless of your web design and development experience, you need to start with Chapter 1 and Appendix B, so that you can learn to "speak Joomla!" fluently and learn how to install Joomla! on your server or on a test server on your computer. The chapters on building a template and advanced tips and tricks require at least a basic working knowledge of HTML, CSS, and PHP to really get a full understanding of what they are trying to teach. Every chapter in between is foundational to understanding how to build a web site with Joomla!, and readers of all levels should take the time to read through and understand the concepts presented in those chapters.

What This Book Covers

This book covers the concepts related to building and managing a web site with Joomla! version 1.5. I have referenced some differences between Joomla! version 1.0 inasmuch as they relate to your understanding of version 1.5, but the book is geared toward building web sites with Joomla! version 1.5.

How This Book Is Structured

This book is organized to help a beginner gain the greatest understanding of the concepts involved in building a Joomla!-powered web site. The purpose of the structure of this book is to take you step-by-step through the thought processes taken during the typical development cycle of a web site with Joomla!. It begins by teaching you the language of Joomla! and some of the things that can be done with an out-of-the-box installation of Joomla!. It then takes you through the process of configuring Joomla! and setting up and managing content and menus before jumping into the more advanced concepts of extending Joomla!'s core functionality, syndicating content, and building a custom template. Finally, the book goes through the last stage of development, testing and troubleshooting, before teaching some tips and tricks for more advanced users.

Beginning in Chapter 4, this book takes you through building a real-world example of a web site with Joomla!. This sample site is a local wedding-related web site that serves as a community of brides, grooms, and local wedding vendors. As you progress through the book, you will see how different concepts covered in the book relate to building an actual web site.

The book includes the following chapters:

❑ *Chapter 1: "Joomla! Jargon: Understanding the Language of Joomla!"* — As with any industry or technology, Joomla! has a language all its own. This chapter covers the most commonly used words and phrases that are part of Joomla!'s jargon to help you learn to speak fluent Joomla!.

❑ *Chapter 2: "Taking a Look Under the Hood"* — Joomla! is a powerful system for building interactive web sites out-of-the-box. This chapter examines the core features of Joomla! to help you get a feel for what can be accomplished with a plain installation of the system.

❑ *Chapter 3: "Configuring Joomla!"* — This chapter covers all of the configuration options for Joomla!. It walks you through Joomla!'s global configuration, explaining each configuration parameter in detail. It then takes you through the configuration of each component in the system.

❑ *Chapter 4: "Managing Content"* — This chapter examines Joomla!'s content structure, and shows you how to set up sections, categories, and articles. It covers the importance of establishing an information architecture that is consistent with Joomla!'s content structure, so that your content works within the system hierarchy.

❑ *Chapter 5: "Managing Menus"* — This chapter covers Joomla!'s menu management system, which is used to create and manage your site's navigation. It takes you step-by-step through the process of building menus and menu items in Joomla!.

❑ *Chapter 6: "Extending Joomla!"* — This chapter examines each type of extension that can be used to extend Joomla!'s functionality: components, modules, plugins, templates, and languages. It also takes you through the process of installing extensions, shows you where to find extensions, and lists some of the most popular extensions.

❑ *Chapter 7: "Syndication in Joomla! 1.5"* — This chapter teaches you about how Joomla! 1.5 handles content syndication and shows you how to syndicate content in your site.

❑ *Chapter 8: "Building a Custom Template"* — This chapter covers the important concepts involved in building custom Joomla! templates. It walks you through the process of building a template as you follow the development of a custom template. To get the most out of this chapter, you should have a working knowledge of HTML, CSS, and PHP.

❑ *Chapter 9: "Troubleshooting Your Site"* — Once you have built your site, it is important to test your site and troubleshoot any issues that may have arisen during development. This chapter discusses this concept, and shows you some of the common pitfalls that developers experience while building a Joomla!-powered site.

❑ *Chapter 10: "Advanced Tips and Tricks"* — This chapter covers some advanced techniques for accomplishing tasks or achieving non-standard functionality in Joomla!. You should have a working understanding of PHP if you are going to attempt some of the tricks in this chapter.

What You Need to Use This Book

To get the most out of this book, you need to have access to a web server that supports PHP and MySQL so that you can follow the instructions in Appendix B to install your own copy of Joomla!. Many shared web hosting services support PHP and MySQL and offer very affordable plans, so you should have no trouble finding a hosting provider on which you can install Joomla!.

If you want to install Joomla! on your local computer, you will also need to download an Apache/MySQL/PHP package that you can install on your system, such as XAMPP from http://www.apachefriends.org or WAMP from http://www.wampserver.com.

Conventions

To help you get the most from the text and keep track of what's happening, we've used a number of conventions throughout the book.

Try It Out

The *Try It Out* is an exercise you should work through, following the text in the book.

1. They usually consist of a set of steps.

2. Each step has a number.

3. Follow the steps through with your copy of the database.

How It Works

After each *Try It Out*, the code you've typed will be explained in detail.

> Boxes like this one hold important, not-to-be forgotten information that is directly relevant to the surrounding text.

Notes, tips, hints, tricks, and asides to the current discussion are offset and placed in italics like this.

As for styles in the text:

❑ We *highlight* new terms and important words when we introduce them.

❑ We show keyboard strokes like this: Ctrl+A.

❑ We show file names, URLs, and code within the text like so: `persistence.properties`.

❑ We present code in two different ways:

```
We use a monofont type with no highlighting for most code examples.
We use gray highlighting to emphasize code that's particularly important in the
present context.
```

Source Code

As you work through the examples in this book, you may choose either to type in all the code manually or to use the source code files that accompany the book. All of the source code used in this book is available for download at `http://www.wrox.com`. Once at the site, simply locate the book's title (either by using the Search box or by using one of the title lists) and click the Download Code link on the book's detail page to obtain all the source code for the book.

Because many books have similar titles, you may find it easiest to search by ISBN; this book's ISBN is 978-0-470-43853-4.

Once you download the code, just decompress it with your favorite compression tool. Alternatively, you can go to the main Wrox code download page at `http://www.wrox.com/dynamic/books/download.aspx` to see the code available for this book and all other Wrox books.

Errata

We make every effort to ensure that there are no errors in the text or in the code. However, no one is perfect, and mistakes do occur. If you find an error in one of our books, like a spelling mistake or faulty piece of code, we would be very grateful for your feedback. By sending in errata you may save another reader hours of frustration and at the same time you will be helping us provide even higher quality information.

To find the errata page for this book, go to http://www.wrox.com and locate the title using the Search box or one of the title lists. Then, on the book details page, click the Book Errata link. On this page you can view all errata that has been submitted for this book and posted by Wrox editors. A complete book list including links to each book's errata is also available at www.wrox.com/misc-pages/booklist .shtml.

If you don't spot "your" error on the Book Errata page, go to www.wrox.com/contact/techsupport .shtml and complete the form there to send us the error you have found. We'll check the information and, if appropriate, post a message to the book's errata page and fix the problem in subsequent editions of the book.

p2p.wrox.com

For author and peer discussion, join the P2P forums at p2p.wrox.com. The forums are a Web-based system for you to post messages relating to Wrox books and related technologies and interact with other readers and technology users. The forums offer a subscription feature to e-mail you topics of interest of your choosing when new posts are made to the forums. Wrox authors, editors, other industry experts, and your fellow readers are present on these forums.

At http://p2p.wrox.com you will find a number of different forums that will help you not only as you read this book, but also as you develop your own applications. To join the forums, just follow these steps:

1. Go to p2p.wrox.com and click the Register link.

2. Read the terms of use and click Agree.

3. Complete the required information to join as well as any optional information you wish to provide and click Submit.

4. You will receive an e-mail with information describing how to verify your account and complete the joining process.

You can read messages in the forums without joining P2P but in order to post your own messages, you must join.

Once you join, you can post new messages and respond to messages other users post. You can read messages at any time on the Web. If you would like to have new messages from a particular forum e-mailed to you, click the Subscribe to this Forum icon by the forum name in the forum listing.

For more information about how to use the Wrox P2P, be sure to read the P2P FAQs for answers to questions about how the forum software works as well as many common questions specific to P2P and Wrox books. To read the FAQs, click the FAQ link on any P2P page.

Joomla! Jargon: Understanding the Language of Joomla!

Everything in life has a language of its own. If you want to speak intelligently about a subject, you first need to learn its language. For instance, if you want to talk to someone about baseball, you wouldn't say "I hit a touchdown over the fence!" because by doing so you immediately inform everyone within hearing distance that you know nothing about baseball.

Like any other product, industry, hobby, or niche, Joomla! has its own language (a.k.a. jargon). Seasoned veterans are fluent in Joomla! jargon, but if you are new to Joomla!, the jargon can often sound like gibberish.

Glossaries normally come at the end of a book, but understanding Joomla! begins with understanding its jargon. You cannot have a meaningful conversation about Joomla! without using words that are common in the Joomla! language. If you want to understand the rest of this book, you need to have a firm grasp on the meanings of the terms that are used. This list is grouped into the following headings:

❑ **Framework:** Joomla! is more than just a content management system. It is a framework for rapidly building web applications. This section covers terms associated with the Joomla! framework.

❑ **Installation:** This section first explains the difference between an installation of Joomla! and the installation of a Joomla! extension. Then, it covers common terms you will encounter during the process of installing Joomla!.

❑ **Extensions:** This section explains the meaning of the term "extensions" as it relates to Joomla!, and then it lists and defines the various types of extensions available for Joomla!.

❑ **Content:** This section defines the specific meaning of the word "content" as it is used in Joomla!. Then it covers words associated with content in Joomla!.

❑ **Menus:** In this section, you learn about terms relating to Joomla!'s primary system of navigation: menus.

❑ **Users:** This section explains the concept of users as it relates to Joomla!. It then defines user groups and access levels and how they are implemented in Joomla!.

❑ **More Jargon:** This section covers more terms within the lexicon of Joomla! jargon.

Framework

If you spend enough time in the forums or reading Joomla!-related blogs, you will probably see multiple references to the "Joomla! framework." Although Joomla! is a world-class content management system, it goes far beyond traditional content management by giving developers the ability to easily create extensions to perform a potentially infinite number of tasks. The framework is a sophisticated system of code libraries that perform common tasks and tie everything together in Joomla! In fact, the Joomla! CMS is just one of several applications built upon the Joomla! framework.

❑ **Application:** In general terms, an application is a piece of software developed to perform a task or set of tasks. In Joomla!, this is no different, although the word "application" has a more specific meaning. An application in Joomla! is a layer in the Joomla! framework, and extensions are built to extend the functionality of applications. The Joomla! package actually has four applications built in: the site application (the front end of your site); the administrator application (the backend); the installer; and an application called XML-RPC, which basically allows other systems to interact directly with the server without the need for a web browser.

❑ **API:** API stands for Application Programming Interface, and it is a set of procedures that programs can use to interact with another program or operating system. Joomla! has an API that enables developers to build extensions that interact with the Joomla! system. This allows for integration of all extensions built specifically for Joomla!, because they all use a common API.

Installation

Installation is the process of taking a piece of software and setting it up to work on your system. It can also be used to refer to the software once it has been installed (for example, "I have two installations of Joomla! on my server.) In Joomla!, there are two types of installations: Joomla! installation and extension installation. A helpful way to think about it is to think of Joomla! as an operating system like Windows or Mac OSX, and think of extensions as programs installed on your operating system. You learn how to install Joomla! in Appendix B, and you learn how to install extensions in Chapter 6.

❑ **Sample Data:** Whenever you install Joomla!, you have the option to install sample data. The sample data is a set of preconfigured menus, menu items, modules, components, and content sections, categories, and articles. You learn about the pros and cons of installing sample data in Chapter 7. You can see the installation screen where you have the option to install sample data in Figure 1-1.

❑ **Table Prefix:** The Joomla! database is made up of several tables that store data for a Joomla! installation. When you install Joomla!, you are given the option to set a table prefix, which is basically just a set of letters and an underscore character that precedes each data table name. The default table prefix is `jos_`. For example, with `jos_` as the table prefix, the core content data table would be named `jos_content`.

The benefit of a table prefix is that you can have multiple installations of Joomla! using the same database without the data from installations interfering with each other. For example, your first installation could have a table prefix of `jos_`, and your second installation could use a table prefix of `jos2_`, and their data will not interfere with each other because they will have separate tables.

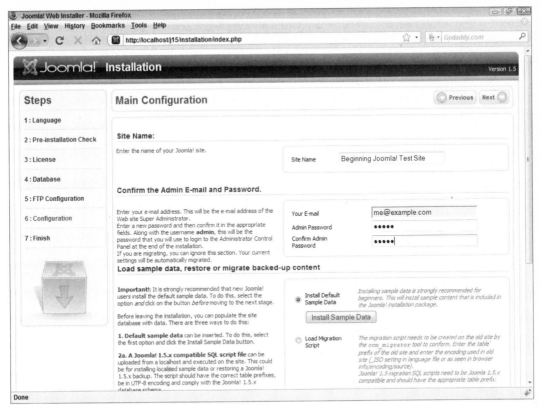

Figure 1-1

❏ **Installation Folder:** The Joomla! installation application is one of the four applications that come with Joomla!. It is located in a directory named `installation`, and it is automatically launched the first time you access your site after you upload the Joomla! files to your server. After you have installed Joomla!, the system will ask you to remove the `installation` folder because leaving this folder in place causes a security risk for your site.

Extensions

Extensions are essentially mini-applications that enhance Joomla! by adding new functionality that is not present in the core. Five types of extensions are available for Joomla!: Components, Modules, Plugins, Templates, and Languages. You learn more about extensions in Chapter 6.

❏ **Components:** A component can be thought of as an application within an application. Components are applications built upon the Joomla! framework. Going with the analogy of Joomla! as an operating system like Windows, and components as programs that run on the operating system, I like to think of the Joomla! content component (com_content) as the word processor (like Microsoft Word).

Only one component is loaded in your Joomla! website at a time, and it handles the major tasks that occur on a given page in your site. This is one way in which the operating system analogy breaks down, because in most modern operating systems, you can have several applications open at one time.

3

❑ **Modules:** A module further extends your Joomla! site by performing side functions outside of the component. Modules can be used to perform just about any task you can think of. They are typically used to display menus, lists, banners, and other little tidbits of content. I like to think of modules as being like little widgets that perform a simple, specific, necessary task that cannot be handled efficiently by components. See Figure 1-2 to see a typical configuration of modules and the component on a Joomla! page.

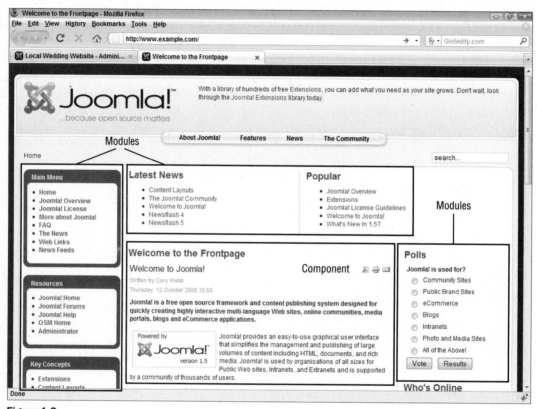

Figure 1-2

❑ **Plugins/Mambots:** Plugins have a variety of uses, but they typically perform a specific function to extend the functionality of a component. For example, the Content – Load Module plugin makes it possible to load a module position within an article. By default, eight different types of plugins are available: authentication, content, editors, editors-xtd, search, system, user, and xml-rpc.

   ❑ **Authentication plugins** are used to enable different methods of authentication for Joomla!. Joomla! comes with four different types of authentication: Joomla! core authentication, LDAP authentication, OpenID authentication, and Gmail authentication.

   ❑ **Content plugins** extend the functionality of the core content component. For example, there is a plugin called Content – Rating that enables a rating system for your articles.

❑ **Editor plugins** provide what-you-see-is-what-you-get (WYSIWYG) editors (discussed later in this chapter) for entering content.

❑ **Editors-xtd plugins** are used to extend the functionality of content creation in the core content component.

❑ **Search plugins** are used to make components searchable by the core search component.

❑ **System plugins** perform functions that most people will not directly see the results of. They offer tools for making components, modules, and even other plugins more powerful.

❑ **User plugins** can be used to tie Joomla!'s user database to other systems. For example, the bridge between Joomla! and phpBB3 uses a user plugin.

❑ **XML-RPC plugins** load APIs for use with the XML-RPC application.

In Joomla! 1.0, plugins were called "mambots," which was a carryover from the Mambo days. This word is still used occasionally, but since the release of Joomla! 1.5 it has been deprecated in favor of the term "plugins."

❑ **Templates:** Many people think of a template as their website, but that is an incorrect way of seeing templates. Templates are used for providing a layout and design within which all of the pieces of your Joomla! site come together.

Here's an analogy that might help. Think of your Joomla! website as a house. It is made up of brick, stone, wood, dry wall, and so on. The template is the blueprint that puts all of those pieces in the most logical locations for what your house needs to be, and it is also the decorations that make your house look nice once it is completely built.

You learn how to build a custom template in Chapter 8.

❑ **Module Position:** A module position is a location within a template that is set aside for containing modules. Module positions normally have names like left, right, top, bottom, header, footer, user1, user2, and so on, but can have any name that the template designer chooses to give them. The name of a module position usually, but not always, corresponds with its location on the page. For example, the left module position can usually be found on the left side of the page.

❑ **Language:** Joomla! is a multilingual content management system, which means that the user interface can be translated into any language using custom language packs. Language extensions can be found for many different languages.

❑ **Core:** Core refers to that basic Joomla! installation without any third-party extensions installed. It is all of the code for the Joomla! framework along with a set of core applications and extensions that come with the Joomla! installation.

❑ **Third Party:** Third party refers to any application or extension that is not part of the core.

❑ **Joomla! Extension Directory (JED):** The Joomla! Extension Directory (JED) is a very valuable resource that lists 3,651 Joomla! extensions at the time of this writing. You can find the JED at http://extensions.joomla.org. Bookmark that site, because it will be one of the most valuable resources available to you as you build your website. You can see the JED in Figure 1-3.

❑ **Bridge:** A bridge is code that ties Joomla! to another system. For example, there is a bridge that ties Joomla! to a popular stand-alone forum application called phpBB3. The most common use of a bridge is to tie Joomla!'s user information to the user information in other systems, giving users a single sign-on.

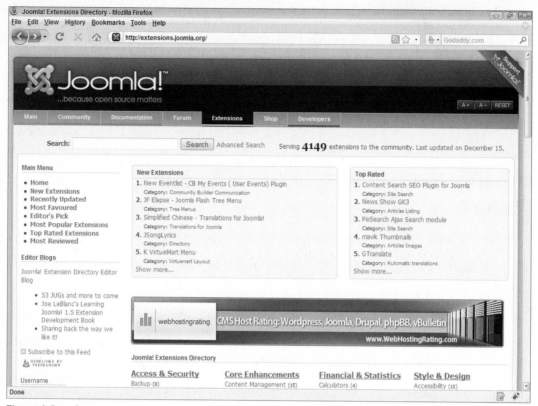

Figure 1-3

Content

Technically, content is every piece of text and media that is distributed/displayed via your site, whether in the component, module, plugin, or template. In Joomla!, when someone says content, they are probably referring to the core content component and the articles that are entered into that component and displayed on your site. You learn more about managing content in Chapter 4.

❑ **Sections:** A section is the highest level in the Joomla! content organization hierarchy. Sections contain categories, and categories contain articles.

❑ **Categories:** A category is the second level in the Joomla! content organization hierarchy. Categories are contained within sections, and categories contain articles. At this time, it is not possible to assign the same category to multiple sections, assign multiple categories to a single article, or contain categories within categories.

❑ **Article/Content Item:** An article is the main way that content is displayed in a Joomla! site. Articles can be organized into categories and sections, or they can be uncategorized. The term "content item" was used in Joomla! 1.0, but that phrase has been deprecated in favor of the term "article."

❑ **Blog:** In general, the term "blog" (short for "web log") refers to an online journal usually listed in reverse chronological order and updated on a regular basis. In Joomla!, the term blog refers to a specific style of layout for content sections and categories. Blog layouts can be ordered chronologically or by several other ordering choices available in the component's parameters.

❑ **Front Page:** The front page view of the content component is a blog-style layout. It works exactly the same as the blog layout for sections and categories, but with the front page view you can assign multiple sections and categories. Another distinction is that you must explicitly publish an article to the front page in order for it to display there. It is called the front page view because it is by default the front page of your site when you install Joomla!; however, the system does not require that the front page view be the actual front page of your site. This can be set using the menu manager (See "Default Menu Item" in the following section).

Menus

A menu is a piece of paper, a booklet, or a sign at a restaurant that lists possible food choices for the restaurant's patrons. Now that I know that you're paying attention, a menu in Joomla! is a list of links that direct your visitors to the various parts of your site. You learn more about menus later in Chapter 5.

❑ **Menu Items:** Menu items are the links that make up a menu.

❑ **Item IDs:** The item ID is perhaps the single most important piece of information in Joomla!, because it helps determine when and where modules load, what parameters are used by a component, which piece of a component is loaded, what template is used, and so on. An item ID is automatically assigned to a menu item when it is created.

❑ **Default Menu Item:** The default menu item is a new concept in Joomla! 1.5. In previous versions of Joomla!, the front page of your site could only be the first menu item in the "mainmenu" menu. Recognizing the obvious limitations of this approach, the core team (defined later in this chapter) decided to introduce the concept of the default menu item. In the menu manager, you can now set any menu item in any menu as the default menu item, and this menu item will become the front page of your site. There can be only one default menu item for your site.

Users

A user is anyone who visits a Joomla! site. A user can be a guest or an authenticated user. Authenticated users are users who have a user account for your site and are logged in to the site. These users fall into one of seven predefined user groups.

❑ **User Group:** A user group is a predefined access level group in Joomla! Every Joomla! installation has seven predefined user groups: Registered, Author, Editor, Publisher, Manager, Administrator, and Super Administrator.

❑ **Access Level:** Modules, articles, categories, sections, and menu items can be published for one of three access levels: Public, Registered, and Special. If an item is public, anyone who visits your site can access it. If an item is published as registered, anyone who has a user account can access it. If an item is published as special, only users in the Author, Editor, Publisher, Manager, Administrator, and Super Administrator groups can access it.

More Jargon

❑ **Content Management System (CMS):** Joomla! is known primarily as a web content management system (CMS). A CMS is a computer application that is built for the efficient organization, management, and presentation of content. A CMS can be built to manage articles, images, audio, video, files, applications, or almost any other type of digital content. Joomla! is a web content management system built for managing web content, such as articles, media, contacts, links, and more.

❑ **Administrator:** In Joomla!, the term "administrator" has multiple meanings. Administrator and Super Administrator are two of the seven predefined user groups. These two groups have the highest access level of any of the user groups. Administrator also refers to one of the four core applications (See "Application" earlier in the chapter). The administrator application is the back-end application used to manage every aspect of your site. You can find the administrator application at `yoursite.com/administrator`.

❑ **SEF URL:** SEF URL is an acronym that stands for Search Engine Friendly URL. For you web acronym trivia buffs, URL stands for Uniform Resource Locater, but that's the last time this book will refer to it as anything other than URL.

By default, Joomla!'s URLs are not search engine friendly or people friendly for that matter. A URL for an article might look something like this: `http://www.example.com/index .php?option=com_content&view=article&id=3:article-title&catid=5:category-name& Itemid=7`. Did you follow that? Neither will your visitors, and it's not very useful when Google is indexing your site. That's where the SEF URLs come in.

An SEF URL will look something like this: `http://www.example.com/menu-item/5-category- name/3-article-title.html`. This is not only easier to remember, but it is also better for search engine optimization. You can take more control of your SEF URLs with third-party components like sh404SEF, which you can find at `http://extensions.siliana.com/`.

You learn more about SEF URLs later in Chapter 3.

❑ **WYSIWYG Editor:** WYSIWYG is an acronym that stands for "What You See Is What You Get." A WYSIWYG editor is text area with special functionality built in so that you can edit content just like you would in a word processor. This makes adding and editing content easier because it makes it possible to add or edit content without knowing HTML.

Joomla! comes with one pre-installed WYSIWYG editor called TinyMCE, but you can easily install one of the third-party WYSIWYG editor plugins available in the JED. You can set which WYSIWYG editor you want to use in the global configuration or in your user profile in the user manager, or you can choose to use no WYSIWYG editor. Choosing no WYSIWYG editor means you will have to hand-code all of the HTML in your articles.

❑ **Open Source:** When people hear the phrase "open source," the first thing that usually comes to mind is software developed by some sucker who decided to give it away for free. Although this is partially true, open source actually refers to a widely adopted methodology for software development and distribution. Open source software is not necessarily free, although it is usually distributed for free depending on the license applied to the software. The defining characteristic of open source software is that the source code of the software is distributed with the software, and the end user has the right and ability to modify the software's source as he or she sees fit. This methodology opens up the possibility for users of the software to become active participants in the development of the software, and development teams are often spread out all over the world.

❑ **GNU/GPL:** GNU is a recursive acronym that stands for "GNU is Not Unix," and GPL is an acronym that stands for "General Public License." GNU is an open source operating system built on the Linux kernel, and it has set several standards for open source projects. The GNU/GPL is a license established by GNU under which many open source projects, including Joomla!, freely release their software to the public. Software released under the GNU/GPL may be freely modified and redistributed as long as you abide by the stipulations set forth in the license. The main stipulation is that any derivatives of the software must also be released under the GNU/GPL and a copy of the GNU/GPL must be distributed with the software. You can read the GNU/GPL here: `http://www.gnu.org/licenses/gpl.html`.

❑ **Core Team:** The Joomla! core team is an exceptional group of individuals who have volunteered countless hours to developing Joomla! into what it is today. Everyone who uses Joomla! owes these people a tremendous debt of gratitude.

Summary

Learning the language is important in any endeavor you undertake, which is why this book starts with a chapter that teaches the jargon associated with Joomla!. This chapter has covered many of the most commonly used words and phrases in the Joomla! community:

❑ Framework
  ❑ Application
  ❑ API
  ❑ Bridge
❑ Installation
  ❑ Sample Data
  ❑ Table Prefix
  ❑ Installation Folder
❑ Extensions
  ❑ Components
  ❑ Modules
  ❑ Plugins/Mambots
  ❑ Templates
  ❑ Module Positions
  ❑ Language
  ❑ Core
  ❑ Third Party
  ❑ Joomla! Extension Directory (JED)
❑ Content
  ❑ Sections
  ❑ Categories

- ❑ Article/Content Item
- ❑ Blog
- ❑ Front Page
- ❑ Menus
  - ❑ Menu Items
  - ❑ Item IDs
  - ❑ Default Menu Item
- ❑ Users
  - ❑ User Groups
  - ❑ Access Levels
- ❑ More Jargon
  - ❑ Content Management System (CMS)
  - ❑ Administrator
  - ❑ SEF URL
  - ❑ WYSIWYG Editor
  - ❑ Open Source
  - ❑ GNU/GPL
  - ❑ Core Team

Now that you are completely fluent in Joomlese, you can proceed with learning how your newly learned language can be applied to building a Joomla!-powered site. In the next chapter, you learn how to install Joomla!, but before you move on, work through the following exercises to test your understanding of Joomla! jargon. You can find the solutions to these exercises in Appendix A.

Exercises

1. What is the highest level in the content hierarchy? What is the next highest level?
2. What is the difference between a module and a module position?
3. What are the four applications that come with Joomla!?
4. What is the benefit of having a table prefix?
5. What is automatically assigned to a menu item when it is created?

Taking a Look Under the Hood

One of the biggest selling points of Joomla! is the fact that you can extend it to do just about anything you want. Thousands of extensions are available in the JED you learned about in Chapter 1, and you can use those extensions to turn your Joomla! site into anything ranging from a business directory to a sports league manager to a social network.

With all of the great options available to you in the JED, it is easy to overlook the fact that Joomla! has a feature-packed set of core extensions that you can use to build an attractive, interactive site. In this chapter, you take a look under the hood to see what Joomla! can do out of the box. You learn about some of the core components, modules, plugins, and templates available in every Joomla! installation package. You also learn about the pros and cons of some of the core extensions.

Core Components

As you learned in Chapter 1, components are applications that are built upon the Joomla! framework. There is a set of core components that perform several functions within a Joomla!-powered site. In this section, you learn about content, banners, contacts, media manager, news feeds, polls, search, and web links. You learn what each of these components does and some of the pros and cons of each component.

Content

The content component (sometimes referred to as "com_content") is arguably the most important of all the core components. It even has its own link in the main menu bar of the administrator panel as shown in Figure 2-1. This component is used for creating, editing, and managing articles and pages on your site. Articles can be uncategorized or grouped together in categories. Categories are grouped together into top-level categories called sections.

Joomla!'s content hierarchy, which you learn more about in Chapter 4, can be thought of as a filing cabinet. The cabinet represents the content component itself. Each drawer represents a section, and each folder within a drawer represents a category. The files within each folder represent articles. As with a filing cabinet, where a file can exist only within one folder and a folder can exist only within one drawer, an article can exist only within one category and a category can exist only within one section. Uncategorized articles are filed in a folder labeled "Uncategorized," which is the only folder within the drawer labeled "Uncategorized."

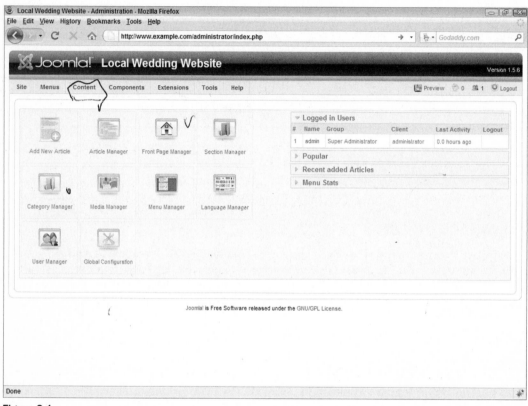

Figure 2-1

The content component has several layout options: Section Blog Layout, Category Blog Layout, Front Page Blog Layout, Section Table Layout, Category Table Layout, and the Article Layout. The blog and table layouts are just lists of recent articles from sections and/or categories, where the blog layout is formatted like a blog with introduction text for each article and a link to the full text, and the table layout is a table of titles linked to the full text of the article.

Benefits: The core content component has many benefits. Here are just a few of the benefits of using the core content component:

❑ This component makes it easy to create and organize content. Creating sections, categories, and articles is as easy as filling out a form.

❑ The core component is still the de facto standard for managing in Joomla!. Some developers have attempted other means of managing articles such as a Wordpress component, but the content component is still the clear choice for managing content for most people.

❑ Ample core and third-party modules and plugins are available that support and extend the functionality of the core content component, such as latest news, most read, and syndication modules, and rating and commenting plugins.

❑ The new layout overrides in Joomla! 1.5 allow for overriding default HTML output of the component, giving you unprecedented flexibility in how your content is presented to your visitors. You learn more about this in Chapter 8.

Room for Improvement: Although the core content component has a lot of useful features, it is also has room for improvement. Fortunately, the following limitations can be overcome with third-party extensions (see Appendix C):

❑ The content component has a very limited organizational hierarchy. With only sections and categories, you have very few options for how you organize your content. You cannot create nested categories, so you are stuck with a 2-tiered structure.

❑ You cannot apply more than one category to an article like you can in other systems.

❑ The core content component does not have built-in commenting functionality, which is a crucial feature for running an interactive blog.

❑ The default HTML output uses tables for the layout, which goes against web standards. Fortunately, as you learned earlier, this can easily be overcome by utilizing HTML layout overrides.

Banners

The banners component is an advertising banner management system. It works with the banners module, which you learn about in the next section, to manage and display ad banners throughout your site. You can manage your banners by organizing them by category and by client. You then create a banner module and assign it to a specific set of categories and/or clients, and ads from those categories and/or clients will display in that module.

Benefits: Here are some of the benefits of the banners component:

❑ The main benefit of the core banners component is that it is built into Joomla!, and no extra installation is required to use it.

❑ The banners component is a great tool for simple ad management if you do not require an extensive feature set.

❑ The component supports ad codes like Google Adsense.

❑ It supports any size banner, so you can use standard banner sizes or any other size you choose.

❑ It also supports impression limits, so you can control the number of times an ad is seen before it is disabled.

❑ The component also tracks ad impressions and clicks, so you can track how many times an ad has been viewed and clicked.

Room for Improvement: In terms of ad management, the core banners component leaves a lot to be desired. The following items are areas for improvement in the banners component:

❑ The banners component has a limited feature set compared to other ad management systems like OpenX.

❑ It has no functionality that enables your clients to control their own ads.

❑   Image management is handled outside of the component, so adding banners is not as intuitive as it should be.

❑   This component cannot be used to serve ads for other sites.

❑   It cannot be used to serve Flash-based ads.

Contacts

The contacts component is used for managing contacts within your company to be displayed to your site's visitors. Each contact is placed in a contact category, and information such as the contact's position, address, phone number, and e-mail address is stored. You can optionally display all of the contact's details on the front end of your site, or you can choose to display an e-mail form so that your site's visitors can contact that person directly from the site.

Benefits: Here are some of the benefits of the contacts component:

❑   The main benefit is that this component is built into Joomla!, so no extra installation is required.

❑   It provides a contact form, so your visitors can send you an e-mail directly from your site.

❑   You can use this component to manage multiple contacts within multiple categories, so you can display as many contacts as you need in a well-organized manner.

Room for Improvement: The contacts component is a very useful component for managing your contact information and making your site more interactive by allowing your visitors to contact you directly through the site. However, there is some room for improvement in the contacts component:

❑   When a visitor contacts you through the form, the data entered by the visitor is not stored in the database anywhere. It only sends an e-mail to the designated recipient. Therefore, you cannot maintain an archive of past contacts in the database.

❑   This component has no anti-SPAM measures to protect you from receiving unwanted e-mails.

Media Manager

The media manager, as shown in Figure 2-2, is accessible only through the administrator application, and is used for managing all of the media files on your site. A media file can be any file type as long as its type has been specified as a legal file type in the site configuration, which you learn about in Chapter 3. If you are familiar with standard Windows PC folders, you can think of the media manager as the "My Pictures" folder on a PC.

The media manager stores all of your files in the images directory of your Joomla! installation and all subdirectories of the images directory. With this interface, you can upload and delete files to and from the images directory, and you can create and delete directories in and from the images directory.

Benefits: Here are a few of the many benefits that the media manager offers:

❑   The media manager offers an easy way to manage all of the images on your site.

❑   It displays image thumbnails so that you can easily find the images you are looking for.

❑ The component offers an improved interface over its Joomla! 1.0 predecessor with a directory tree in the left column and an AJAX-based interface for uploading files.

❑ It offers two directory views: thumbnails and details. The details view displays file sizes and dimensions, so you can scan the list of available images to determine this information.

Figure 2-2

Room for Improvement: The media manager is a great tool for managing your images, but it is lacking in some areas that would make it a much more useful utility:

❑ The component is limited to the images directory, so you have little option for where you can restore and retrieve images.

❑ You cannot use the media manager as a general file manager because the number of file types are limited.

❑ With the media manager, you cannot move, copy, or rename files. The only things you can do are upload and remove files.

News Feeds

The news feeds component is essentially an RSS (Real Simple Syndication) aggregator. You can manage a set of news feeds to display on your site with links back to the originating site. News feeds can be grouped into categories and displayed in a blog-like layout.

Benefits: The news feeds component is a great tool for displaying syndicated content on your site. Here are some of the benefits for the news feeds component:

❏ You can use the news feeds component to turn your site into a simple news aggregator.

❏ It enables you to manage an unlimited number of categories and news feeds.

Room for Improvement: The news feeds component has some useful features, but it can be improved in a couple of areas:

❏ In the category layout, lists only link to each news feed layout within that category. In other words, the category layout does not show individual articles from each news feed within that category. To access articles in a particular news feed, your visitors would need to click through to the news feed layout.

❏ The component does not store articles to keep displaying them after they have expired from the news feed. News feeds are usually limited in the number of articles they syndicate, so once there are too many articles in a feed, the first one in is bumped out. If you want to continue displaying that article, you could not do that with the news feeds component because it does not store the data.

Polls

The polls component is a basic tool for building polls to get a feel for what your site's visitors are thinking. It works in conjunction with the polls module to display a poll in a module position. It displays the results in the form of a bar graph that shows what number and percentage of visitors supplied each answer.

Benefits: The polls component has a couple of great benefits:

❏ The main benefit of the polls component is that it is bundled with Joomla!, so you get that functionality without having to install a third-party component.

❏ Another benefit is that it is a great way to get a feel for what your visitors are thinking on a particular subject.

❏ Another nice feature is that it has a method to prevent people from voting more than once in the same poll.

Room for Improvement: This component is far from being a full-featured website polling system. Although it has some nice features, there is some room for improvement:

❏ Although it does have ways to prevent users from voting multiple times, these methods are not advanced enough to guarantee that voters are not voting more than once. Therefore, the results of each poll cannot be trusted as being 100% accurate, and they are subject to cheating.

❏   The number of answer choices for each poll is limited to twelve.

❏   Polls cannot be categorized, so there is no way to easily organize your polls.

Search

The search component is used to search the contents of all of the other components on the system. It uses search plugins built for each component to search data fields specific to each component and display the search results in a standardized way. In this way, it removes the need for each component to have a separate, stand-alone search function, because any component can be tied to the search component via the search plugins.

Benefits: The search component has many benefits. Here are just a few of them:

❏   The greatest benefit of the search component is that it provides a single interface for searching the contents of each component on your site.

❏   This component makes it possible to integrate third-party components using search plugins.

❏   It also has an optional statistics gathering feature, so you can easily see and track what your visitors are searching for.

Room for Improvement: The search component is a great tool for enabling your visitors to search your site, but here are some areas in which this component can improve:

❏   The system is prone to inaccurate search results. When users are accustomed to powerful search engines like Google, they might find that getting a list of irrelevant results is a bit frustrating.

❏   The component does not index the site's content, so it is not as efficient in querying the database as it could be.

❏   Although it provides a mechanism for integrating third-party components, not all third-party developers have adopted this means of searching the contents of their components. In fact, many third-party components actually have their own built-in search engines and bypass the core search component altogether.

Web Links

The web links component is used to manage links to other sites on the web, hence the name "web links." It enables you to store the name and a description of a site, and links the name to the site. Web links can be grouped by category, and the web links manager counts the number of hits that each link gets.

Benefits: The web links component is a great tool for compiling and organizing a list of links to resources across the web. Here are some of the benefits of this component:

❏   The component tracks each time someone clicks a link, so you can track which links are clicked most often.

❏   With the web links component, you can organize your links by category for easier management.

❑ It offers a measurable way to link to outside resources for your visitors, so you can see which resources are most interesting to your visitors.

❑ It allows for opening links in a new browser window, so when your visitors click a link they are not taken away from your site.

Room for Improvement: This component is a very useful tool, but it does have room for improvement in these areas:

❑ You can add a short description for each web link, but you cannot add any HTML to the description. You are limited to adding plain text.

❑ Each link can be added to only one category, so there is little flexibility in the organization of your links.

❑ You cannot have nested categories for your links, so there is only one possible level of hierarchy.

Core Modules

As you learned in Chapter 1, a module further extends your Joomla! site by performing side functions outside of the component. Modules can be used to perform just about any task you can think of. They are typically used to display menus, lists, banners, and other little tidbits of content. In this section, you learn about some of the most commonly used core modules.

Banner

The banner module works in conjunction with the banners component to display ad banners. In the banner module, you can specify the number of banners you want to display, the client, and the category. The banner module has the same pros and cons as the banners component because they work together to provide their functionality. You can see an example of the banner module in Figure 2-3.

Breadcrumbs

The breadcrumbs module displays a breadcrumb trail to let your visitor know where he or she is in relation to the hierarchy of your site's navigation. You can see an example of the breadcrumbs module in Figure 2-4.

Benefits: Here are the benefits of the breadcrumbs module:

❑ It provides an easy, standardized way of providing a breadcrumb trail for your website, so your visitors can tell at a glance where they are within the site's hierarchy.

❑ It is all automatic, so no configuration is necessary. All you have to do is publish it to whichever module position you want.

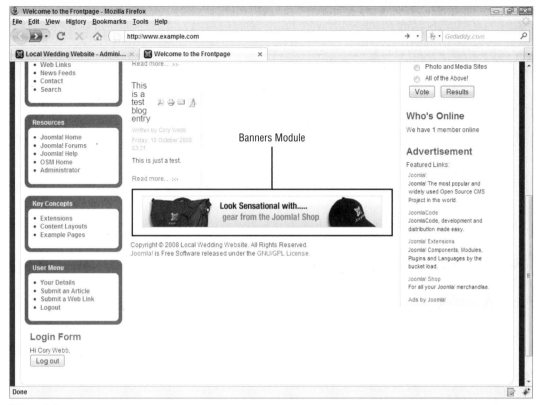

Figure 2-3

Room for Improvement: The breadcrumbs module is a great tool if you need to have this functionality for your website. However, here is an area in which it could improve:

❑   The breadcrumbs are tied to the menu system, and sometimes it can give undesired results depending on how your menus are structured. See Figure 2-4.

Custom HTML

The custom HTML module is perhaps my favorite of all the modules because it is so versatile. This module gives you a text editor and allows you to enter any HTML code you wish to display in a given module position.

Figure 2-4

Benefits: The custom HTML module is very useful tool for displaying content on your site. Here are some of the benefits of this module:

❑   This module is very versatile. You can add any HTML to the module to display content in virtually any format you can think of.

❑   You have total control over what is displayed in this module. If you want to add an image, some text, a list of items, or anything else, you can easily add that through the module manager.

Room for Improvement: The custom HTML module is one of the most useful weapons in your Joomla! arsenal, but there are still some areas in which it can improve:

❑   There is no automated functionality in this module. It is basically just a static content module for displaying whatever content you add to it in the module manager. If you want to update the content in a custom HTML module, you have to manually edit it.

❑   There is no way to add PHP code to a custom HTML module. Any PHP added to the module will be stripped out because the module allows only HTML and JavaScript.

Latest News

The latest news module displays a set number of the most recent articles from specified categories and sections. You can see an example of the latest news module in Figure 2-5.

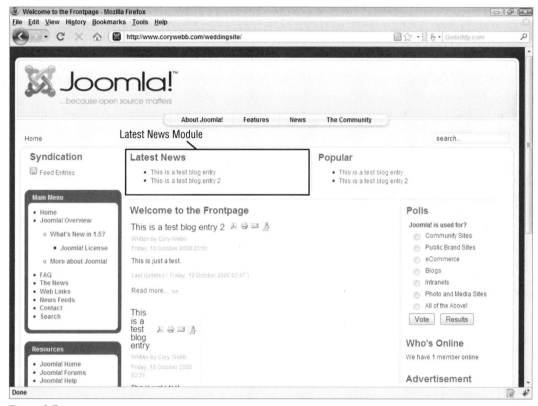

Figure 2-5

Benefits: The latest news module is very useful in a number of ways. Here are a couple of benefits to this module:

❑ The module is automatically updated each time you add a new article to your site, so you do not have to manually add each new article to the list of new articles in this module.

❑ It is a great way to alert your site's visitors of new articles on your site.

Room for Improvement: Although this module is very useful, here are some ways in which it could improve:

❑ The module has limited display options. It only displays a list of titles of recent articles from a specified section or category with links to the full article.

❑   It is not possible with this module to display the introductory text to an article.

❑   The module does not have an option for displaying the name of the article's author or the date it was written.

Login

The login module displays a login form with options links to lost username, lost password, and registration forms. If the user is logged in to your site, the login form displays a Logout button to give the visitor the opportunity to log out of the site. You can see an example of the login module in Figure 2-6.

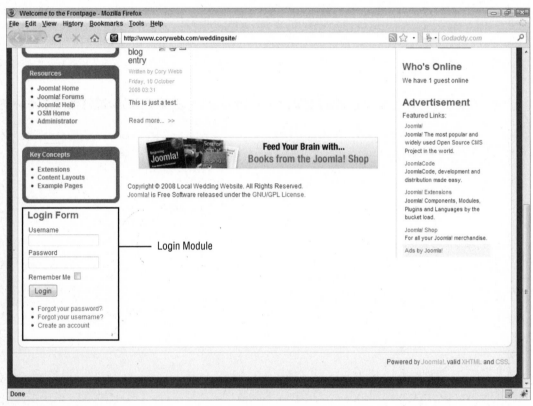

Figure 2-6

Benefits: The login module has several benefits, and here are a couple of them:

❑   This module enables your users to log in from any page on the site. You can publish the login module anywhere on the site, so your visitors do not have to navigate to a different page just to log in.

❑   Besides the default Joomla! user authentication method, it also supports other means of authenticating users based on which authentication plugins are enabled on your site.

Room for Improvement: The login module has very little room for improvement because it is so useful and versatile. However, here is an area in which this module could improve:

❑ The module is very limited in how you can display it. You could override the module's template to display it any way you wish, which you learn more about in Chapter 8, but that is not easy to do for beginners.

Menu Man Ag

The menu module displays a menu that has been created in the menu manager. This module offers four options for displaying a menu: List, Legacy – Horizontal, Legacy – Vertical, and Legacy – Flat List. The best way to display a menu using HTML best practices is to use the List layout in conjunction with CSS styling. Look at Figure 2-7 to see an example of the menu module.

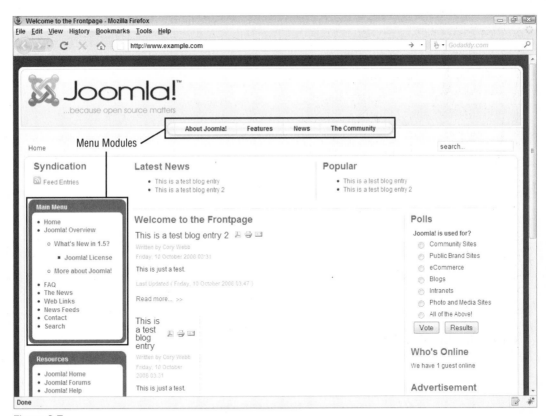

Figure 2-7

Benefits: The menu module has several benefits, and here are a few of them:

❑ The module allows for multiple menus. You can display as many menus as you need to on any page in your site, and they will not interfere with each other.

❑ The default menu style uses XHTML best practices by displaying your menu as nested unordered lists.

❑ You can easily add your own custom styles to your menus using CSS techniques for styling unordered lists.

Room for Improvement: The core menu module has improved dramatically over its predecessor from Joomla! 1.0, but there is still room for improvement:

❑ The options for how your menus are rendered in HTML are still limited. Your only options are the new nested unordered list format and the legacy styles that render menus in non-nested unordered lists or tables. You can customize the HTML that is rendered using HTML overrides, but this option is useful only for very advanced users.

Most Read Content

The most read content module displays a set number of articles from specified categories and sections based on which articles have the most page views. You can see an example of the most read content module in Figure 2-8.

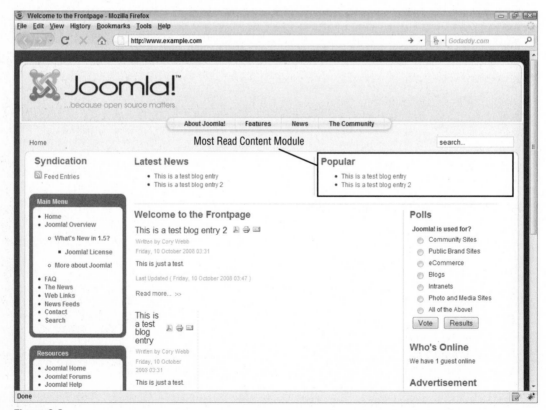

Figure 2-8

Benefits: The most read content module is a very useful tool for displaying your most popular articles. Here are some of the benefits of this module:

❑ This module is a great way to showcase popular articles. By showcasing your popular articles, you give them more visibility.

❑ It is also a great way to track which articles are the most popular. You can look at the most read content module and quickly see which articles your users have viewed the most.

Room for Improvement: This module can be a very useful tool, but it does have some room for improvement:

❑ Popular articles stay on the list longer than perhaps they should because by being on the list, they have more visibility than other articles on the site. With more visibility, they get more hits than other articles, so they remain popular longer than they might be if they were not promoted.

Newsflash

The newsflash module displays either one randomly selected article or a set number of articles from a specified category. You can see an example of the newsflash module in Figure 2-9.

Figure 2-9

Benefits: The newsflash module has the following benefits:

❏ With this module, you can easily display randomized news from a selected category.

❏ It displays more than just the article title. It also displays the introductory text of the article.

Room for Improvement: Here are some ways that the newsflash module could be improved:

❏ It currently relies on a page refresh to rotate through articles. There is no way to dynamically rotate through newsflash articles without requiring a page refresh.

❏ The module does not handle images well. Ideally, it should load images from each article at a size that fits into the position where the module is loaded.

Poll

The poll module works with the polls component to display a specific poll. This module has the same pros and cons as the polls component, with the additional con that you must manually specify a poll to be displayed in this module rather than automatically having new polls replace the existing poll. You can see an example of the poll module in Figure 2-10.

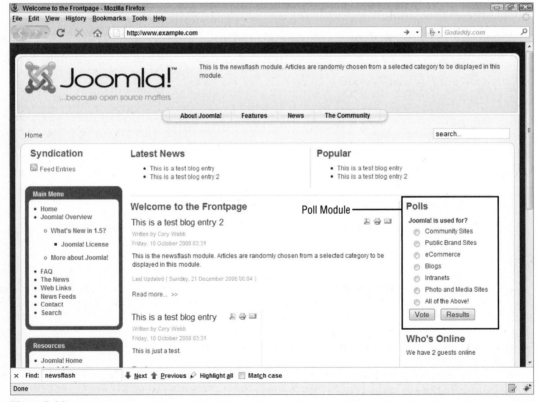

Figure 2-10

Random Image

The random image module displays a randomly selected image from the directory of your choice.

Benefits: The random image module really only performs one simple task, but it does it very well. Here are some of the benefits of having the random image module:

❑   It is a great way to display a different, randomly selected header image each time the page refreshes, which adds some visual interest to the page.

❑   It automatically pulls images from a directory you select, so it is easy to set up. You do not have to tell it which images to load. You just need to add the images that you wish to use into the selected directory.

Room for Improvement: Here are some ways that the random image module could be improved:

❑   The module only displays a static image. It doesn't do anything else like rotate the images as a slideshow with JavaScript or Flash.

❑   It uses every image from the selected directory. It doesn't allow you to pick and choose which images you want to use from the directory.

Related Articles

The related articles module displays a list of articles related to the current article you are viewing based on meta keywords that you enter when creating each article.

Benefits: The related articles module has the following benefits:

❑   The module ties together articles from different parts of the site.

❑   It also helps keep visitors on the site longer by suggesting other articles related to the current one they are reading.

Room for Improvement: This module could be improved in the following ways:

❑   It only compares meta key-words to determine if articles are related.

❑   It does not compare the full text of the article to determine if other articles are related.

Search

The search module provides a search box that ties to the search component. This enables you to give your visitors the ability to search your site from any page on the site. You can see an example of the search module in Figure 2-11.

Benefits: Here are some of the benefits to having the search module:

❑   This module provides a simple search field that can be displayed anywhere on your site, so users do not have to navigate to the search component to be able to search for content.

❑   It offers multiple display options to suit the needs of your site.

Room for Improvement: Here is one way in which this module could be improved:

❑ If a search box resides on a particular page, you would expect that it might search content related to the content on that page. However, the search module has no way to customize the search results so that they are relevant to the page from which the query was entered.

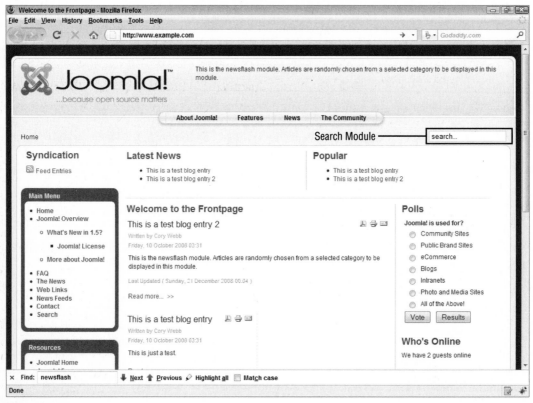

Figure 2-11

Syndicate

The syndicate module displays a link to the RSS feed for the category or section you are viewing. You learn more about syndication in Joomla! in Chapter 7. You can see an example of the syndicate module in Figure 2-12.

Benefits: Here are some of the benefits of having the syndicate module:

❑ The syndicate module makes it easy for your visitors to find your RSS feeds. You can use this module to place a link to your RSS feed anywhere on your site, so you can make it as conspicuous or inconspicuous as you want it to be.

❑ It automatically generates the feed URL based on the component, section, or category that the visitor is viewing on the page where the module is displayed.

Room for Improvement: Here are some ways in which the syndicate module could be improved:

❑   It only displays feeds on pages where a section or category is displayed. You cannot have a persistent and consistent link to your feed throughout the site using this module because it will not display on pages where a section or category is not displayed.

❑   It cannot be directly integrated with third-party feed services like FeedBurner.com.

Figure 2-12

Who's Online

The who's online module displays the number of guests and registered users currently on your site. You can see an example of the who's online module in Figure 2-13.

Benefits: Here are the benefits of having the who's online module:

❑   The module displays the number of people on your site at any given time.

❑   You can use it to see how many people are currently on your site, so you can know whether or not now would be a good time to make a change to the site or if it should wait until later.

Room for Improvement: Here is a way in which this module could be improved:

❑   The module only shows a number. It does not give specific data about who is on your site. For example, it could display a list of usernames of the users who are logged in.

Figure 2-13

Wrapper

The wrapper module displays any web page within an iframe at a specified module position.

Benefits: Here is one of the benefits of having the wrapper module:

❑   This module is a great way to incorporate content from a separate system on your server, or from other sites into your site.

Room for Improvement: Here are a couple of ways in which this module could be improved:

❑   With the wrapper module, it is difficult to control the layout of content from another system. It is impossible to control the layout from another site that you do not manage.

❑   If the other site or system that you are wrapping into an iframe is larger than the size that is allotted for it, the module might either add unwanted scroll bars or simply cut off the content.

Core Plugins

As you learned in Chapter 1, plugins have a variety of uses, but they typically perform a specific function to extend the functionality of a component. By default, eight different types of plugins are available: authentication, content, editors, editors-xtd, search, system, user, and xml-rpc. In this section, you read about each plugin type and a selection of plugins for each type.

Authentication Plugins

Authentication plugins are used to enable different methods of authentication for Joomla!. Joomla! comes with four different types of authentication: Joomla! core authentication, LDAP authentication, OpenID authentication, and Gmail authentication. In this section, you learn about the Joomla! authentication plugin and the OpenID authentication plugin.

Authentication — Joomla!

The Joomla! authentication plugin handles basic Joomla! authentication, meaning when a user logs in to your site, this plugin checks his or her credentials against your site's user database.

Authentication — OpenID

The OpenID authentication plugin enables your visitors to log in to your site with their OpenID credentials. OpenID is a decentralized framework for establishing an identity on the web that can be used to log in to any website that supports OpenID. With an OpenID, you log in to your OpenID provider, and then you can use that ID to log in anywhere that supports OpenID. You can learn more about OpenID at `http://openid.net`. Enabling your site to support OpenID is as simple as enabling this plugin.

If a user logs in with OpenID, a user account is automatically created with the user's OpenID as the username and no password, because no password is required with OpenID authentication.

Benefits: Here are some of the benefits of having the OpenID plugin:

❑   This plugin leverages OpenID, which is an increasingly popular authentication method.

❑   It gives users another option for how they log in to your site. Having more options makes it easier for visitors to access member-only parts of your site, which makes your site more usable and improves the overall user experience.

❑   It does not require a password to enable users to log in, so they do not have to worry about whether or not they can remember their password.

Room for Improvement: Here is an area in which this plugin could improve:

❑   OpenID has not achieved the kind of mainstream popularity it needs for this to be a heavily used option for authentication.

Content Plugins

Content plugins extend the functionality of the core content component. In this section, you read about the rating and e-mail cloaking content plugins.

Content — Rating

The content rating plugin places a rating form in each article that allows your visitors to rate each article. It also displays the average rating and the number of times an article was rated.

Content — E-mail Cloaking

The e-mail cloaking plugin automatically searches an article for e-mail addresses and "cloaks" each address using JavaScript so that web crawlers that search the web for e-mail addresses for use by spammers cannot find the e-mail addresses in your articles.

Benefits: Here are some of the benefits of the e-mail cloaking plugin:

❏ This plugin offers a great way to hide e-mail addresses from spammers.

❏ It works automatically, so there is no configuration required.

Room for Improvement: Here is a way in which this plugin could be improved:

❏ There is no way to opt out of this plugin for a specific address. It cloaks all e-mail addresses displayed in articles. The only way to prevent it from cloaking an address is to disable it, but that removes the functionality from the site completely.

Editors

Editor plugins are used to provide WYSIWYG editors (see the "WYSIWYG Editor" definition in Chapter 1) for entering content. In this section, you learn about the No Editor and the TinyMCE 2.0 editor plugins.

Editor — No Editor

The No Editor editor plugin removes the WYSIWYG editor from any place that might use an editor and provides a plain text area for typing content. With this option enabled, the user must manually enter all of the HTML code.

Editor — TinyMCE 2.0

TinyMCE 2.0 is the default WYSIWYG editor that comes with Joomla!. It is a full-featured editor that enables you to enter content and see it as it will appear on the site. It automatically generates the necessary HTML behind the scenes, so you don't have to.

Benefits: Here are some of the benefits of the TinyMCE editor plugin:

❏ Being a WYSIWYG editor, it provides an easy way to add and style content without knowing HTML.

❏ It also provides useful tools for adding things like pictures, links, ordered and unordered lists, and more.

Room for Improvement: The TinyMCE editor plugin has some room for improvement:

❏ The WYSIWYG editor is not as feature-rich as some other third-party WYSIWYG editors. You can see a list of recommended third-party WYSIWYG editor plugins in Appendix C.

❏ Sometimes the editor modifies the underlying HTML of an article in unintended ways.

Editors-XTD

Editors-xtd plugins are used to extend the functionality of content creation in the core content component. In this section you read about the Image and Read more editors-xtd plugins.

Editor Button — Image

The Image button sits just beneath the editor when you are entering content for an article or a custom HTML module, and it provides an interface for searching the images directory using the media manager component and inserting an image into the content. You can see an example of the Image button in Figure 2-14.

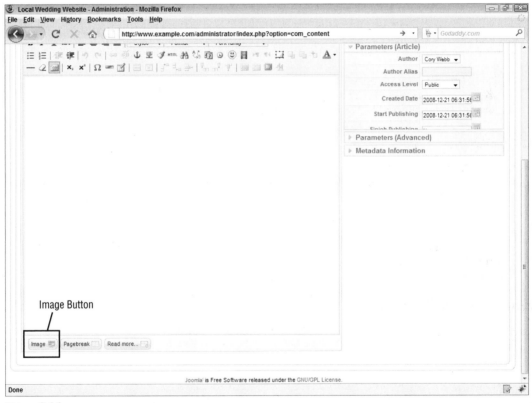

Figure 2-14

Benefits: Here are some of the benefits of the Image button:

❑ This button offers improved image handling over what was available in Joomla! 1.0.

❑ The button launches a mini media manager, so you can browse available images to select which one to add to an article, or you can upload an image to use in the article all from the same interface.

Room for Improvement: Here are a couple of ways that this plugin could be improved:

❑ There is no way to scale the image dimensions with this plugin. You have to add an image at its current size and then manually edit the dimensions either in the HTML code or using the image handler built into the WYSIWYG editor.

❑ The mini media manager loads slowly because it has to load all of the images in your image directory.

Editor Button — Read More

The Read more button is a new feature to Joomla! 1.5. In Joomla! 1.0, there were two editor areas when adding or editing a content item. The first was for introductory text, and the second was for the full text. In Joomla! 1.5, they have removed the second box and added the Read more button. When you click the Read more button, it adds a special tag to the content item in the specified location that tells Joomla! that any text above that tag is the introductory text, and any text below that tag is the full text. You can see the Read more button in Figure 2-15.

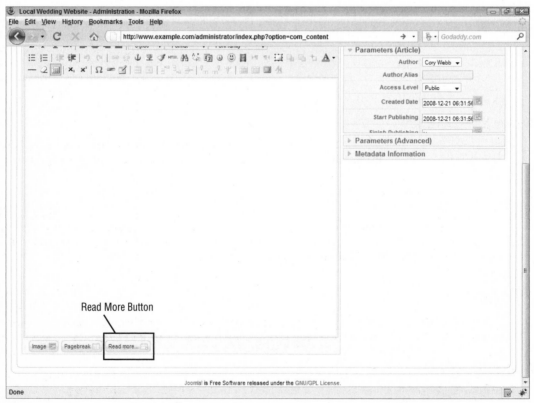

Figure 2-15

Benefits: Here are some of the benefits of the Read more button:

❑   This button streamlines the content editing screen by making it possible to get rid of the second editor on the screen.

❑   It automatically inserts a Read more line into the content with the proper syntax so that Joomla! knows which part of the text is introductory text, so you do not have to know the proper syntax.

Room for Improvement: Here are some ways in which the Read more button could be improved:

❑   It is less intuitive than having two editors for introductory and full text. Someone unfamiliar with Joomla! might not even recognize that it is there or understand its purpose.

❑   It is possible that this button could get confused with the Pagebreak button because they have very similar but different purposes.

Search

Search plugins are used to make components searchable by the core search component. Plugins are necessary for this task because each component's data is structured differently, and therefore they must be searched differently. Building all of the possibilities into one component would be impossible, but making the component extensible with the use of plugins makes it possible to search a virtually unlimited number of components. In this section, you learn about the content search plugin and the contacts search plugin.

Search — Content

The content search plugin makes it possible to search all articles in the core content component. This is arguably the most important search plugin because typically your visitors are most interested in searching your content.

Search — Contacts

The contacts search plugin makes it possible to search every field in the contacts component's data set. For example, if a visitor does a search for "Main St.," and one of the contacts on your site is listed as living on Main St., that contact will come up in the search results.

System

System plugins perform functions that most people will not directly see the results of. They are used to make other tools available for making components, modules, and even other plugins more powerful.

System — SEF

The SEF plugin handles links within your website. It finds links that are not search-engine–friendly and converts them to the SEF version before displaying your page in the browser.

System — Legacy

The legacy plugin loads the Joomla! 1.0 libraries so that Joomla! 1.5 can install and use components that are compatible with Joomla! 1.0.

Benefits: Here are some of the benefits of the legacy plugin:

❑   This plugin makes it possible to run many third-party extensions that were built for Joomla! 1.0. Having this ability means that you can upgrade your site from 1.0 to 1.5 and continue to use mission-critical extensions that may not be compatible with 1.5 yet.

❑   It provides a bridge from 1.0 to 1.5 for developers because it makes their extensions work on 1.5 without forcing them to completely re-write the extensions. That lets their users continue to use their extensions and gives the developers time to re-work their extensions for 1.5.

❑   It only loads the Joomla! 1.0 libraries for extensions that need them, so you do not see a hit in the site's overall performance.

Room for Improvement: Here are some ways in which this plugin could be improved:

❑   The legacy plugin does not work with all extensions built for Joomla! 1.0. Having this plugin is no guarantee that the extension you need will work.

❑   It makes people complacent because it enables extensions that are not optimized for Joomla! 1.5. People should be encouraging developers to upgrade their extensions to work with 1.5 or seeking extensions that are optimized to work with 1.5.

User

User plugins can be used to tie Joomla!'s user database to other systems. For example, the bridge between Joomla! and phpBB3 uses a user plugin. There is only one user plugin, the Joomla! user plugin, and it is used to handle the default user synchronization in Joomla!.

XML-RPC

XML-RPC plugins load APIs for use with the XML-RPC application. They make it possible to manage your website from an interface other than the web browser.

XML-RPC — Blogger API

The Blogger API makes it possible to manage your Joomla! content with any client that can be used to manage a blog at blogspot.com.

Core Templates

Joomla! comes with three pre-installed templates, so you can easily choose a template and start building your site right away. These templates are Rhuk_Milkyway, Beez, and JA_Purity. Although these templates are very high quality, I recommend looking for other templates because most people tend to use one of these core templates for their sites. Of course, if you want to be just like everyone else, then go ahead and use one of these templates.

Rhuk_Milkyway

Rhuk_Milkyway was the first Joomla! 1.5 template. It was built early in the development process of Joomla! 1.5 for the purposes of having a template to test the front end of the site and to give the front end of Joomla! 1.5 a face.

The template, as shown in Figure 2-16, is blue by default, but it comes with five other color options: red, green, orange, black, and white. When you install Joomla! 1.5, Rhuk_Milkyway is the default template until you set a different template as default.

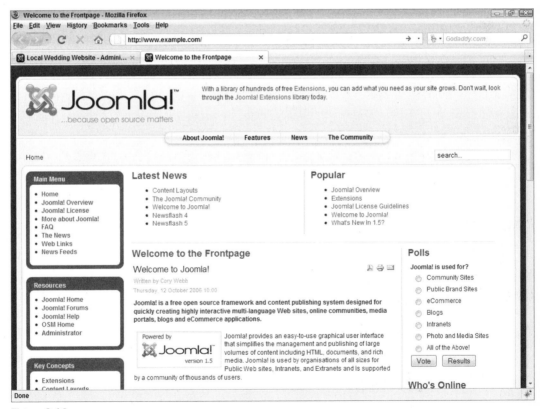

Figure 2-16

Beez

The Beez template, as shown in Figure 2-17, was designed and developed primarily as a demonstration of what can be accomplished with the new layout overrides available in the Joomla! 1.5 template framework. You read more about overrides in Chapter 9. Beez was developed as a fully accessible, standards-compliant template, getting rid of the tables used for layout in the core components by overriding their default HTML output.

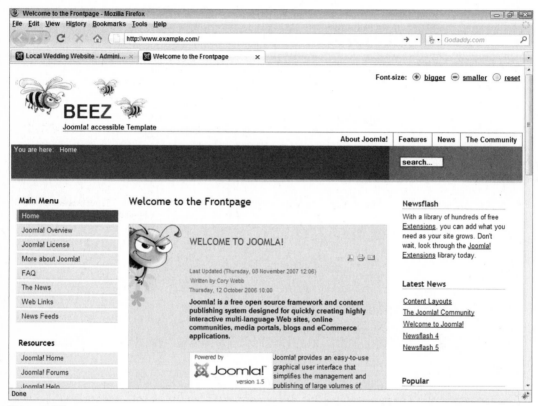

Figure 2-17

JA_Purity

JA_Purity, as shown in Figure 2-18, was the winning entry in a contest held to develop a template for Joomla! 1.5. By becoming the winning entry, JA_Purity earned a place in the Joomla! 1.5 distribution. This template offers the most customization parameters of any of the core templates.

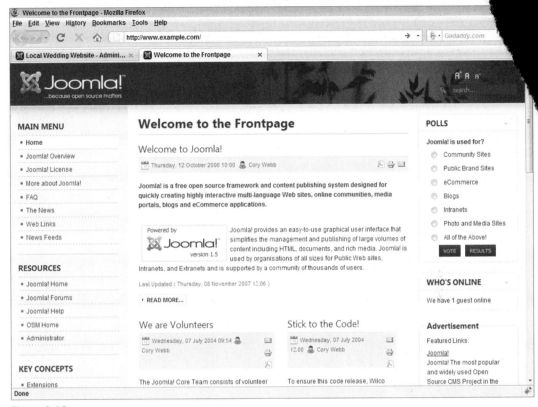

Figure 2-18

Summary

Besides being one of the most easily extensible content management systems on the planet, Joomla! also comes with a load of great tools built right in. With just a standard installation of Joomla!, you have the tools necessary to build an attractive, interactive site in no time at all.

In the next chapter, you learn how to configure Joomla!. Take a few moments and work through the following exercises to test your knowledge of what's under the hood in Joomla!. You can find the solutions to these exercises in Appendix A.

cises

1. List three layouts for the core content component.

2. Why does the search component use search plugins to handle searching each component?

3. What does the e-mail cloaking plugin do?

4. Which template is in the Joomla! distribution as a result of winning a contest?

Configuring Joomla!

When you install Joomla!, it comes preset with a standard configuration. You should always change Joomla!'s default configuration because it is never set in such a way that it will work perfectly for your site. For example, the site's metadata (keywords and description) are set to information about Joomla! by default, and unless your site is about Joomla! you should always change this information as soon as possible.

Configuration in Joomla! 1.5 is handled differently than in Joomla! 1.0. The main difference is that the management of many of the component-specific configuration parameters has been moved to within each component's back-end manager. In Joomla! 1.0, all core configuration was handled in the global configuration, but now only parameters that affect the entire system are managed in the global configuration.

In this chapter, you learn about the global configuration parameters and how they affect your site. Then, you learn about component-specific configuration parameters and how they affect your site.

Global Configuration

The global configuration of your site is the first thing you should modify. The parameters in the global configuration are stored in `configuration.php`, which you can read more about in Appendix B. Fortunately, Joomla! provides an easy-to-use interface for modifying your configuration settings. If the FTP layer is not enabled, you must make sure that `configuration.php` is writable before you can change the global configuration. Once you are finished making changes to the global configuration, for security purposes, best practices dictate that you should always return the `configuration.php` file to an unwritable state, and make it writable only when you need to make a modification.

To access the global configuration manager, you first need to log in to your site administrator, located at `www.yoursite.com/administrator/` (replace `yoursite.com` with the domain name of your site). Your administrator username is `admin` by default, and your password is the one you set up during installation.

Once you have logged in to your site administrator, you can access the global configuration manager in one of two ways, as shown in Figure 3-1. You can access it by clicking Site ➪ Global

Configuration in the administrator main menu, or by clicking the Global Configuration button on your site administrator home page.

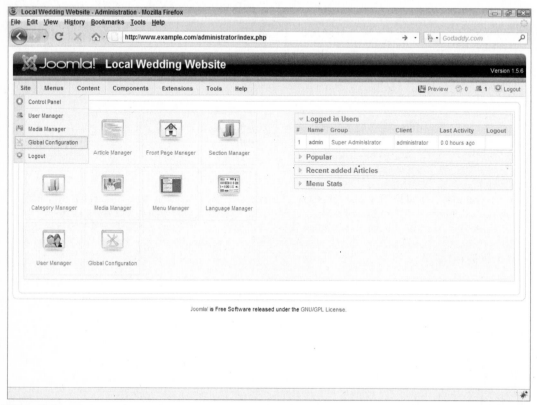

Figure 3-1

After you have accessed the global configuration manager, you have three main categories of global configuration: site, system, and server. In this section, you learn about the configuration settings in these categories.

Site Settings

The site settings, as shown in Figure 3-2, are the first settings you see when you access the global configuration manager. Under site settings are three groups of settings: Site Settings, Metadata Settings, and SEO Settings.

Site Settings

The first group of settings is called "Site Settings." This group contains six basic settings: Site Offline, Offline Message, Site Name, Default WYSIWYG Editor, List Length, and Feed Length. These are discussed in the following table.

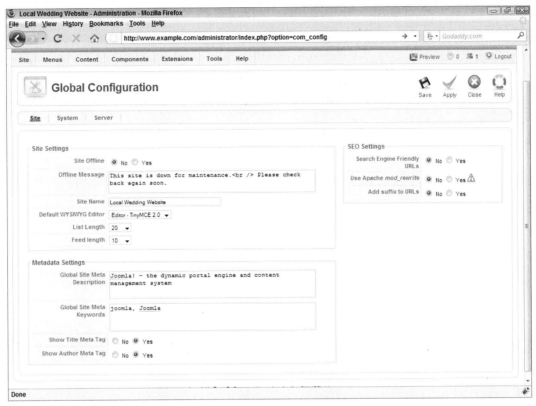

Figure 3-2

Setting	Definition
Site Offline	This setting gives you the ability to turn access to the site on and off. For example, if your site is under construction, you can set this to "yes" so that anyone who happens to come across your site will see a screen that says that the site is offline.
	The offline screen gives you the opportunity to log in to the front end, so as the site's administrator, you can see the site even though the rest of the world cannot see it. You learn how to customize the offline screen in Chapter 8.
Offline Message	This is the message the visitors to your site see when you have set the site offline.
Site Name	This is the name of your site. For example, if your site is a blog, you might give it the name "Cory's Blog" (if your name happened to be Cory).

(continued)

(continued)

Setting	Definition
Default WYSIWYG Editor	You learned about WYSIWYG editors in Chapter 1 and in Chapter 2. This setting is where you set the global WYSIWYG editor for the site. By default, you have two choices here: Editor – No Editor, and Editor – TinyMCE 2.0. To add more editor choices, you need to install third-party WYSIWYG editor plugins. You learn how to install plugins in Chapter 6.
List Length	Joomla! has a lot of lists: article lists, module lists, plugin lists, and so on. Some of these lists could potentially be extremely long, so Joomla! has a method called "pagination" that splits these lists up into pages so that you don't have to wait for the entire list to load. The List Length setting lets you set a default length (number of items) for each page. I like to set this number as high as it will go (100) because I don't like clicking through pages.
Feed Length	Most modern content management systems offer the ability to syndicate content through RSS or news feeds, and Joomla! is no exception. The Feed Length setting enables you to limit the number of articles that will be displayed in your RSS feeds. You learn more about syndication in Joomla! in Chapter 7.

Metadata Settings

Metadata is data that describes data. Each web page contains data, and metadata is used to describe the data that exists on each page. HTML has several types of metadata, but two of the main types are description and keywords. It is important that you set your metadata keywords and description to something other than the default information that is loaded upon installation. Metadata keywords and description are important elements in search engine optimization (SEO) because they describe the information that is found in your site. Joomla! allows you to set default global values for these two sets of metadata, as shown in the following table.

Setting	Definition
Global Site Meta Description	This is the global metadata description for your site. This description will be placed on each page of your site.
Global Site Meta Keywords	This is the list of global metadata keywords for your site. This list will be placed on each page of your site.
Show Title Meta Tag	This setting tells Joomla! whether to show the title meta tag when viewing articles. If set to Yes, Joomla! automatically populates this tag with the title of the article and adds this tag to your site's metadata.
Show Author Meta Tag	This setting tells Joomla! whether to show the author meta tag when viewing articles. If set to Yes, Joomla! automatically populates this tag with the name of the article's author and adds this tag to your site's metadata.

SEO Settings

The SEO Settings are used to enable or disable SEF URLs and to apply two specific settings that dictate how SEF URLs will be rendered on your site. See the following table.

Setting	Definition
Search Engine Friendly URLs	This setting is used to turn SEF URLs on and off. By default, this is set to No, but I recommend always setting this to Yes.
Use Apache `mod_rewrite`	This setting tells Joomla! whether or not to use Apache's `mod_rewrite` module when handling SEF URLs. If this is set to No when SEF URLs are turned on, the URLs will look something like this: `http://www.yoursite.com/index.php/some/url/`. If this is set to Yes, the URLs will look something like this: `http://www.yoursite.com/some/url/`. The only difference is that without `mod_rewrite` the URL contains `index.php`, and with `mod_rewrite` the URL does not contain `index.php`.
Add suffix to URLs	This parameter tells Joomla! whether to add a suffix such as `.html` or `.feed` to the SEF URL. With a suffix, the URL would look like this: `http://www.yoursite.com/some/url.html` Without a suffix, the URL would look like this: `http://www.yoursite.com/some/url/`.

System Settings

The system settings, as shown in Figure 3-3, are managed by clicking the System link in the global configuration menu bar. Under system settings are six groups of settings: System Settings, User Settings, Media Settings, Debug Settings, Cache Settings, and Session Settings.

System Settings

Your System Settings are used for security, logging, enabling XML-RPC, and determining which server is to be used for getting help documentation. The settings are discussed in the following table.

Setting	Definition
Secret Word	This is a set of numbers and letters that is used for security functions within Joomla!. The value of this setting is automatically set when you install Joomla! and cannot be changed from this interface.
Path to Log folder	This is the folder where Joomla! writes log files. This value is automatically set when you install Joomla!. There is likely no reason to ever change this value.
Enable Web Services	This is used to enable the use of the XML-RPC application you learned about in Chapters 1 and 2.
Help Server	This setting tells Joomla! where to pull help documentation from. The two options are Local and English (GB) – help.joomla.org by default. Local uses the set of help files that came with your Joomla! installation, and English (GB) – help.joomla.org uses help files directly from help.joomla.org.

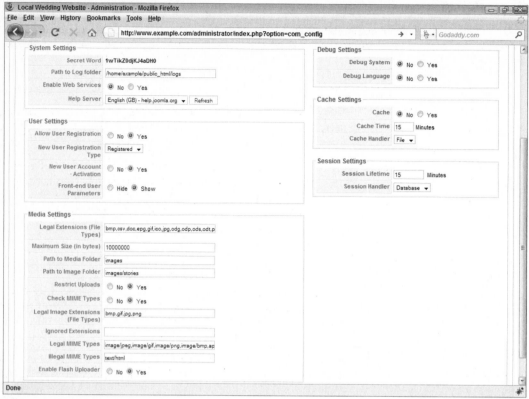

Figure 3-3

User Settings

The User Settings, discussed in the following table, are used to determine how a user registers and maintains his or her account.

Setting	Definition
Allow User Registration	This setting is used to allow or disallow users from registering on the front end of the site. This is useful if you want to allow user logins, but you want to control via the back-end user manager who has a user account and therefore has access to the site.
New User Registration Type	This is the default user type when a user registers. By default, this is set to Registered, but you could set it such that anyone who registers for the site is automatically an author, editor, or publisher.
New User Account Activation	Enabling new user account activation causes the system to send an e-mail to new users with an account activation code. They must use this code to then activate their account before being able to access the sections of the site that require the user to be logged in. This is useful for verifying that the user submits a valid e-mail address during registration.
Front-end User Parameters	If this is enabled, users can select their language (if you have multiple languages set up in the system), WYSIWYG editor, and help site preferences.

Media Settings

The Media Settings, discussed in the following table, are properties for managing media files through Joomla!. These settings control the size and types of files that can be uploaded to your site through Joomla!.

Setting	Definition
Legal Extensions (File Types)	This is a list of file extensions that users may upload to your site. If a user tries to upload a file through Joomla! that does not have one of these extensions, the upload will not be allowed.
Maximum Size (in bytes)	This is the maximum size of a file that can be uploaded. Setting this to zero means there is no limit. Your PHP settings will have a maximum file size regardless of what you set this to, so you may need to consult your web host for the maximum file upload size allowed in your server's PHP settings.
Path to Media Folder	This is the path to the media folder that is managed through the media manager.
Path to Image Folder	This is the path to the image folder. This is the path that is used to determine where Joomla! starts looking for image files when you click the Image editor-xtd button that you learned about in Chapter 2.
Restrict Uploads	This setting is used to restrict uploads based on the type of user attempting to upload a file and the MIME (Multipurpose Internet Mail Extensions) type of the file. MIME is a protocol used to describe content types.
Check MIME Types	This setting tells Joomla! whether or not to check the MIME types of uploaded files. Checking MIME types helps prevent users from uploading malicious files to the server.
	If this is enabled and your server does not support MIME magic or Fileinfo, you will get MIME errors. If you get MIME errors, you should set this setting to No.
Legal Image Extensions (File Types)	This setting is used to limit the types of images that a user can upload to the server through Joomla!. It is a list of file extensions separated by commas.
Ignored Extensions	This is a list of file extensions that are ignored for MIME checking when files are uploaded.
Legal MIME Types	This is a list of MIME types that are allowed for uploading. Joomla! includes a standard list by default, and you should not add to or remove from this list unless you know what you are doing.
Illegal MIME Types	This is a list of MIME types that are not allowed for uploading. Joomla! blocks the upload of HTML file types by default, and you should not modify this setting unless you know what you are doing.
Enable Flash Uploader	This setting tells Joomla! whether or not to use the Flash uploader for uploading media through the media manager.

Debug Settings

The Debug Settings are used to enable or disable system and language debugging. They are discussed in the following table.

Setting	Definition
Debug System	This is used to enable or disable system debugging. If system debugging is enabled, the system will display diagnostic information, language translations, and any potential SQL errors. If your site is live, you should disable debugging because this will display debug messages at the bottom of each page.
Debug Language	This is used to turn language indicators on and off for the purpose of debugging language files. This works even if system debugging is disabled, but you will not get detailed information without system debugging enabled.

Cache Settings

Caching is used in Joomla! to improve your site's performance. Caching is a process by which the system saves a (cached) copy of a file to the system to minimize the number of calls to the database server. The Cache Settings, which are discussed in the following table, are used to enable or disable caching and to determine how caching operates in Joomla!.

Setting	Definition
Cache	This setting is used to turn caching on and off.
Cache Time	This setting tells Joomla! how long to store a cache file before refreshing it with content from the database. If the content on your site is relatively static, meaning it is not updated often, you can set this to a higher value. If, however, your site is constantly updated, you should consider carefully how high this number should be set, balancing performance with accurate content.
Cache Handler	This setting sets how Joomla! handles caching. The only option is file-based. This option is here for the possibility that other cache handlers might be added to the system later.

Server Settings

The server settings, as shown in Figure 3-4, are managed by clicking the "Server" link in the global configuration menu bar. Under server settings are five groups of settings: Server Settings, Locale Settings, FTP Settings, Database Settings, and Mail Settings.

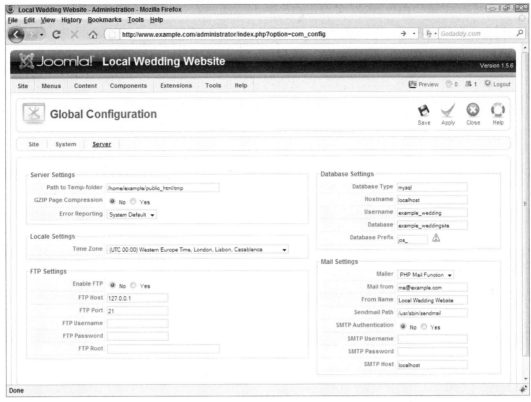

Figure 3-4

Server Settings

The Server Settings, outlined in the following table, are a group of settings that control general server configuration parameters.

Setting	Definition
Path to Temp-folder	This is the path to a folder where files are stored temporarily. Joomla! sets this automatically during installation, and there is usually no need to change this.
GZIP Page Compression	If your server supports GZIP compression, this setting is used to enable or disable GZIP page compression. GZIP page compression compresses the buffered output of each page, which can improve your site's speed.
Error Reporting	This sets the level of error reporting for your site. The four choices are System Default, None, Simple, and Maximum. Unless you know what you are doing, you should leave this on System Default.

Locale Settings

The Locale Settings contain the time zone for your site, as discussed in the following table.

Setting	Definition
Time Zone	This is the time zone for your site. For example, if your company operates in US Central Time Zone, you would set this parameter to (UTC -06:00) Central Time (US & Canada), Mexico City.

FTP Settings

The FTP Settings are covered in the following table. You can read more about these settings in Appendix B. If you do not set your FTP Settings during installation, you can set them here.

Setting	Definition
Enable FTP	This setting tells Joomla! whether or not to turn on the FTP layer for handling file uploads.
FTP Host	This is the URL or IP address of the FTP host server. In most cases, this will be 127.0.0.1. Consult your hosting provider if you are unsure of this value.
FTP Port	FTP servers use a port for allowing outside computers to connect to the server. The FTP port is usually 21, so this value defaults to 21.
FTP Username	This is the username of the FTP user account that you are using for the FTP layer.
FTP Password	This is the password of the FTP user account that you are using for the FTP layer.
FTP Root	This is the root server path that your FTP user has access to.

Database Settings

The Database Settings are the parameters that Joomla! uses to connect to your database server. These parameters are set during installation, but you can change them here if you choose to migrate your database to a different server. Most of the time, you should just leave these settings as they are. Nevertheless, they are detailed in the following table.

Setting	Definition
Database Type	This is the type of database server you are using. This value defaults to MySQL.
Hostname	This is the name of the host server for your database server. If your database is hosted on the same server as your website files, this value is localhost. This is the most common value for this setting in a shared hosting environment. Ask your hosting provider if you are unsure of this value.

Setting	Definition
Username	This is the username of the database user account that is used to access your database.
Database	This is the name of your database.
Database Prefix	This is the table prefix you learned about in Chapter 1. The most common value for this setting is jos_.

Mail Settings

The Mail Settings are used by Joomla! to determine how it should send e-mails. These settings, discussed in the following table, are set during installation, and you should only change them if you know what you are doing.

Setting	Definition
Mailer	This setting tells Joomla! which mail function to use to send e-mails. The PHP Mail Function is the default value. The other choices are Sendmail and the SMTP Server.
Mail from	This is the e-mail address that is used in the From setting in e-mail headers for messages sent from your site. This is usually the e-mail address of the site's administrator, but you can set this to any value.
From Name	This is the name that is used in the From setting in e-mail headers for messages sent from your site. This is set to the name of the site by default, but you can set this to any value.
Sendmail Path	If your host server has the Sendmail program, this parameter is where you set the path to this program on your server. Ask your hosting provider if you are unsure if this program is available on your server. This is only necessary if you set the value of Mailer to Sendmail.
SMTP Authentication	This setting tells Joomla! whether or not your SMTP server requires authentication. Consult your hosting provider if you are unsure of this. This is only necessary if you set the value of Mailer to SMTP Server.
SMTP Username	If your SMTP server requires authentication, this is the username of the SMTP user account that has access to use the server.
SMTP Password	If your SMTP server requires authentication, this is the password of the SMTP user account that has access to use the server.

All three methods of sending e-mail from your site have pros and cons. The default PHP Mail function is the easiest to set up because it requires no special configuration, but with this function you run more of a risk of your messages getting caught in a spam filter. The Sendmail option is a binary application that resides on your server and is used for sending e-mails. This is similar to the PHP Mail function, but it requires you to know where Sendmail is installed on the server. The SMTP method for sending e-mail requires the most setup because you must know the SMTP host, username, and password in order to use SMTP authentication. However, with SMTP, you have less chance of your messages being caught up in a spam filter.

Saving Your Changes

Once you have made the changes you wish to make to the global configuration, you need to save your changes. You have two options for saving your changes in the global configuration toolbar, as shown in Figure 3-5. The first option is the Save button, which saves your configuration and returns you to the administrator control panel. The second option is the Apply button, which saves your changes but keeps you in the global configuration manager to make more changes.

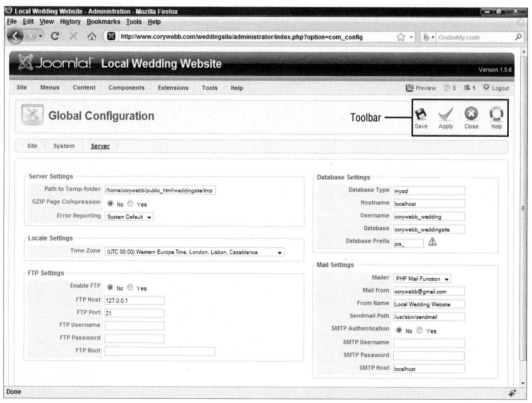

Figure 3-5

Core Component Configuration

Most of the core components have their own configuration settings that you can manage from the core component manager specific to that component. In this section, you learn how to access the configuration of six core components, their configuration settings, and how each setting affects your site. The components covered in this section are content, banners, contact, news feed, search, and web links. This section only covers the global configuration for each core component. In most cases, the global configuration can be overridden within menu item parameters. You learn more about menu items and their parameters in Chapter 5.

It is important to note that third-party components usually have their own configuration, and they may or may not handle configuration in the same way that core components handle it. Please refer to the documentation of any third-party component you use for information on how to configure that component.

Content Settings

The core content component has the longest list of parameters, and you should carefully consider each parameter and how it will affect the display of your content. You can access the content configuration by clicking Content ⇨ Article Manager in the administrator menu as shown in Figure 3-6, and clicking the Parameters button in the article manager toolbar as seen in Figure 3-7. The Parameters button is in the same respective location for each core component.

Figure 3-6

After you have clicked the Parameters button, the parameters window pops up on top of the page with a semi-transparent black screen covering the content of the page, as seen in Figure 3-8.

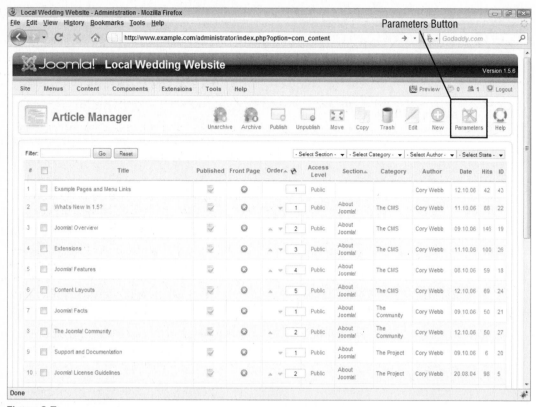

Figure 3-7

The content setting details are discussed in the following table.

Setting	Definition
Show Unauthorized Links	Each article has an access level: Public, Registered, or Special. Use this parameter to set whether links to an article with a Registered or Special access level will be displayed even when the user is not logged in. If you choose to show unauthorized links, the user can click the link to navigate to that page but will see a message that he or she can't access the content on that page.
Show Article Title	This sets whether each article's title is displayed. This setting can be overridden for each article.
Title Linkable	This sets whether each article's title links to the full article text. This is useful in the category and section blog and table layouts. This setting can be overridden for each blog or table layout.

Setting	Definition
Show Intro Text	Use this setting to show or hide the introductory text in the full article display. Hiding the introductory text can be useful if you wish to show the introductory text in a blog layout as an excerpt of the full text, and then show the full text in the article layout. This setting can be overridden for each article, category and section blog layout, and front page layout.
Section Name	Use this setting to show or hide the section name, usually under the article title. It can be useful to show the section name in a blog layout with multiple sections or in the article layout. This setting can be overridden for each article, category and section blog layout, and front page layout.
Section Title Linkable	This sets whether the section name links to a list of articles in a blog or table layout for that section. This setting can be overridden for each article, category and section blog layout, and front page layout.
Category Title	Use this setting to show or hide the category title, usually under the article title and next to the section name. It can be useful to show the category title in a blog layout with multiple categories or in the article layout. This setting can be overridden for each article, category and section blog layout, and front page layout.
Category Title Linkable	This sets whether the category title links to a list of articles in a blog or table layout for that category. This setting can be overridden for each article, category and section blog layout, and front page layout.
Author Name	Each article has an author, and this setting is used to show or hide the author's name with the article. Usually, the author's name is displayed below the article title. This setting can be overridden for each article, category and section blog layout, and front page layout.
Created Date and Time	Use this setting to show or hide the date and time that each article was created. This setting can be overridden for each article, category and section blog layout, and front page layout.
Modified Date and Time	Use this setting to show or hide the last date and time that each article was modified. The modified date will not display if an article has not been modified. This setting can be overridden for each article, category and section blog layout, and front page layout.
Show Navigation	Use this setting to show or hide navigation between articles. For example, if you are viewing the second article in a list of three or more articles, there will be previous and next links at the bottom of the article that link to the previous and next articles, respectively. This setting can be overridden for each category and section blog layout, and front page layout.
Read more... Link	Use this setting to show or hide the Read more link at the bottom of each article in a section or category blog layout. This link serves two purposes: it lets the reader know that there is more text in the article, and it links to the full text of the article. This setting can be overridden for each category and section blog layout, and front page layout.

(continued)

(continued)

Setting	Definition
Article Rating/Voting	Use this setting to enable or disable article rating. If article rating is enabled, a rating form is displayed with each article that allows readers to rate each article on a scale of 1 to 5. It also shows each article's rating and how many people have voted on that article. This setting can be overridden for each article, category and section blog layout, and front page layout.
Icons	Each article can be automatically converted to a PDF, viewed in a printable format, or shared via e-mail. This parameter controls whether the icons for these three functions are displayed for each article. This setting can be overridden for each category and section blog layout, and front page layout.
PDF Icon	This parameter controls whether the icon for enabling automatic conversion of the article to a PDF is displayed. This setting can be overridden for each article, category and section blog layout, and front page layout.
Print Icon	This parameter sets whether the icon for enabling the function to display the article in a printable format is displayed. This setting can be overridden for each article, category and section blog layout, and front page layout.
E-mail Icon	This parameter sets whether the icon for enabling the function to share the article via e-mail is displayed. This setting can be overridden for each article, category and section blog layout, and front page layout.
Hits	Use this setting to show or hide the number of times an article has been "hit," or viewed. The number of hits is displayed in the section or category table layout. This setting can be overridden for each category and section table layout.
For each feed item show	This setting is a syndication, or RSS, setting. You use it to determine whether each RSS feed item displays just the introductory text of an article or the full text of an article. This setting can be overridden for each category and section table or blog layout.
Filtering options	The filtering options are a set of options for filtering out certain HTML tags when a user adds or edits an article.
Filter groups	The filter groups are the user access level groups for which the filters are applied. Groups that are not selected here will have no filters on them.
Filter type	There are three filter types: blacklist (default), whitelist, and no html. Blacklist filters out only the HTML tags and attributes that you deem unsafe for your site. Whitelist filters out everything but the HTML tags and attributes that you deem safe for your site. No HTML filters out all HTML tags. Blacklist is the recommended setting here.
Filter tags	This is the list of HTML tags, separated by commas, that you either allow or disallow depending on whether you set the filter type to blacklist or whitelist.
Filter attributes	This is the list of attributes, separated by commas, that you either allow or disallow depending on whether you set the filter type to blacklist or whitelist.

Figure 3-8

Banner Settings

You can access the banner configuration by clicking Components ⇨ Banner ⇨ Banners in the administrator menu, and clicking the Parameters button in the banner manager toolbar. The following options are available.

Setting	Definition
Track Banner Impression Times	Banner impressions are instances when a particular banner is displayed on a page in your site. It is usually a good idea to track this so that you can measure how many times a banner is displayed.
Track Banner Click Times	This is the measure of how many times a banner is clicked. It is also a good idea to measure this so your advertising clients can know how many times their ads have been clicked.
Tag Prefix	Banners can be displayed for particular articles by matching banner tags to article keywords. The tag prefix forces the system to search only for tags with this prefix, which improves performance because it narrows the scope of the tags to be searched.

Contact Settings

You access the contact configuration by clicking Components ⇨ Contacts ⇨ Contacts in the administrator menu, and clicking the Parameters button in the contact manager toolbar. Choose among the following options.

Setting	Definition
Icons/Text	This controls how each line item is labeled in the contact form. The three options are Icons, Text, or None. For example, if Icons is selected, a picture of a telephone might be used to indicate which item is the phone number. If Text is selected, the word Phone would be used to label the phone number. If None is selected, no labels or icons are used for any line item. This setting can be overridden for each contact.
Address Icon	This controls the image used for the address icon. This setting can be overridden for each contact.
E-mail Icon	This controls the image used for the e-mail icon. This setting can be overridden for each contact.
Telephone Icon	This controls the image used for the telephone icon. This setting can be overridden for each contact.
Mobile Icon	This controls the image used for the mobile icon. This setting can be overridden for each contact.
Fax Icon	This controls the image used for the fax icon. This setting can be overridden for each contact.
Miscellaneous Icon	This controls the image used for the miscellaneous icon. This setting can be overridden for each contact.
Show Table Headings	This controls whether table headings are displayed in the contact category view. This can be overridden for each category.
Show Contact's Position	This determines whether you show or hide the contact's position. This can be overridden for each contact.
Show E-mail Address	This determines whether you show or hide the contact's e-mail address. This can be overridden for each contact.
Show Telephone Number	This controls whether you show or hide the contact's telephone number. This can be overridden for each contact.
Show Mobile Number	This controls whether you show or hide the contact's mobile number. This can be overridden for each contact.
Show Fax Number	This controls whether you show or hide the contact's fax number. This can be overridden for each contact.
Enable vCard	A vCard is a file that can be downloaded with a contact's information. It is in a standard electronic business card format that can be imported into popular contact systems such as Microsoft Outlook. This can be overridden for each contact.

Setting	Definition
Banned E-mail	E-mail addresses that contain any of the text in this comma-separated list are banned.
Banned Subject	E-mail subjects that contain any of the text in this comma-separated list are banned.
Banned Text	E-mail text that contains any of the text in this comma-separated list are banned.
Session Check	A session check checks for a session cookie before the user is able to send an e-mail. If cookies are not enabled in the user's browser and session check is enabled, the user will not be able to submit an e-mail.
Custom Reply	Enabling the custom reply turns of the automated reply. This allows for the possibility of using plugins to develop a custom reply to contacts.

News Feed Settings

You can access the news feed configuration by clicking Components ⇨ News Feeds ⇨ Feeds in the administrator menu, and clicking the Parameters button in the news feed manager toolbar. The following News Feed settings are available.

Setting	Definition
Table Headings	This controls whether table headings in a list of news feeds are hidden or shown. This setting can be overridden for each news feed category.
Name Column	This controls whether you show or hide the name of each news feed in a list of news feeds. This setting can be overridden for each news feed category.
# Articles Column	Use this to show or hide the number of articles for each news feed in a list of news feeds. This setting can be overridden for each news feed category.
Link Column	Use this to show or hide a link to the news feed.
Category Description	This controls whether you show or hide each category's description. This can be overridden for each category.
# Category Items	This controls whether you show or hide the number of news feeds in each category. This can be overridden for each category.
Feed Image	News feeds usually have an image associated with them from the original publisher of the feed. This parameter controls whether to show or hide the feed image. This can be overridden for each category or news feed.
Feed Description	News feeds also have a description from the original publisher. This parameter sets whether to show or hide the feed description. This can be overridden for each category or news feed.

(continued)

(continued)

Setting	Definition
Item Description	This parameter controls whether you show or hide the item description or introductory text. When set to hide, only the title of each feed item and a link to the original item will be displayed. This can be overridden for each category or news feed.
Word Count	This limits the number of words you display in the item description. This can be overridden for each category or news feed.

Search Parameters

You can access the search configuration by clicking Components ⇨ Search in the administrator menu, and clicking the Parameters button in the search statistics toolbar. The search parameter options are discussed in the following table.

Setting	Definition
Gather Search Statistics	Use this to control whether to gather search statistics. If set to Yes, every time someone does a search on your site the search words are recorded for statistical purposes. This can be useful in determining what people are looking for when they visit your site, but it can also use up a lot of resources as more and more searches are recorded.
Show Created Date	This controls whether to show or hide the created date for an article when it appears in the search results. This can be overridden in the search component menu item or for each article.

Web Links Parameters

You can access the web links configuration by clicking Components ⇨ Web Links ⇨ Links in the administrator menu, and clicking the Parameters button in the web link manager toolbar. The options are listed in the following table.

Setting	Definition
Description	This controls whether to show or hide the description entered in the Web Links Introduction parameter.
Web Links Introduction	This is an introductory description that is displayed at the top of the web links category list.
Hits	This controls whether you show or hide the number of hits received by each web link. This can be overridden for each web link category.
Link Descriptions	This controls whether you show or hide the description of each web link. This can be overridden for each web link category.

Setting	Definition
Other Categories	This controls whether you show or hide other web link categories with a category's list of links. This can be overridden for each web link category.
Table Headings	This controls whether you show or hide table headings in a list of web links. This can be overridden for each web link category.
Target	This sets the target window for each web link item. The options are Parent Window with Browser Navigation, New Window with Browser Navigation, or New Window without Browser Navigation. This can be overridden for each web link category.
Icon	This sets the icon to be used to the left of each web link in the list of web links.

Summary

Joomla! configuration is divided into global configuration and component configuration at the top level. Each menu item, article, web link, category, and so on can have its own specific configuration that overrides certain global or component configuration settings, but it is important to know where and how to set the global configuration and component configuration settings so that your site operates in a consistent manner.

Now that you know how to configure your installation of Joomla!, it is time to think about how to manage content in Joomla! and how to plan your content structure so that it works with Joomla!'s content structure. First, work through the following exercises to test your knowledge of Joomla! configuration. You can find the answers to these exercises in Appendix A.

Exercises

1. What are the three main categories in the global configuration?

2. What is the purpose of caching?

3. What two purposes do the "Read more . . . " link serve?

4. What are one pro and one con of gathering search statistics?

Managing Content

I know what you're probably thinking, "Wait. Doesn't Joomla! do that for me? Why do I need to learn about this?" That's what I thought when I first started using content management systems, and in a way it's true. The temptation is to just jump right in and start writing articles and static pages because Joomla! makes it so easy. If you take the shoot-first-and-ask-questions-later route, you will learn quickly that you should have taken some time to learn how to manage content with Joomla! or any content management system (CMS) for that matter, because often you're left with a disorganized mess of a website.

Every CMS has its own unique way of organizing and managing content. Some systems use tags, which are a set of keywords, to categorize content. Others use the concept of folders, or nested categories. Others use a combination of techniques for organizing content. Joomla! has a clearly defined, somewhat rigid hierarchy for managing content, and it is important to understand this hierarchy before you begin adding content to your site.

In this chapter, you learn about Joomla!'s content structure and how content is organized into sections, categories, articles, and uncategorized articles. You also learn about planning your content, why content planning is important, and how your content plan might fit into Joomla!'s architecture. Finally, you see an example of content management in the sample site for this book.

Understanding Joomla!'s Content Structure

Joomla! has a fairly rigid content structure. The top level of the hierarchy is a content section. Sections do not contain articles directly, but rather they contain the next level in the hierarchy — categories. Categories contain articles, and each article can belong to only one category. If an article does not require categorization, it can be set up as an uncategorized article, which (confusingly enough) simply means that it is categorized in the uncategorized category. Head spinning yet? Don't worry. In this section, you learn about content sections, categories, and articles (both categorized and uncategorized).

Sections

As you learned in Chapter 1, a section is the highest level in the Joomla! content organization hierarchy. Sections contain categories, and categories contain articles. For example, a section might be something like "Automobiles," and it would contain categories such as "Cars," "Trucks," and "SUVs."

Try It Out   Creating a Section

To create a section:

1. Navigate to the section manager in your Joomla! administrator. You can access the Section Manager from the Content menu, as shown in Figure 4-1.

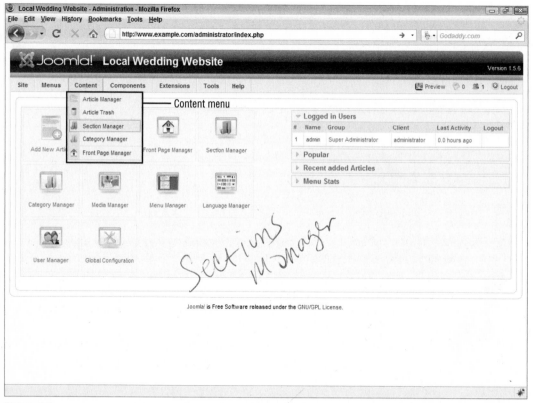

Figure 4-1

2. In the Section Manager toolbar, click New to open the form to create a new section, which you can see in Figure 4-2.

3. Enter a title for your section. This is a mandatory field.

4. Enter an alias for your section. This is not mandatory, but if you do not enter an alias, one will be generated automatically.

Figure 4-2

5.   Set the value of Published to Yes if you want the section to be published, or set it to No if you do not want the section to be published.

6.   Select the access level of the section. Select Public if you want anyone who visits your site to view content in this section. Select Registered if you only want registered users to be able to access content in this section. Select Special if you want only users with at least author access to be able to access this section.

7.   Select an image that you want to be associated with this section. This is not a mandatory field.

8.   Select an image position. This determines how the image appears on the section page. This is not a mandatory field.

9.   Enter a description for the section. This also is not a mandatory field.

10.   Click the Save button in the toolbar to save your new section and return to the Section Manager. If you want to save your new section, but remain in the section form, click the Apply button.

How It Works

On the new section form, shown in Figure 4-2, the most important fields are Title, Alias, Published, and Access Level. The first field is the title of the section. The title should be short and descriptive of the contents of that section (for example, "Automobiles"). The alias is usually the same as the title, and it is typically used for the purposes of Search Engine Friendly (SEF) URLs, which you learned about in Chapter 1. The value of Published determines whether or not the section and its contents are viewable by visitors to your site. Access Level is used to control what level of user access is required to view the contents of the section.

The other fields are Order, Image, Image Position, and Description. You cannot set the order value for a new section until after the section is created. A new section defaults to the last place in the order of sections. Each section can have an image associated with it, and the Image drop-down list is where you select that image. The list of images comes from the images located at `yoursite.com/images/stories/`. The image position is used to determine how the image is displayed along with the section description, if you choose to display the description or the image. The description can contain any text, images, or other media that you deem necessary to describe the section.

Categories

As you also learned in Chapter 1, a category is the second level in the Joomla! content organization hierarchy. Categories are contained within sections, and categories contain articles. At this time, it is not possible to assign the same category to multiple sections, assign multiple categories to a single article, or contain categories within categories. Going with the previous example, the category "Cars" might contain articles such as "Honda Accord," "Toyota Camry," and "Nissan Altima."

Try It Out   Creating a Category

To create a category:

1. Make sure you have at least one section in the system. Before you can create a category, you must create at least one section to contain that category.

2. Navigate to the Category Manager in your Joomla! administrator. You can access the Category Manager from the Content menu, as shown in Figure 4-1.

3. In the Category Manager toolbar, click New to open the form to create a new category, which you can see in Figure 4-3. The new category form is almost identical to the new section form, with the addition of a Section drop-down list with which you select a section to contain the category.

4. Enter a title for your category. This field is mandatory.

5. Enter an alias for your category. Like the section alias, this field is not mandatory, but if you do not enter an alias one will be generated automatically.

6. Set the value of Published to Yes if you want the category to be published, or set it to No if you do not want the category to be published.

7. Select the section in which you want the category to reside.

8. Select the access level of the category. Select Public if you want anyone who visits your site to view content in this category. Select Registered if you only want registered users to be able to access content in this category. Select Special if you want only users with at least author access to be able to access this category.

9. Select an image that you want to be associated with this category. This is not a mandatory field.

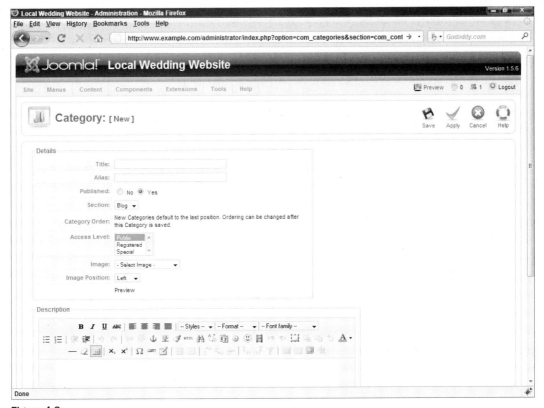

Figure 4-3

10. Select an image position. This determines how the image appears on the category page. This is not a mandatory field.

11. Enter a description for the section. This also is not a mandatory field.

12. Click the Save button in the toolbar to save your new category and return to the Category Manager. If you want to save your new category, but remain in the category form, click the Apply button.

How It Works

On the new category form, shown in Figure 4-3, the most important fields are Title, Alias, Published, Section, and Access Level. The first field is the title of the category. The title should be short and descriptive of the contents of that category (for example, ''Cars''). The alias is usually the same as the title, and it is typically used for the purposes of SEF URLs, which you learned about in Chapter 1. The value of Published determines whether or not the category and its contents are viewable by visitors to your site. The value of Section is the section in which the category resides. A category must belong to one and only one section. Access Level is used to control what level of user access is required to view the contents of the category.

The other fields are Order, Image, Image Position, and Description. Categories are ordered within their selected sections. You cannot set the order value for a new category until after the category is created. A new category defaults to the last place in the order of categories within the selected section. Like sections, each category can have an image associated with it, and the Image drop-down list is where you select that image. The list of images comes from the images located at `yoursite.com/images/stories/`. The image position is used to determine how the image is displayed along with the category description, if you choose to display the description or the image. The description can contain any text, images, or other media that you deem necessary to describe the category. Selecting a section does not lock the category into that section. You can move the category to any available section at any time. You can move a category to a different section in two ways. The first is to edit the category. To do this, navigate to the Category Manager and click the title of the category you wish to move or check the box next to the category title and click the Edit button in the Category Manager toolbar as shown in Figure 4-4. Then in the category editor form, just like the new category form shown in Figure 4-3, select a different section in the Section drop-down list.

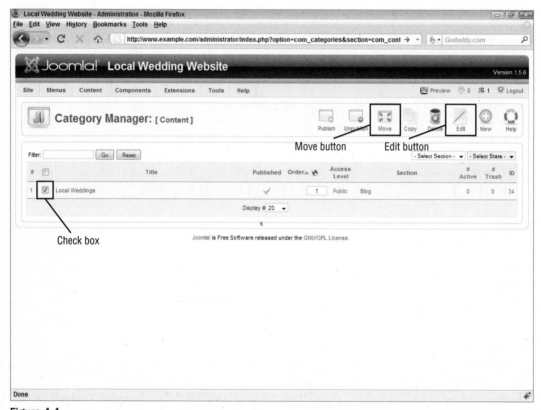

Figure 4-4

The second way to move a category to a different section is to check the box next to the category title in the Category Manager, and click the Move button as shown in Figure 4-4. Then, on the move category screen shown in Figure 4-5, select the section to which you want to move the category, and click the Save button in the toolbar. When you move a category from one section to another, all of the articles in that category are moved along with the category.

Figure 4-5

Articles

In Chapter 1, you also learned that an article is the main way that content is displayed in a Joomla! site. Articles can be organized into categories and sections, or they can be uncategorized. The term "content item" was used in Joomla! 1.0, but that phrase has been deprecated in favor of the term "article." You will often catch people like me, who have been around Joomla! since before it was Joomla!, still referring to articles as content items. Just know that they are one in the same.

Try It Out   **Creating an Article**

To create an article:

1. Navigate to the Article Manager in your Joomla! administrator. You can access the Article Manager from the Content menu, as shown earlier in Figure 4-1.

2. Once you are in the Article Manager, click the New button in the toolbar to open the new article form. You can see the new article form in Figures 4-6, 4-7, 4-8, and 4-9.

3. Enter a title for your article. This field is mandatory.

4. Enter an alias for your article. This field is not mandatory, but if you do not enter an alias, one will be generated automatically.

5. Set the value of Published to Yes if you want the article to be published, or set it to No if you do not want the article to be published.

6. Set the value of Front Page to Yes if you want the article to display in the Front Page view of the content component, or set it to No if you do not want it to display in the Front Page view.

7. Select the section to which you want this article to belong. You must select a section before you select a category, because selecting a section will pre-populate the Category drop-down list with categories that belong to that section. Selecting a section is mandatory, although you could select "Uncategorized" as your section.

8. Select the category to which you want this article to belong. Selecting a category is mandatory. If you selected "Uncategorized" for your section, then "Uncategorized" is automatically selected as your category.

9. In the main text editor, begin to enter your content.

10. Click the Read more button below the content editor to add a breaking point in the article that separates introductory text from the rest of the text. You can add only one Read more separator per article. This is useful if the article is going into a blog or news-style category or section because on the category or section page, only the introductory text is displayed and a Read more link is included to direct the reader to the rest of the article.

11. Add pictures to your article using the Image button below the main text editor. This button will pop up a window that gives you access to the media manager, shown in Figure 4-7, and thumbnails of each image in your images directory. With that, you can select an image, set its alignment, and add alternate text, a title, and a caption to the image, and the image will then be added to your article when you click the Insert button.

12. To add page breaks to your article, click the Pagebreak button, shown in Figure 4-8, just beneath the main text editor. You can add as many page breaks as you want to split up your article into as many pages as you want.

13. In the right column, set your parameters and metadata information however you need them to be set. You can see an explanation of each parameter and metadata information in the Article Parameters, Advanced Parameters, and Metadata Information tables.

14. Click the Save button in the toolbar to save your new article and return to the Article Manager. If you want to save your new article, but remain in the article form, click the Apply button.

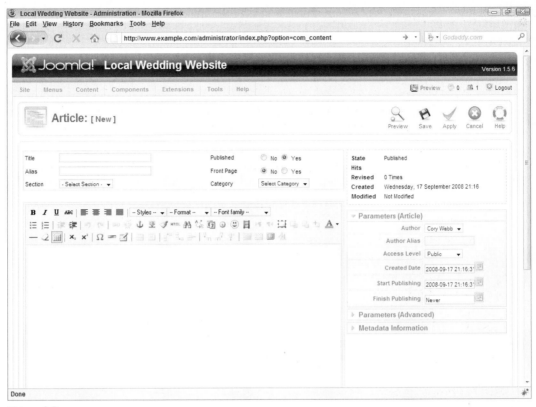

Figure 4-6

How It Works

In Figure 4-6, you can see the key elements of creating a new article in the left column. These elements are Title, Alias, Published, Front Page, Section, Category, and Text (not labeled, but it's hard to miss it...it's the one with the big text area WYSIWYG editor). The Title is just the title of the article, and the Alias is used primarily for SEF URLs. The Front Page parameter tells whether or not the article will be published in the Front Page view, which is a blog-style layout of all sections and categories that you learn more about in Chapter 5. You must select a Section and a Category before you can save your article. If you have not set up any sections or categories yet, the only options available in these drop-downs will be Uncategorized. Once you select a Section, the Category drop-down will be populated with the available categories in the selected Section. You can move an article from one section and category to another at any time with this form, so you are not locked in, which is good if you have a fear of commitment.

The ability to use WYSIWYG editors makes adding text and pictures to your content as easy as using a modern word processor. As you learned in Chapter 1, in Joomla!, WYSIWYG editors are plugins that load a word-processor–style text editor so that you can easily make changes to the look and feel of the content and see the content in the editor as it would appear on a page in your site. You can use one of the core WYSIWYG editors, which you learned about in Chapter 2, or you can install a third-party WYSIWYG editor, some of which are listed in Appendix C.

At the bottom of the Text WYSIWYG editor, there is a Read more button as shown in Figure 4-8. This button is used to add a divider between introductory text and the rest of the text of the article. The Read more divider is optional, and leaving it out simply means that all of the content of the article will be treated as introductory text. The divider is important for blog layouts of sections and categories because it provides a way to display a short excerpt of an article in the blog layout while displaying a Read more link that links to the rest of the text.

Another button beneath the WYSIWYG editor is the Image button, which provides a way to upload images and select from your site's image directory to add to pictures your article. This uses an AJAX pop-up window to give you access to your site's media manager, shown in Figure 4-7.

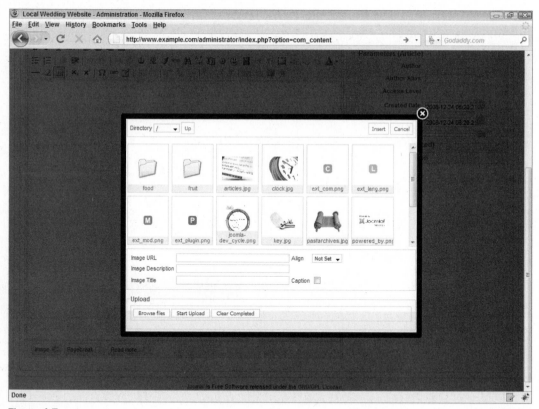

Figure 4-7

The other button beneath the WYSIWYG editor is the Pagebreak button. This gives you the ability to split your article into pages. This can be particularly useful for really long articles. You simply place your cursor within the text where you want to add a page break, and click the button. This uses an AJAX pop-up window to bring up a form in which you add a page title and a table of contents alias for the new page. The WYSIWYG editor will display a visual indicator of where you added the page break.

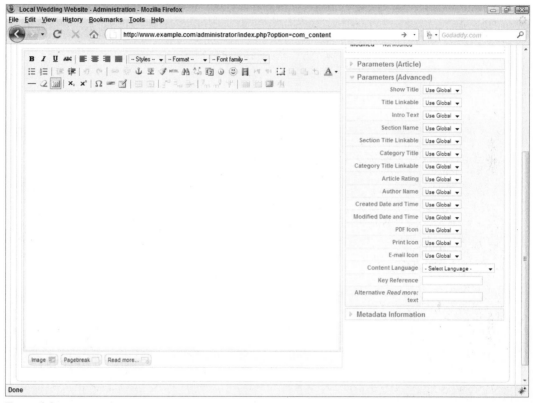

Figure 4-8

The right column, as seen in Figures 4-6, 4-7, 4-8, and 4-9 contains three "sliding drawers" with parameters for your article. The first drawer has article parameters; the second has advanced parameters, and the third has metadata information (keywords and description). The following tables show what each parameter means.

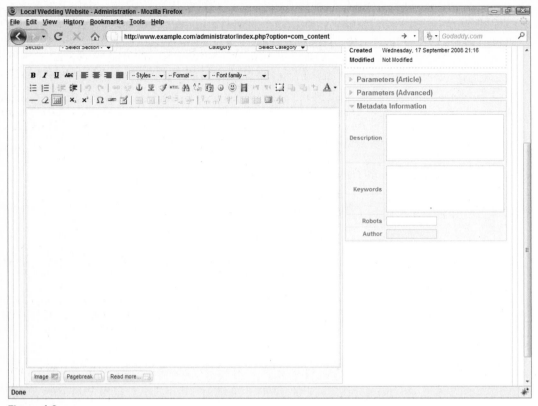

Figure 4-9

Setting	Definition
Author	This is the author of the article. This defaults to the user account id of the person who originally creates the article, but you can change this value if the actual author is a different user.
Author Alias	The author alias can be used to display a different name for the author other than the name associated with his or her user account. This can be especially useful if the author does not have a user account for your site.
Access Level	This is the level of access that a user must have to be able to access this article. Public means anyone can access it. Registered means anyone with a user account can access it. Special means anyone with author level access or above can access the article.
Created Date	This is the actual date and time that the article is created. It is automatically set to the date and time that the article is first saved, but this value can be overridden here.

Setting	Definition
Start Publishing	This is the date and time to start publishing the article. This is useful if you have time-sensitive material that can only be published starting on a specific date. This is optional, and by default it will be the same as the Created Date.
Finish Publishing	This is the date and time to finish publishing the article. This is useful if you have time-sensitive material that can only be published up to a specific date. This is optional, and by default it is set to Never, which means there is no end date to when the article is published.

The advanced parameters are shown in the following table.

Setting	Definition
Show Title	This sets whether to show the article title on the article layout page.
Title Linkable	This sets whether the title will link to the full text of the article from a blog layout.
Intro Text	This is used to show or hide the introductory text in the article layout. This is useful if you want to use the introductory text as an excerpt of the article in a blog layout, but hide the text when you are in the article layout.
Section Name	This sets whether to show the name of the section to which the article belongs. The section name is usually displayed just below the article title.
Section Title Linkable	This sets whether the section name links to the page on the site that is a blog or list/table layout of the articles in this article's section.
Category Title	This sets whether to show the name of the category to which the article belongs. The category name is usually displayed just below the article title.
Category Title Linkable	This sets whether the category name links to the page on the site that is a blog or list/table layout of the articles in this article's category.
Article Rating	This enables or disables the built-in article rating system for the article.
Author Name	This sets whether to display the author's name along with the article.
Created Date and Time	This sets whether to display the created date and time along with the article.
Modified Date and Time	This sets whether to display the date and time of the last time the article was modified along with the article.
PDF Icon	This sets whether to display the PDF icon with the article. The PDF icon links to the system that automatically generates a PDF file of the content of the article.

(continued)

(continued)

Setting	Definition
Print Icon	This sets whether to display the print icon with the article. The print icon links to a printer-friendly page from which the visitor can easily print the article.
E-mail Icon	This sets whether to display the e-mail icon with the article. The e-mail icon links to a form from which the visitor can e-mail a link to the article to his or her friends.
Content Language	This sets the language in which the article is written. This is necessary only if the language is different from the default language of the site.
Key Reference	This is a keyword by which the article can be referenced.

The following table contains the metadata information.

Setting	Definition
Description	This is the description that will be used in the meta tags in the `<head>` area of your site.
Keywords	This is the set of keywords that will be used in the meta tags in the `<head>` area of your site.
Robots	This is the set of keywords for robots that will be used in the meta tags in the `<head>` area of your site. These keywords are used to tell search engine robots if they can or cannot index the content of the article, and if they can or cannot follow links from the page that the article is on.
Author	This is the name of the author that will be used in the meta tags in the `<head>` area of your site.

Uncategorized Articles

An uncategorized article is an article that has been categorized in the Uncategorized category. Say that five times fast. Joomla! 1.0 did not have the concept of uncategorized articles because it used something it called *static content items*. These are basically the same thing, but treating static content items as uncategorized articles is more in line with how the data is actually stored in the database.

Uncategorized articles are content items that do not fit into a hierarchy, but stand alone in and of themselves. For example, you might have a simple About Us page that doesn't really fit neatly into a category. In that case, you would just leave it as uncategorized. I have built entire sites with nothing but uncategorized articles because that structure made sense for those sites, but in many cases you will want to use these sparingly.

Creating an uncategorized article is exactly the same as creating a categorized article except that you categorize the article in the Uncategorized category. There, I've said it again. Hopefully it makes more sense to you now and is more than just a tongue twister.

Try It Out — Adding Sections, Categories, and Articles

Now that you know how to add sections, categories, and articles, take some time to add them to your site. Try to build the following structure on your site following these steps:

1. Create a new section titled **Animals**.

2. Set Published to Yes, and set the access level to Public. Let the system automatically generate an alias for you.

3. Create the categories **Dogs**, **Cats**, and **Dolphins**.

4. Set the section for each category to **Animals**.

5. Set Published to Yes for each category, and set the access level to Public. Again, let the system automatically generate an alias for you.

6. Create the articles "I Like Dogs" and "My Favorite Breed is the Lhasa Apso." Set the section to Animals and the category to Dogs for each of these articles. Set Published to Yes and Front Page to No. Be sure and add some content to each article. Try to add an image or two while you're at it.

7. Create the articles "I Don't Like Cats" and "My Friend's Cat Scratched Me When I was Thirteen." Set the section to Animals and the category to Cats for each of these articles. Set Published to Yes and Front Page to No. Be sure and add some content. Just for fun, take a break from reading about Joomla! and write a short story for the article, "My Friend's Cat Scratched Me When I was Thirteen." Come back when you're finished. The book will still be here.

8. Welcome back. Now that you're finished expressing yourself through prose, create the articles "Flipper was a Dolphin Who Lived in a World Full of Wonder" and "Killer Whales are in the Dolphin Family, and Other Things I Learned at Sea World." Set the section to Animals and the category to Dolphins for each of these articles. Set Published to Yes and Front Page to No. Be sure and add some content to each article.

Details of the Category and Article structure are shown in the following table.

Section	Category	Article
Animals	Dogs	I Like Dogs
		My Favorite Breed is the Lhasa Apso
	Cats	I Don't Like Cats
		My Friend's Cat Scratched Me When I was Thirteen
	Dolphins	Flipper was a Dolphin Who Lived in a World Full of Wonder
		Killer Whales are in the Dolphin Family, and Other Things I Learned at Sea World

How It Works

Joomla! has a very rigid content structure, and as such, it is necessary to follow a certain order when you create content. Before you can create your categories, you must first create a section in which those categories can reside. After you have created your categories, you can then move on to creating articles for those categories.

You could always create all of your articles as uncategorized articles, and then add them to sections and categories after you've finished writing all of the articles. There is technically nothing wrong with this approach, but it is a lot easier to put an article in a section and category when it is written rather than adding it to a section and category later.

Planning Your Content

Now that you know how to add content to your site, don't do it. Not yet anyway. Joomla! makes adding articles so easy, it can be tough to resist the temptation to act like a kid in a candy store and start adding articles all over the place. Don't be that person. You're better than that. In this section, you learn why planning your content is important and how to plan your content for the purpose of your site. You also learn how to plan your content to fit into Joomla!'s content structure. Some people might categorize this practice as "information architecture." I just call it a common-sense approach to developing a website.

Why Is Planning Important?

As you learned earlier in this chapter, Joomla!'s content hierarchy is somewhat rigid, and it's important to tailor your content to fit into that architecture, or determine whether you need to take a different approach to organizing your content than Joomla! offers.

The design of your site should be based upon the structure of your content and not the other way around. Everything from the menu structure, which you learn about in Chapter 5, to the design of your template is based on how you structure your content. Once you start adding content and building menus and designing templates, it's very time-consuming to go back and re-do everything because you suddenly realize that your content structure doesn't make any sense. Take a little extra time at the beginning of your project to do some proper planning, and you will save yourself a lot of time and a lot of headaches later on in the project.

Planning for Purpose

Every website should have a purpose. Whatever your site's purpose is, you need to have a clear understanding of what you want to communicate and plan your content structure accordingly. It's common sense, but you'd be surprised how often this gets overlooked. This approach has a lot less to do with actual web design than it does with creating a marketing plan or business plan.

For example, if you are building a site as a personal blog, you probably don't need a lot of sections, but you do need some categories for your blog posts and a couple of uncategorized articles for things like the obligatory About Me page and your Pictures of My Dog Rufus page. Or, if you are building a newspaper site, you will likely need several sections like Local, Politics, Sports, and Weather, and within those sections you would need some categories. In the Sports section, for example, you might need categories like Football, Baseball, Basketball, Hockey, and Tennis, just to name a few.

If you want to build a simple brochure-style site that basically tells a little bit about your product or company, you might need only one uncategorized article. In that case, Joomla! might be overkill for your project, but if you chose to use Joomla! to "future-proof" your site, you certainly wouldn't want to waste time building a section and category for one article.

Never lose sight of the purpose of your website, and take the time to plan your content according to that purpose. You will be glad you spent the time developing the right structure in order that you can more effectively communicate what you want to communicate with your site.

For example, I created a site called HowToJoomla.net, which contains tips, tricks and tutorials for building sites with Joomla!. Before I wrote my first article, I set out the purpose of the site, which was to share instructional information about Joomla!. To that end, I created the following content structure:

- ❏ How-Tos (Section)
  - ❏ Installation (Category)
  - ❏ Components (Category)
  - ❏ Modules (Category)
  - ❏ Templates (Category)
  - ❏ Mambots/Plugins (Category)
  - ❏ Content Management (Category)
  - ❏ Menu Management (Category)
  - ❏ User Management (Category)
  - ❏ Miscellaneous (Category)
  - ❏ Links (Uncategorized Article)
  - ❏ Disclaimer (Uncategorized Article)

The purpose of the site is simple, so the content structure is simple. There was no need to build an elaborately woven web of sections and categories when the purpose of the site only called for a section and a few categories. Keeping the content structure simple makes the site easy to navigate and easy to read.

How Does Your Plan Fit into Joomla!'s Content Architecture?

Joomla!'s content architecture is rigid. The hierarchy consists of sections, categories, and articles. Each article belongs to one category, and each category belongs to one section. If your content structure does not fit into this architecture, you have some decisions to make. You can either adapt your planned content structure or make some compromises, find third-party components to help you accomplish the structure you are planning, or (and I know this may sound like heresy) consider using a different CMS that will handle your planned structure out-of-the-box.

Consider a newspaper site. I broke down the Sports section earlier into a few categories, but the reality is that there would probably be nested categories (categories within categories), and Joomla!'s architecture does not allow for this out of the box. For example, within Football, you might have the categories High School Football, College Football, and Professional Football.

In this case, it's decision time. One compromise would be that perhaps you don't need to categorize your football-related stories down to that level and just go with one all-encompassing Football category. Another option would be to use a third-party component like Joomla! tags that enable you to add virtually unlimited keyword tags to an article allowing for infinite levels of categorization. The last option would be to scrap Joomla! altogether and go with another CMS that can handle unlimited nested categories.

Content for the Sample Site

As you learned in the Introduction of the book, you will be building a sample website to accompany the content of this book to help illustrate what you are learning. The sample website is a local wedding-related website that serves as a community of brides, grooms, and local wedding vendors. The purpose of the site's content is three-fold: share expert tips and advice to local brides and grooms; present information about the site; and share news related to the local wedding industry.

The following table shows the content for the sample wedding website.

Section	Category	Article
Expert Tips	Ceremony	Which music is right for your wedding ceremony?
		How to incorporate all of your little nieces and nephews into your ceremony
	Fashion	Wedding dress dos and don'ts
		How to pick a bridesmaid dress that won't make your bridesmaids hate you
	Reception	How to decide what type of food to serve at your reception
		Should you have live music or a DJ?
Uncategorized	Uncategorized	About Us
		Sponsors
		Privacy Policy
		Terms & Conditions
News	Recent Weddings	Joanie and Chachi
		Fred and Wilma
		Jim and Pam

Section	Category	Article
	Vendor News	ABC Catering hires a new chef
		XYZ Photography offers 2 for 1 prints for the month of October
		Local church damaged in fire, cancels all scheduled weddings for three weeks

Summary

Managing content in Joomla! comes down to understanding three basic elements: sections, categories, and articles. Once you have a firm grasp on adding and modifying these elements and moving them around, you have a solid understanding of setting up content within Joomla!'s content structure.

Joomla! makes managing content easy, but as you learned in this chapter, proper planning can help you avoid some of the pitfalls of being overly eager to add content to your site. Your site has a purpose, and you should plan your content according to that purpose while trying to keep in line with Joomla!'s content architecture.

Now that you know how to manage content in Joomla!, in the next chapter you learn how to manage menus. First, take a few moments and work the following exercises. You can find the answers to these exercises in Appendix A.

Exercises

1. How many categories can an article belong to at one time?

2. Describe two ways to move a category from one section to another.

3. Say "Categorize the article in the uncategorized category" five times fast, and then create an uncategorized article.

4. What are three options if your planned content structure does not fit into Joomla!'s content architecture? Can you think of any more options?

Managing Menus

Menus form the main navigation of any Joomla!-powered website. They influence not only how your visitors locate content on your site, but they also help determine which component gets loaded for a particular page, where and when modules are published throughout your site, which template is used for a particular page, and which parameters are active for a particular component on a specific page.

In Joomla!, you can have one menu or hundreds of menus, depending on the needs of your site. Like your content structure, you should plan your menu structure carefully. Creating a proper menu structure is like creating a site map for your website, because your menus and menu items determine how the site is structured. In this chapter you learn how to create menus and menu items.

Creating Menus

In Joomla!, you must have at least one menu and at least one menu item within that menu. All access to the site is based on what the menu items tell Joomla! to load, so there is no way to avoid having menus. OK, maybe there is a way, but this book is called "Beginning Joomla!," not "Crazy Joomla! That Even Advanced Joomla! Users Shouldn't Try." Menus are displayed in modules, so it is possible to have a menu that is not visible to your site's visitors by simply disabling the modules that are used to display that menu. The most important thing is that the menu exists in the back end of the site to determine how your site is organized.

Because you need at least one menu and one menu item, the kind-hearted members of the core team have kind-heartedly made it so that installing Joomla! automatically installs one menu called Main Menu and one menu item within Main Menu called Home even if you do not install the sample content. In this section, you learn how to create new menus in Joomla!, as well as how you should name your menus.

How Should I Name My Menus?

Technically, you can name your menus any way you want to name them, but you should always name your menus in a way that is descriptive of the purpose of each particular menu. For example, the main menu of your site should be called something like Main Menu. A menu with tools for registered users should be called something like User Menu.

As you learn in Appendix B, installing Joomla! automatically creates a menu called Main Menu, and if you install the sample content, a menu called User Menu is installed that contains tools for registered users. You might also want to name a menu based on its visible location on the page; for example, Top Menu, Side Menu, or Footer Menu. Note that you don't have to use the word Menu in your menu's name, and the name you give your menu will not necessarily be displayed on the site.

The bottom line is that you should name your menus in such a way that their names make sense to you and anyone else working on your site. As long as your naming convention is understood by you and the other people working with you to manage your site, you can name your menus whatever you want to name them.

Try It Out   Creating a Menu

To create a menu in Joomla!:

1. Access the menu manager by clicking Menus ➪ Menu Manager from your administrator control panel as shown in Figure 5-1.

2. In the menu manager toolbar, as shown in Figure 5-2, click the New button to open the Menu [New] form, which you can see in Figure 5-3.

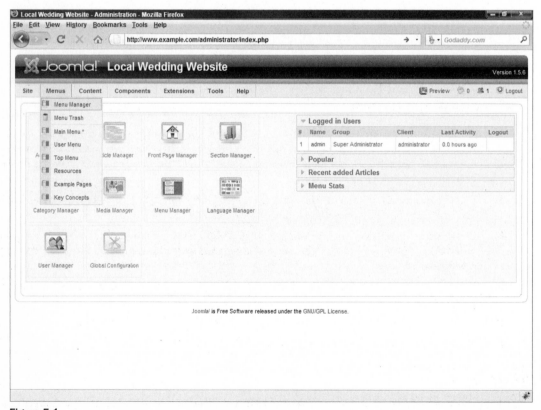

Figure 5-1

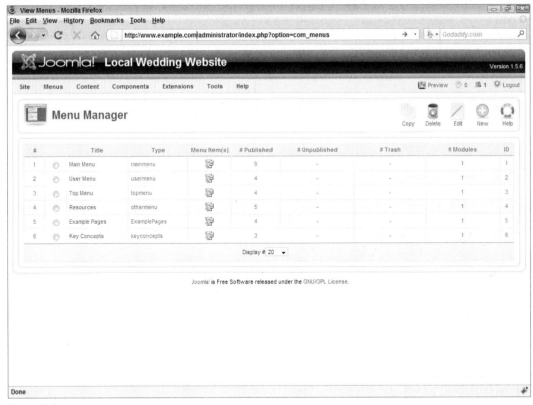

Figure 5-2

As you can see in Figure 5-2, several menus are already set up in the menu manager. These menus are the ones that are automatically set up if you choose to install the sample data when you install Joomla!. Obviously, these menus are not there if you do not install the sample data when you install Joomla!.

3. Enter a unique name for your menu in the Unique Name field. Do not use spaces or special characters in your unique name. Only use numbers and letters.

4. Enter a title for your menu in the Title field. This field does not have the same restrictions, so you can use spaces and special characters, although you should use special characters only if you absolutely have to.

5. Enter a description for your menu. This can be just a short sentence describing the purpose of the menu.

6. Enter a title for the module that is automatically created to display your menu.

7. Click Save to save your new menu and return to the menu manager.

How It Works

In Figure 5-3, you can see that you must fill out four fields to create a new form: Unique Name, Title, Description, and Module Title.

Figure 5-3

The Unique Name field is only used to identify each menu from within Joomla!'s code, so you can name this whatever you want to name it as long as it is different than all of the other menus' unique names. It is recommended that you do not have any spaces or special characters in the unique names, and that you just stick to letters and numbers. A common practice is to simply take the spaces and special characters out of the menu's title and use that for the unique name.

The Title is simply the title of the menu. This is the value you see in the Menus drop-down that you can see in Figure 5-1. It is a good idea to make this descriptive of the purpose or position of the menu, as you have already learned.

The Description is simply a way to describe the purpose of the menu. Honestly, I'm not sure what the purpose of this field is because it is not used anywhere on the site other than in this form. I usually just copy my menu's title into the Description field.

The Module Title is the title of the menu module that is automatically created to display your new menu. You learned about the menu module in Chapter 2, and it is used to display your menu to your site's visitors. When you configure your menu module, you can choose whether or not the Module Title is displayed, and you can change the Module Title at any time. It is important that you give your Module Title an appropriate value for being displayed on your site. This is usually the same as your menu's title, but it does not have to be.

Once you have entered these four values, click the Save button in the toolbar to save your new menu. You will then be returned to your menu manager and see your new menu added to the list. You can also go to your module manager to see the new module that has been created. You learn more about the module manager in Chapter 6. Now that you have created a new menu, it is time to add some menu items to your menu.

Creating Menu Items

Each menu can have one menu item or hundreds of menu items. A menu item is a link or a placeholder in your menu that performs a specific, predefined function. A menu item can be almost anything, depending on the components that are installed on your site. It can be an external link to a web page on a different site, a link to a content item, category, or section, a link to a component or a specific part of a component, a separator or placeholder, a link to a link, and the list goes on and on.

In this section you learn how to create a menu item. You also learn about some of the many menu item types, menu item parameters, the default menu item, and menu item IDs.

Try It Out   **Creating a Menu Item**

To create a menu item:

1.   Navigate to the menu item manager, shown in Figure 5-4, for the menu in which you want to create the menu item.

Figure 5-4

2. Click the New button in the Menu Item Manager toolbar, as shown in Figure 5-4.

3. Select a menu item type on the screen shown in Figure 5-5.

Figure 5-5

4. Click the menu item type to open the new menu item form. For the purposes of explanation, take a closer look at the Section Blog Layout menu item type. You can see the form in Figure 5-6.

5. Enter a title for your new menu item. This title can be anything you want it to be, but keep in mind how a long or short title would look within your menu as it is displayed on the page. The title is a mandatory field.

6. Enter an alias. This is not a mandatory field, but if you do not add an alias the system will automatically generate one.

7. Unless you are creating an external link menu item, you do not need to enter a link. If you are creating an external link, enter that link in the Link field.

8. Select the parent menu item. If you want this menu item to be at the top level of this menu's hierarchy, just leave Top selected.

9. Set Published to Yes if you want to publish the menu item, or set it to No if you do not want to publish the menu item.

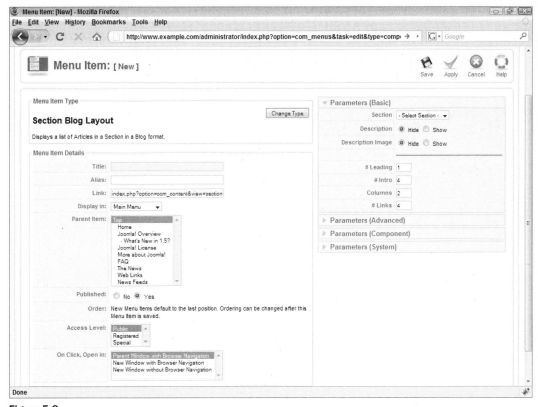

Figure 5-6

10. Select the access level for the menu item. Select Public if you want to allow anyone to view the menu item, Registered if you only want users who are logged in to be able to see the menu item, and Special if you want only users with Author level access or above to be able to see the menu item.

11. Select how you want the menu item to open the page that it links to when the user clicks the item. By default, the menu item will open in the same window, but you can choose to open the menu item in a new window with or without browser navigation.

12. Set the menu item's parameters to your desired settings. Each menu item type has different parameters.

13. Click Save in the toolbar to save your new menu item and return to the Menu Item Manager.

How It Works

Four different groups of menu item types exist: Internal Link, External Link, Separator, and Alias. Internal Links are links to components or specific parts of components installed on your site. External Links are links to web pages usually outside of your site (for example, http://www.google.com), although it is possible to use this to link to a page in your site. Separators are used to add a line of separation between one menu item and another. The separator can be any text you choose, but is usually something like "|" so that your menu can render like this: link 1 | link 2 | link 3. An alias is a copy of an already existing menu item in your site. The purpose of this is so that the alias takes on all of the properties and the ID of the existing menu item, so if you ever change the menu item, the alias takes on those changes.

Internal Links

Internal links are links to components or specific parts (called "views") of components. To see the available views for a particular component, click the Internal Link menu item type category. That will expand the category to display the available views if there are any. A standard Joomla! installation has the following Internal Link categories:

❑ **Articles** — This contains menu item types that link to specific views in the core content component. These views are an Archived Article List, an Article Layout, an Article Submission Layout, a Category Blog Layout, a Category List Layout, a Front Page Blog Layout, a Section Blog Layout, and a Section Layout.

❑ **Contacts** — This contains menu item types that link to views in the core contact component. These views are the Contact Category Layout and the Standard Contact Layout.

❑ **News Feeds** — This contains menu item types that link to views in the core news feeds component. The views are the Category List Layout, the Category Layout, and the Single Feed Layout.

❑ **Polls** — This contains only one menu item type, which is the Poll Layout.

❑ **Search** — This contains only one menu item type, which is the Search view. This view displays both the search form and search results if a search term is submitted.

❑ **User** — This contains menu item types that link to views in the user component. The views are the Default Login Layout, the Default Registration Layout, the Default Remind Layout (for reminding the user of his or her username), the Default Reset Layout (for allowing the user to reset his or her password and have the new password sent to the e-mail address on record), the Default User Layout, and the User Form Layout (for modifying the user's account information).

❑ **Web Links** — This contains menu item types that link to views in the core web links component. The views are the Web Link Category List Layout (a list of Web Link categories), the Category List Layout (a single Web Link category and its list of web links), and the Web Links Submission Layout (for allowing registered users to submit web links).

❑ **Wrapper** — This contains one menu item type, which is the Wrapper view. The Wrapper view "wraps" an external site within your Joomla! site by loading it in an iframe.

Each time you install a new component, a new Internal Link type category is added to the list. The developers of third-party components determine what view types appear in this list and the options and parameters available for a view.

After you have selected which type of menu item you are creating, you are not locked into that particular menu item type. You can change menu item types by clicking the Change Types button. This returns you to the menu item types selection screen you saw in Figure 5-5. You can change the menu item type of any menu item at any time. The main advantage of changing the menu item type over simply deleting the menu item and creating a new one is that you maintain a consistent menu item ID.

Menu Item Details

Once you have committed to a menu item type, it's time to start filling out the menu item details. In the left column, a box labeled Menu Item Details contains all of the detail fields. A list of these fields along with an explanation of each field is in the following table.

Field	Description
Title	This is the visible portion of your menu item. It is the word or words that a visitor will click to navigate to the menu item link. This should be short but descriptive of the content that it links to. An example would be something like Home, Contact Us, or About Us.
Alias	This field is primarily used for SEF URLs. A common practice is to use the title without spaces. For example, you might use something like home, contact-us, or about-us. When Joomla! automatically generates SEF URLs, it uses the alias to determine the URLs, like `http://www.yoursite.com/contact-us.html`.
Link	This is the actual link that this menu item creates minus a few parameters. This value is automatically set, and you couldn't change it even if you wanted to.
Display in	This is the menu where you want to display the menu item.
Parent Item	Each menu item can have a parent menu item and multiple child menu items. This allows for creating nested menu items, which helps establish your site's content hierarchy. Nested menu items are displayed along with parent menu items in the menu module if the module is set to display nested menu items. The way that these menu items are displayed depends on the settings for the module that displays the menu and the CSS styles that you or your template applies to the menu's HTML markup.
Published	This sets whether or not the menu item is published to your site.
Order	This is the order in which your menu item is displayed in the menu. For a new menu item, you can't set the order, so don't even try it.
Access Level	This sets who is allowed to access this menu item: Public (anyone), Registered (anyone logged in with a user account), or Special (anyone logged in with at least "Author" level access to the site) users. You learned about access levels in Chapter 1.
On Click, Open in	This sets where the menu item is opened when a user clicks it: in the same window, in a pop-up window with regular browser navigation, or in a pop-up window without browser navigation. For an internal link, it is *almost always* a good idea to set it to open in the same window. You might open an internal link in a pop-up window if you are displaying a small form, or a small bit of information that does not require all of the page modules and styles, but it is usually a good idea to keep it all in the same window. You are more likely to use one of the pop-up window options with external links, because with external links your users are navigating away from your site. (Opening the link in a pop-up window keeps your site active in the current window.)

Menu Item Parameters

Once you have filled in your menu item details, you fill in the menu item parameters. As you can see in the right column in Figure 5-6, there are *usually* (but not always) four sets of parameters: Basic, Advanced, Component, and System. A third-party component developer can add as many parameter sets as he or she deems necessary to support the functionality of the component.

The Basic parameters are different for each component, and are usually parameters that must be set in order for the view to work properly. The basic parameters for the Section Blog Layout are listed in the following table.

Parameter	Description
Section	This is the section whose categories and articles are displayed in the view.
Description	This determines whether or not to display the section's description in the view.
Description Image	This determines whether or not to display the section's image in the view along with the description.
# Leading	This sets the number of leading article introductions to display in the view. Leading article introductions can be set apart in the site's template and displayed differently than regular article introductions.
# Intro	This determines the number of non-leading article introductions to display in the view.
Columns	This determines the number of columns to use to display the non-leading article introductions. Leading article introductions are displayed in one column by default, but this can be overridden in the template. Template overrides are covered in more detail in Chapter 8.
# Links	This determines the number of article title links to be displayed at the end of the view. These links are displayed as a list after all of the leading and non-leading article introductions are displayed.

The Advanced parameters are also different for each component. These are used for applying advanced settings to the view to allow for things like changing the order in which articles are displayed. The advanced parameters for the Section Blog Layout are listed in the following table.

Parameter	Description
Category Order	This determines the order in which categories are displayed in the section if you choose to order your articles by category. By default, articles are not ordered by category but by the Primary Order parameter.
Primary Order	This is the order in which articles are displayed in the view, unless the articles are displayed by category. For blogs, a common setting for this parameter is "Most recent first," and this is the default setting for this parameter.
Pagination	This is used to determine whether linked page numbers are used if and when the number of articles in the section exceeds the number of leading, introduction, and links set to display per page in the Basic parameters.

Parameter	Description
Pagination Results	This is used to tell Joomla! whether or not to display the current page number and the total number of pages in the section.
Show a Feed Link	This is used to tell Joomla! whether or not to show a feed link in the head of your site along with the metadata. Showing a feed link enables browsers like Firefox to display a feed icon in the browser bar so your visitors can subscribe to your RSS feed from the browser. You learn more about RSS syndication in Chapter 7.

The Component parameters are usually the same as the parameters you can set in the component's configuration. You learned about configuring the content component and other components in Chapter 4. The Component parameters can be set in the menu item to override the component's global configuration.

The System parameters are the same for every component. These parameters are listed in the following table.

Parameter	Description
Page Title	This is used only if you intend for the page title to be different from the menu item title. It determines the title that will be displayed as the browser title and in the page if the component displays page titles.
Show Page Title	This is used to set whether or not the page title will be displayed on the page. Not all components display page titles, so this is not always necessary. The content component does display page titles, so for the Section Blog Layout example, you need to set whether or not you want the page title to be displayed.
Page Class Suffix	Page Class Suffix is used to add a suffix to certain CSS classes in HTML tags on the page. This can be used to give a custom look to different pages on the site. Menu Image is used to set an image to be displayed next to the menu item title in the menu.
Menu Image	This sets an image to be displayed along with the menu item in the menu.
SSL Enabled	SSL Enabled is used to set whether or not SSL (Secure Socket Layer) is to be enabled for this menu item. SSL typically means that the URL begins with `https://` instead of `http://` and that your server is using a secure connection for the page. You should use this option only if you have a proper security certificate for your site, and if your hosting service supports SSL.
	The three options for this parameter are Off, Ignore, and On. If you set it to Off, you are explicitly turning off SSL for this menu item if it was previously enabled in a different menu item. If you set it to Ignore, the SSL state of this menu item will be whatever the SSL state of the site is when the menu item is clicked. If you set it to On, you are explicitly turning on SSL for this menu item.
	If you are unsure of how SSL works, leave it set to Ignore.

Save Your New Menu Item

Once you save your new menu item, you will be returned to the menu item manager for your menu, where you have the option to re-order its menu items, move menu items to a different menu, edit, publish, or trash menu items, or set the default menu item.

The Default Menu Item

The default menu item is the menu item of the component view that is the first thing a visitor sees when he or she visits your site at www.yoursite.com. This is a new concept in Joomla! 1.5. In version 1.0, the default menu item could only be the first menu item in the Main Menu. This provided little flexibility because you had to have a link to your home page in the Main Menu, even if you wanted to arrange your menus differently.

When you install Joomla!, the default menu item is a link to the Front Page Blog Layout of the content component, which is why that view is called Front Page Blog Layout instead of something more descriptive of what it actually is, like Multi-Section Blog Layout, but I digress. This convention goes back to the early days before Joomla!. Fortunately, it gives you the option to change this by setting a new default menu item. The default menu item is the menu item that contains a star icon in the Default column of the menu item manager, as shown in Figure 5-7.

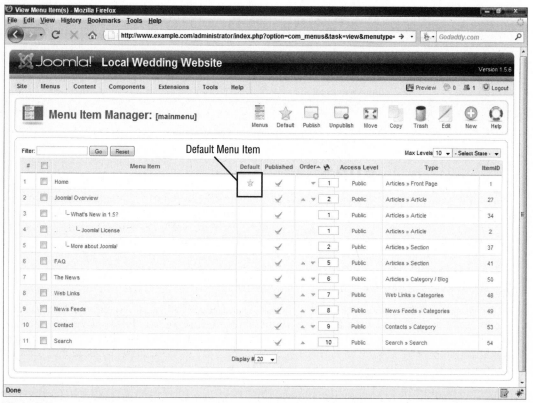

Figure 5-7

Try It Out   Changing the Default Menu Item

To change the default menu item:

1. Navigate to the Menu Item Manager of the menu that contains the menu you wish to make the default menu item.

2. Check the box for the item you want to make the default menu item.

3. Click the Default button in the toolbar of the Menu Item Manager, as shown in Figure 5-7.

How It Works

By simply selecting a menu item and clicking the Default button, you can change which menu item acts as the default menu item. Making this change sets a menu item as the page that is displayed whenever a user visits your site at www.yoursite.com.

Menu Item IDs — The Life Blood of Your Joomla! Site

Each menu item has a unique ID in the database, commonly referred to as the Item ID. This ID is perhaps the most important piece of information on any page in your site. The Item ID is always passed through the URL (even SEF URLs, even though you can't see it), and it helps Joomla! determine a number of things that could not be determined without it.

The Item ID tells Joomla! which menu item is currently active on the site, which tells it which menu items to highlight and which menu item parameters to load in the active view. It also tells Joomla! which modules to display on the site because each module can be set to display for all menu items or for a select few specific menu items.

Displaying Menus

You can display menus on your site in a number of ways. Some templates have built-in menu systems to display your menus. Several third-party menu modules are available that you can use to display a custom-styled menu, although these are arguably obsolete thanks to the flexibility of the menu module in Joomla! 1.5, which is the primary way that menus are displayed in a Joomla! site.

The Menu Module

In Chapter 6, you learn about the Module Manager and how to add, edit, enable, disable, and delete modules. Although this topic is skipping ahead slightly, you learn about the menu module in this section because it is relevant to how menus are displayed in your site. To access the menu module, you first must access the Module Manager. To do this, navigate to Extensions ⇨ Module Manager in the Administrator menu.

The menu module is a core module that offers four ways to render your menus in your site's HTML: List, Legacy – Vertical, Legacy – Horizontal, and Legacy – Flat List. The List style is the newest format, and it is the one that is recommended because it renders your menu in proper XHTML format and according to web accessibility standards. You can see the module editor for the menu module in Figure 5-8.

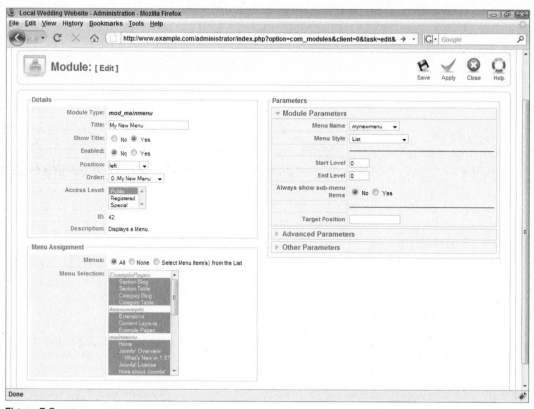

Figure 5-8

In the left column in Figure 5-8, you can see the module details and menu assignments. These are the same for all modules, and you learn about this in Chapter 6. In the right column are the Module Parameters, Advanced Parameters, and Other Parameters. This is where you set the details for how the menu module is displayed. In this section you take a brief look at the Module Parameters, but I will not go into detail on the Advanced Parameters and the Other Parameters.

The Module Parameters are Menu Name, Menu Style, Start Level, End Level, Always show sub-menu items, and Target Position. Menu Name is the name of the menu you wish to display, and you can select the menu name from a drop-down list of all available menus. The Menu Style is where you decide how you want to display the menu: List, Legacy – Vertical, Legacy – Horizontal, or Legacy – Flat List. The recommended setting here is List. You can see an example of a menu module using the List style in Figure 5-9. The List style renders the menu as an unordered list like this:

```
<ul class="menu">

    <li class="item1">
```

```
<a href="menuitemlink">

    <span>Item 1</span>

</a>

</li>

...
</ul>
```

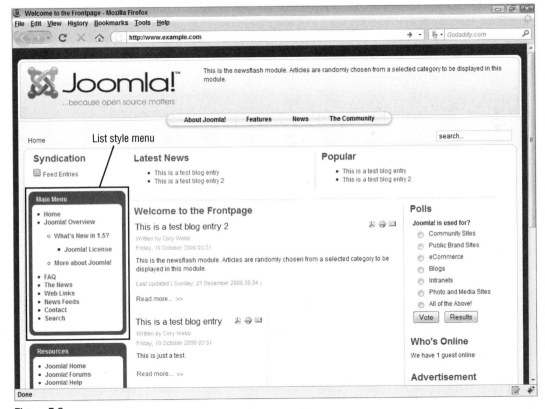

Figure 5-9

The Start and End Level are useful if you have nested menu items. You can choose to show only a certain range of levels in the menu item hierarchy. Always show sub-menu items is used to determine whether or not sub-menu items are displayed for each nested menu item on every page. Target Position is used to set JavaScript window position parameters if any of your menu items are set to open in a new window.

Menus for the Sample Site

The sample site for this book is a wedding-related site that serves as a community of brides, grooms, and local wedding vendors. For now, you will only have a Main Menu, an Expert Tips Menu for the Expert Tips content section created in Chapter 4, and a News Menu for the News content section created in Chapter 4. You add more menus in later chapters as you add third-party components to the site. For the Main Menu, you should add the menu items shown in the following tables.

Sample Site Main Menu Items

Menu Title	Menu Item Type
Home	Articles → Front Page Blog Layout
About Us	Articles → Article Layout
Expert Tips	Articles → Section Blog Layout
News	Articles → Section Blog Layout

Sample Site Expert Tips Menu Items

Menu Title	Menu Item Type
Ceremony	Articles → Category Blog Layout
Fashion	Articles → Category Blog Layout

Sample Site News Menu Items

Menu Title	Menu Item Type
Recent Weddings	Articles → Category Blog Layout
Vendor News	Articles → Category Blog Layout

Summary

Menus are the primary source of navigation for your site. You should take the time to carefully plan and execute your menus because they directly affect the usability and consistency of your site. Creating a menu in Joomla! involves first creating the actual menu, and then creating menu items to be contained within the menu. Menus can be displayed on your site in a number of ways, but the primary way that menus are displayed is through the menu module.

Now that you know how to manage menus in Joomla!, it is time to learn about extending Joomla! with components, modules, plugins, templates, and languages. First, take a few moments to complete the following exercises. You can find the answers to these exercises in Appendix A.

Exercises

1. Is it possible to build a Joomla! site without any menus?

2. What is the "Unique Name" field used for in a menu?

3. What is the default menu item?

4. Name three things that the Item ID is used for.

Extending Joomla!

Out of the box, Joomla! is a powerful, feature-rich web CMS that can be used to build a great website with a lot of functionality with very little effort. However, Joomla! doesn't do everything, nor should it. If they tried to build every possible function into the Joomla! core, the size of the Joomla! installation package would be too big for any web host to handle. That is why the geniuses behind Joomla! and its predecessor, Mambo, decided to make the system extensible.

An extensible system is one that allows and enables the installation of third-party software (called extensions) to extend the functionality of the system or add new functionality. The most common example of an extensible system is an operating system (OS) like Microsoft Windows or Mac OSX. At the risk of oversimplifying what an OS is, it is basically a set of tools that makes it easier for software developers to build applications (extensions) that interact with the computer's hardware using a common interface. Another example of an extensible system is the popular web browser, Firefox. Firefox has an Application Programming Interface (API) that enables software developers to build add-ons (extensions) that enhance the way Firefox users are able to interact with the web beyond simple web browsing. Joomla!, at its core, is basically a platform for enabling software developers to build extensions that bring new and custom functionality to your website.

Every website is different and has a unique purpose. For that reason, not every website needs every possible functionality. An extensible system like Joomla! enables the webmaster (that's you) to tailor his or her website to suit the specific needs of the site.

Joomla! 1.5 has five different types of extensions: components, modules, plugins, templates, and languages. You learned the definitions of each of these in Chapter 1, and in this chapter you learn more about each type of extension. You also learn about some of the most popular extensions available for Joomla! and where you can find other third-party extensions for yourself.

Extensions! What Are They Good For? Absolutely Everything!

One of the most common questions I get asked is "Can Joomla! do (fill in the blank)?" No matter what they ask, my answer is almost always "Yes, if ... " Because Joomla!'s framework is so powerful, you can extend its functionality to do almost anything you want it to do. Three "ifs" go along with my answer to the question of whether or not Joomla! can perform a certain function:

❑ **An extension already exists to perform that function.** Most of the time, this is the case. Literally thousands of third-party extensions are available for Joomla! that perform just about any function you can imagine. If you cannot find an extension to perform the specific function you need, chances are you can find one that comes close, and you can modify the code to suit your specific needs.

❑ **You have the time and skill to build a custom extension to perform that function.** If you cannot find a pre-built extension, you could always build it yourself. The only limitations are time, skill, and creativity.

❑ **You have the time and budget to hire someone who has the skill to build a custom extension to perform that function.** You may have plenty of time, but lack the skill to build a custom extension. In that case, many developers are available who will gladly build your custom extension for a fee.

With an extensible framework like Joomla!, you can accomplish anything as long as an extension already exists that does what you need, or if you have the time and skill or time and budget to develop a custom extension to do what you need it to do. In this section, you learn how to make use of existing extensions on your site.

Figure 6-1

Installing Extensions

Extensions come pre-packaged as a compressed (.zip, .tar, .tar.gz, and so on) set of files called an installation package. The installation package has everything needed to easily install your extension. In Joomla! 1.5, the developers have introduced the concept of a single installer for each extension type, so there is only one place you need to go to install all five types of extensions, which you can see in Figure 6-1. To access the extension installer, log in to your site administrator and click Extensions ➪ Install/Uninstall in the main menu.

You have three ways to install an extension for the installer: uploading your installation package file, installing the extension from a directory on your server, or installing the extension from a URL. Technically there is a fourth option, which is to manually install an extension. However, it is highly unlikely that you will ever need to do this, and that method is well beyond the scope of a beginner-level book.

Uploading Your Installation Package File

The primary method of installing extensions in Joomla! is by uploading an installation package file. It is likely that you will only use this method of extension installation because it is the most common method.

Try It Out   Uploading Your Installation Package File

To upload your installation package file:

1. Make sure the file is available on your computer in an easy-to-find location.

2. If you have not enabled the FTP layer, which you learned about in Chapter 2, you need to make sure the proper permissions are set on these folders:

    ❑   /tmp

    ❑   /components

    ❑   /administrator/components

    ❑   /language/en-GB

    ❑   /administrator/language/en-GB

    ❑   /modules

    ❑   /plugins

    ❑   /templates

    The permissions must be set so that the web server user on the server can write to them. A permissions setting of 757 will suffice. For security best practices, it is a good idea to set the permissions back so that these directories are unwritable after you have installed your extensions.

3. In the extension installer, shown in Figure 6-1, click the Browse button, which opens a file browser window so that you can search your hard drive for your installation package.

4. Once you have found the necessary file, click Open and then click the Upload File & Install button.

How It Works

Each installation package comes with an extension manifest file, which is an XML file that lists the contents of the installation package and tells Joomla! what type of extension you are installing. Joomla! uses this file to determine where to load the extension's files, and it performs any other installation steps that need to take place like creating database tables. All you have to do is upload the package. Joomla! takes care of the rest.

Installing from a Directory

It is possible (but not likely) that you may be unable to upload and install an extension through the upload method. For example, if an extension installation is larger than the allowed size for file uploads in your server's PHP settings, you will not be able to install that extension by uploading it through the installer. In that case, another option is to install the extension from a directory on your server.

Try It Out   **Installing an Extension from a Directory**

To install an extension from a directory on your server:

1. Extract the files from your installation package using a file extractor.
2. Using FTP, upload all of the files from the installation package to the /tmp directory on your server.
3. Type the path to the directory relative to the root of the server in the box labeled Install Directory as shown in Figure 6-1.
4. Click the Install button.

How It Works

The most common directory from which to install an extension is the /tmp directory because this is the temporary directory to which Joomla! uploads and extracts files while preparing to install extensions. You will note that Joomla! already has the path to the /tmp directory entered into this Install Directory box shown in Figure 6-1. Just like with the upload method, all you do is tell Joomla! where to find the installation files and click the Install button, and Joomla! takes care of the rest.

Installing from a URL

The third installation option is to install an extension from a URL. This enables you to install extensions from external servers. It works almost exactly like the upload option except that instead of uploading an installation package to your server, you tell your server where an installation package exists on the web, and the server fetches the file for you. For example, you may keep all of your installation packages on a remote server for use on multiple sites. To install an extension from a URL, you simply enter the direct URL to your installation package (for example, http://www.yourinstallationserver.com/extensionpackage.zip) and click the Install button.

Components

As you learned in Chapter 1, *components* are applications that are built upon the Joomla! framework. You can think of them as programs that run on the Joomla! operating system (although, technically, Joomla! is not an operating system). Thousands of components are available to do almost anything you can think of — social networking components, directory components, forum components, photo gallery components — the list goes on and on.

Once a component is installed, you can access it through the Components menu in the main menu in your Joomla! administrator so that you can manage the component's configuration and data. To make the component visible and usable on the front end of the site, you need to create a menu item of that component's type, which you learned how to do in Chapter 5. You also have other optional configuration parameters in the component's menu item.

Modules

As you also learned in Chapter 1, a *module* further extends your Joomla! site by performing side functions outside of the component. Modules can be used to perform just about any task you can think of. They are typically used to display menus, lists, banners, and other little tidbits of content. I like to think of modules as being like little widgets that perform a simple, specific, necessary task that cannot be handled efficiently by components. Modules are often packaged with a component to give you more options for integrating a component's data into the rest of the site and template layout. The module provides a way to position an interface to a component anywhere on the site.

As you learned in Chapter 1, modules are displayed in module positions, which are set in the site's template, which you learn more about in Chapter 8. You can display a module on every page of your site, or you can pick and choose which pages display a particular module using the module manager. You can also determine the order in which modules are displayed in a specific module position using the module manager.

To manage your modules, you click Extensions ➪ Module Manager in your Joomla! administrator, and that will open the module manager as shown in Figure 6-2. From the module manager, you can enable, disable, copy, delete, reorder, add, or edit a module. Adding a module is different from installing a module because you are simply adding a new instance of a module that has already been installed. You'll notice in the module manager there is a menu that says Site ➪ Administrator, which is there so that you can manage modules for the front end of the site (Site) or the back end of the site (Administrator).

Enabling/Disabling Modules

Enabling and disabling a module simply instructs Joomla! whether or not you want a particular module to be visible on your site. You can enable or disable a module in three ways.

Try It Out   Enabling/Disabling a Module

To enable a module:

1. Navigate to the module manager shown in Figure 6-2.
2. Find a module that is disabled. Look for an icon in the Enabled column of the module manager that is a red circle with a white x.

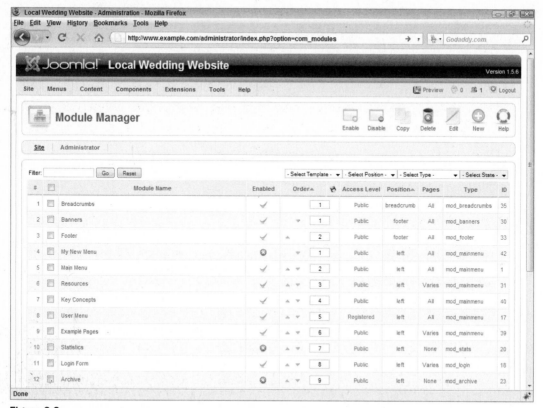

Figure 6-2

3. Click the icon that is a red circle with a white x in the row of the module that you wish to enable.

To disable a module:

1. If you are not already there, navigate to the module manager shown in Figure 6-2.

2. Find a module that is enabled. Look for an icon in the Enabled column of the module manager that is a green check.

3. Click the icon that is a green check.

How It Works

The easiest method of enabling and disabling a module is to click the green check icon or the red circle with a white x icon, which will toggle the state of the module between enabled and disabled. Another method is to check the box or boxes next to the modules you wish to enable or disable, and click the Enable or Disable button in the toolbar. This method is most useful if you intend to enable or disable several modules at one time. The third method is to click the module title or check the box and click the Edit button in the toolbar to open the module editor and change the Enabled parameter to Yes or No.

Copying and Deleting Modules

To copy a module or multiple modules, check the box or boxes next to the module or modules you wish to copy, and click the Copy button. This can be very useful if you are using a module for multiple purposes, and you need multiple instances of the same module. Although multiple instances of a module use the same code for rendering purposes, they can display different data depending on how you set their parameters. For example, you may have two instances of a latest news module on the same page, but one instance could display headlines from one category while the other instance displays headlines from a different category.

To delete a module or multiple modules, check the box or boxes next to the module or modules you wish to delete, and click the Delete button. Deleting a module does not uninstall the module. It simply removes the selected instance of that module from the site.

Reordering Modules

Joomla! allows you to change the order in which modules are displayed in a particular module position. You can see an example of this in Figures 6-3 and 6-4. Note the Order column in Figure 6-3, and then compare the order of the modules to the order in which they are displayed in the left position in Figure 6-4.

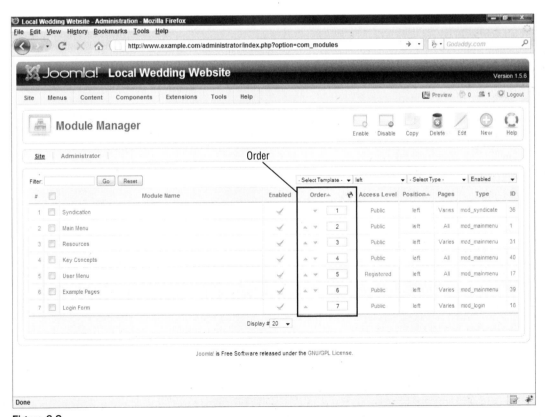

Figure 6-3

Figure 6-4

You can reorder modules in three ways:

❑ Click the up or down green arrows in the Order column of the module manager. This method is the most useful if you just need to switch a couple of modules.

❑ Change the order numbers in the boxes in the Order column. This method is the most useful if you need to rearrange several modules. Once you have changed the numbers, click the Save icon next to the Order column header.

❑ You should understand a couple of things about the order numbers. Due to some potential inconsistencies caused when modules are added or deleted, the order numbers are not always neatly ordered 1, 2, 3, 4, and so on. You will occasionally find that some numbers are skipped and some numbers are repeated. Joomla! will still order based on the lowest number appearing first and the highest number appearing last. Also, if you change the order number of one module so that it is equal to the order number of another module in the same position, the module you change will take on the order number, and the other module's order number and the order number of each subsequent module in that position will be incremented by one.

❑ Click the module title or check the box and click the Edit button in the toolbar to open the module editor and change the Order parameter. This method is really only useful if you are already in the module editor.

Adding and Editing Modules

Adding and editing modules is done through an interface that is very similar to the one used in creating a new menu item on a menu, which you learned about in Chapter 5.

Try It Out   **Adding a Module**

To add a module:

1. Click the New button in the module manager toolbar, as shown in Figure 6-2.

2. Once you have clicked the New button, you will be taken to the Module [New] screen as shown in Figure 6-5.

On this screen, you need to select the type of module you wish to add. The list of module types on this screen is based on the modules that are installed on the system. To select a module type, click the module type name or select the radio button next to the name.

3. Click the Next button in the toolbar. This will take you to the module editor, as shown in Figure 6-6. From this point on, adding a module is exactly the same as editing a module.

4. Enter a title for your module.

5. Set Show Title to Yes if you wish to display the module's title, and set it to No if you do not wish to display the title.

6. Set Enabled to Yes if you wish to display the module, and set it to No if you do not wish to display the module.

Figure 6-5

7. Select the module position in which you wish to display the module. The module position's actual location on the page is determined by the site's template, which you learn about in Chapter 8. The default position is left for new modules if you do not change this parameter.

8. New modules are automatically last in the order for the selected position, so setting the Order parameter is irrelevant for new modules.

9. Under Menu Assignment, select All to display the module on every page of your site; select None to prevent the module from displaying on any page of your site (the same effect as disabling the module), and select Select Menu Item(s) from the List if you want to pick and choose the pages on which to display the module.

10. If you chose Select Menu Item(s) from the List in the previous step, hold the control key while you select all of the menu items on which you wish to display the module from the Menu Selection list.

11. Set the module parameters so that the module works how you need it to work.

12. If you are creating a Custom HTML module, enter your Custom Output.

13. Click Save in the toolbar.

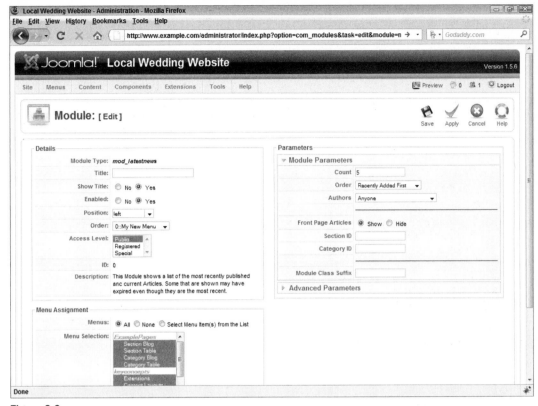

Figure 6-6

How It Works

Like adding a menu item, adding a module first requires that you select the type of module that you are adding. However, unlike with menu items, you cannot change a module's type after you have already created the module. After you select the type of module you are creating, you then enter all of the module's details in the module editor.

In Figure 6-6, you can see that the left column of the menu editor contains the module Details and the Menu Assignment for the module, and the right column contains the module's Parameters. The parameters are different for each module, so we will not cover module parameters in this section. However, you learned about the menu module's parameters in Chapter 5.

The following list tells you what the Module Details settings mean:

❑   **Module Type:** You can't change this value once it has been set, and it was set on the Module [New] screen in Figure 6-5.

❑   **Title:** Here is where you enter the title of the module.

❑ **Show Title:** Sets whether the module title is displayed on the site if the selected module position is set up to display titles.

❑ **Enabled:** Sets whether or not the module will be visible on the site.

❑ **Position:** Sets the position in the template in which the module will be displayed. The position is often named based on its physical location on the page (for example, left, right, top, and so on), but this is not always the case. Be sure you know where each module position is displayed in your template when choosing a position for your module. You learn more about module positions in templates in Chapter 8.

❑ **Order:** Sets the order in which the module will be displayed on the site.

❑ **Access Level:** Sets which groups are allowed to see the module if it is enabled on the site.

❑ **ID:** This parameter is automatically set and can't be changed.

❑ **Description:** Enter information included in the module by its creator to tell you the purpose of the module.

The Menu Assignment section is used to determine on which pages your module will be displayed. You can:

❑ Select All to display the module on every page of the site.

❑ Select None to display the module on none of the pages, which is the same as disabling the module.

❑ Select Select Menu Item(s) from the List, if you want to select specific pages on which to display the module.

The pages in the Menu Selection list are automatically listed based on the published menu items you have created for your site. They are grouped by menu, so you can see a logical grouping of menu items when making your selections.

Once you have set your module details and menu assignment, click the Save or the Apply button in the toolbar to save your module. Clicking Save will save your module and return you to the module manager, and clicking Apply will save your changes and keep the module editor active so you can make more changes if necessary.

Plugins

In Chapter 1, you learned that plugins have a variety of uses, but they typically perform a specific function to extend the functionality of a component. In programming terms, plugins are essentially event handlers that perform a specific task or tasks at predefined event triggers throughout the system. The framework itself triggers several events, and the core content, search, and user components trigger plugin events specific to those components.

Enabling, disabling, and editing plugins all take place through the plugin manager, which you can access via Extensions ➪ Plugin Manager in the administrator of your site. Enabling, disabling, and reordering plugins work exactly the same way as enabling, disabling, and reordering modules. Reordering plugins sets the order in which the plugin is triggered by an event.

By default, eight different types of plugins are available: authentication, content, editors, editors-xtd, search, system, user, and xml-rpc. A new feature in Joomla! 1.5 enables third-party components to trigger their own events, so some third-party components may have their own plugin types.

❑   **Authentication:** Authentication plugins are used to enable different methods of authentication for Joomla!. Joomla! comes with four different types of authentication: Joomla! core authentication, LDAP authentication, OpenID authentication, and Gmail authentication.

❑   **Content:** Content plugins extend the functionality of the core content component. For example, there is a plugin called Content – Rating that enables a rating system for your articles. The rating plugin is triggered by the content component before content is displayed, and it automatically displays the current rating for a given article along with a form that enables the visitor to rate that article. To enable the rating plugin, you must first enable it in the plugin manager, and then you must enable it in the content configuration, which you learned about in Chapter 2. You can see an example of the rating plugin in Figure 6-7.

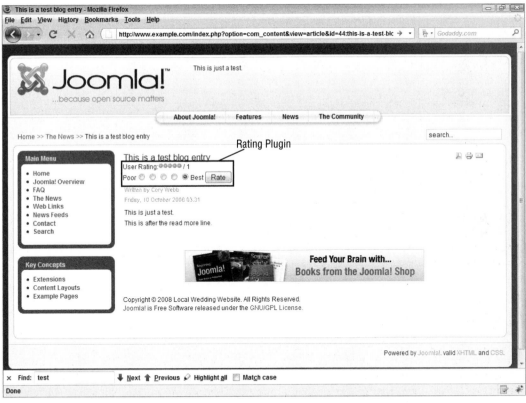

Figure 6-7

❑   **Editor:** Editor plugins are used to provide WYSIWYG editors for entering content. Joomla! comes with two WYSIWYG editor plugins and the No WYSIWYG Editor plugin. Several options are available for editors if you are not satisfied with the options that come pre-installed.

- ❑ **Editors-xtd:** Editor-xtd plugins are used to extend the functionality of content creation in the core content component. By default, three editor-xtd plugins are available: Image, Read more, and Pagebreak. The Image plugin adds a button labeled Image just beneath the article editor. Clicking the Image button pops up a window that enables you to search the default image directory for an image to insert in an article. The Read more plugin adds a button labeled Read more beneath the article editor that enables you to add one and only one Read more separator anywhere in the article. This separator splits the article between introductory text and the rest of the text. The Pagebreak plugin adds a button labeled Pagebreak, which enables you to split your articles into multiple pages by adding page breaks throughout the article. This is especially useful for long articles.

- ❑ **Search:** Search plugins are used to make components searchable by the core search component. Without search modules, Joomla! has no way of knowing how to search each third-party component installed in the system. Search plugins provide a standard method for third-party developers to make their components searchable by Joomla!'s core search component.

- ❑ **System:** System plugins perform functions that most people will not directly see the results of. They are used to make other tools available for making components, modules, and even other plugins more powerful.

- ❑ **User:** User plugins can be used to tie Joomla!'s user database to other systems. For example, the bridge between Joomla! and phpBB3 uses a user plugin.

- ❑ **XML-RPC:** XML-RPC plugins load APIs for use with the XML-RPC application. The XML-RPC application enables remote procedure calls (RPC) so that you can run procedures on your website from outside applications like desktop blogging tools.

Templates

As you also learned in Chapter 1, templates are used for providing a layout and design within which all of the pieces of your Joomla! site come together. A template consists of HTML, CSS, images, JavaScript (sometimes), and PHP code to tie everything together. You learn how to build a custom template in Chapter 8.

Languages

In Chapter 1, you read that Joomla! is a multilingual content management system, which means that the user interface can be translated into any language using custom language packs. Language extensions can be found for many different languages. A language extension cannot and should not translate your site's content. It is only used to translate the user interface of the system. If you want to have multiple translations of your content, you need to use a multilingual content component like JoomFish or Nooku.

Where Can I Find Extensions?

Thousands of extensions are available for Joomla!, and you need to know the best places to look in order to find them. Besides searching Google for "Joomla! Extensions," two main places where you can find almost any extension you can think of are the Joomla! Extension Directory (JED) and JoomlaCode.org:

- ❑ **Joomla! Extension Directory (JED):** The JED was created for the sole purpose of helping the Joomla! community easily find extensions. It is well organized into nested categories, so it is easy to dig through and find exactly what you are looking for. It also provides user ratings and comments, so you can see what other people think about an extension to help you decide whether or not to use it. You can find the JED at `extensions.joomla.org`.

❑ **JoomlaCode.org:** This site is a software development tool used by hundreds of developers to manage the development of their open source extensions. You can find hundreds of open source extensions for Joomla! at JoomlaCode.org, not to mention the Joomla! installation package itself.

Take a few moments to browse through the extensions available at the JED and JoomlaCode.org. You should have no trouble finding one or more extensions in these repositories that suit your needs.

Popular Extensions

Following is a list of some of the most popular Joomla! extensions with a brief description of what each extension does. You can find a larger list of popular extensions in Appendix C. The JED also provides a list of the most popular extensions based on their actual rating in the JED and the number of times they are visited in the directory, so that is a great place to find out what other people are using. It also provides editors' picks, which are the extensions that the editors feel stand out above the rest in terms of quality and usefulness.

Community Builder

Community Builder is a full-featured, extensible component that enables you to build a website with social networking features. This is the best user profile component available for Joomla!, and it's absolutely free! You can use this component to create something as complex as your own version of the popular social networking site, MySpace, or something as simple as an extended user profile for gathering information about your users. At the time of this writing, the Community Builder website has almost 200,000 registered users, making it one of the largest websites of any Joomla! extension. You can find out more about Community Builder at `www.joomlapolis.com`.

FireBoard

FireBoard is the most widely used message board (Forum) component available that is completely integrated into Joomla!. It has been downloaded more than 725,000 times from JoomlaCode.org, making it the fifth most downloaded extension on that site. Its only drawback is that it does not work natively with Joomla! 1.5, which means you have to enable legacy mode for the component to work. You can find out more about FireBoard at `www.bestofjoomla.com`.

NinjaXplorer

NinjaXplorer is the successor of the popular file management component, JoomlaXplorer. NinjaXplorer runs natively in Joomla! 1.5 without the need for the legacy plugin, and JoomlaXplorer does not. This component provides a way for you to manage files on your server through your Joomla! administrator. It can be used to add, edit, or delete files and folders. I often use it to make changes to my sites' templates. NinjaXplorer's predecessor, JoomlaXplorer, is listed as one of the most popular extensions in the JED. You can find out more about NinjaXplorer at `www.ninjaforge.com`.

JomComment

JomComment is the most popular commenting system available for Joomla!. It is commercially supported, which means it is not free, but it is well worth the price. With JomComment, you can enable your users to comment on any article on your site, which gives Joomla! much-needed functionality to make it useful as a blogging platform. JomComment is listed as one of the most popular extensions in the JED. You can find out more about JomComment at `www.azrul.com`.

Mosets Tree

Mosets Tree is a directory component that can be used to build a full-featured directory complete with ratings and comments. You can use it to create a local business directory or any other kind of directory you can think of. For example, the JED is powered by Mosets Tree. It is commercially supported like Jom-Comment, which means it also is not free. You can find out more about Mosets Tree at `www.mosets.com`.

Adding Extensions to Our Sample Site

As you have learned in previous chapters, throughout this book you will be building a sample site to support what you have learned. The sample site is a local wedding community website that caters to local brides, grooms, and wedding vendors. With that in mind, you need to consider the functionality you would like to achieve with the site and then choose your extensions based on the desired functionality. With so many extensions available for Joomla!, it is important to show restraint and use only those extensions you need to achieve the functionality you want to achieve.

Community Builder

For starters, you want to build a community. The first thing you need to install is Community Builder, so that members can have extended user profiles with photographs and information about themselves and their weddings. You can download the latest version of Community Builder from `www.joomlapolis.com`. At the time of this writing, the latest version is Community Builder 1.2 Release Candidate (RC) 4.

Try It Out   **Setting Up Community Builder**

To set up Community Builder:

1.   Download and install the component.

2.   Create a menu item to point to the Community Builder component's User Profile view, and set its title to **Community** and alias to **community**.

3.   Install the Community Builder custom login module.

4.   Publish the login module to the left module position on your site.

5.   Configure Community Builder in the administrator at Components ➪ Community Builder ➪ Configuration.

6.   Create a new tab in which to add extra fields. Call the new tab **Personal Information**. You can create a new tab at Components ➪ Community Builder ➪ Tab Management.

7. Create custom user profile fields in Community Builder at Components ⇨ Community Builder ⇨ Field Management. Add the following fields:

- ❏ About Me (Text Area)
- ❏ My Engagement Story (Text Area)
- ❏ About My Wedding (Text Area)
- ❏ Wedding Date (Date)

You should now be able to register a user account and access your user profile. You can see an example of what a user profile looks like on the sample site in Figure 6-8.

Figure 6-8

FireBoard

To add further community functionality, you need to add a way for members to interact with one another in a forum. The next component you need to add is FireBoard. Another added benefit of using FireBoard is that it has hooks that tie it in with Community Builder, which helps to provide a seamless user experience on the site. You can download the latest version of FireBoard at `http://joomlacode.org/gf/project/fireboard/frs/`. At the time of this writing, the latest version is FireBoard 1.0.5 RC2.

Try It Out **Setting Up FireBoard**

To set up FireBoard:

1. Enable the Legacy plugin in the plugin manager. The Legacy plugin is titled "System – Legacy."

2. Download and install the component.

3. Create a menu item to point to the FireBoard component, and set its title to **Forum** and alias to **forum**.

4. Navigate to the Fireboard Control Panel at Components ⇨ FireBoard Forum as shown in Figure 6-9.

Figure 6-9

5. In the FireBoard Control Panel, click the FireBoard Configuration button to configure FireBoard the way you want it. Under Avatar Integration, set Use Avatar Picture From to Community Builder, and under Profile Settings, be sure to set Profile to Community Builder.

6. In the FireBoard Control Panel, click the Forum Administration button to begin adding forums. A good practice to follow for a new message board is to keep it simple and avoid creating too many forums. For this message board, create the following forums and sub-forums:

❑   Wedding Talk

❑   Wedding Talk ⇨ Ceremony

❑   Wedding Talk ⇨ Fashion

❑   Wedding Talk ⇨ Reception

❑   Wedding Talk ⇨ Miscellaneous

These forums and sub-forums will give your visitors a place to discuss weddings and wedding planning. As your forum grows, you can get a feel for what your users are discussing and create new forums and sub-forums to facilitate those discussions.

How It Works

FireBoard is a full-featured forum component built specifically for Joomla, so it is tightly integrated with Joomla!'s user and template system, and it is easy to install and easy to set up. Setting the avatar and profile information to Community Builder will ensure that the user's avatar and profile information are all handled by Community Builder and not FireBoard's own built-in avatar and profile information. Starting with a small number of forums concentrates the discussions in those areas, and it helps to give the appearance of more activity in the forums.

MyBlog and JomComment

Another feature for a good community website is blogging. To provide a way for each user to have his or her own blog, you cannot rely on the core content component because it does not have that level of access control. For that reason, you need a third-party component to handle user blogs. Azrul.com, the makers of JomComment, has a blogging component called MyBlog that you will use to enable users to have their own blogs. You will also use JomComment to enable commenting on blog posts. Both components are commercially supported, so you will have to pay for them, but this is the best and easiest way to add blogging functionality to the site. You can see a list of other alternatives in Appendix C. You can purchase and download MyBlog and JomComment from Azrul.com.

Try It Out   **Setting Up MyBlog and JomComment**

To set up MyBlog:

1. Download and install MyBlog.
2. Create a menu item to point to MyBlog, and set its title to **Blogs** and its alias to **blogs**.
3. Navigate to the MyBlog Control Panel, shown in Figure 6-10, at Components ⇨ My Blog.
4. Click General Settings in the Admin Panel on the left side of the screen to edit MyBlog's configuration. Under the Workflow tab on the configuration screen, be sure and check the box that says "Integration with JomComment" so that the blogs will work with JomComment after it is installed and set up.

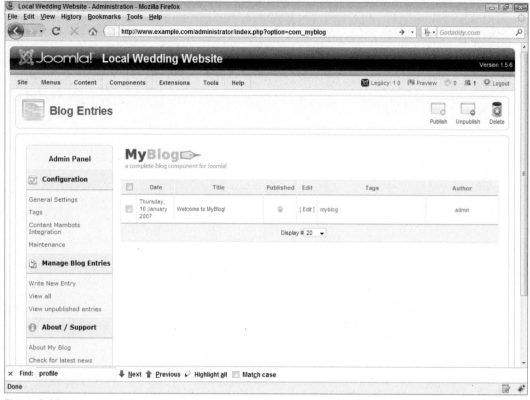

Figure 6-10

How It Works

MyBlog makes it easy for users on your site to create and share blogs. When you install MyBlog, it automatically creates a content section and a content category, both titled MyBlog. All new blog entries submitted through MyBlog are stored in the core content component's data table and posted to the MyBlog category. You can configure other content categories to accept MyBlog posts, but it is easier to restrict it to the MyBlog category, because the component has its own system of categorization called Tags. When you install MyBlog and link to it in a menu, users who are logged in will see a link on the Blogs page that enables them to manage their blog posts, write new blogs, and manage comments made on their posts.

Try It Out   Setting Up JomComment

To set up JomComment:

1.   Download and install JomComment.

2.   Navigate to the JomComment Control Panel, as shown in Figure 6-11, at Components ➪ JomComment.

3.   Click General Settings in the Admin Panel on the left side of the screen to edit JomComment's configuration.

Figure 6-11

How It Works

JomComment is both a component and a content plugin. The plugin is automatically installed along with the plugin. There is no need to create a menu item for JomComment because it was built to interact directly with other components like the content component. When you set up MyBlog, you enable integration with JomComment in the MyBlog configuration so that after JomComment is installed, it starts working with MyBlog automatically. JomComment adds another level of interactivity to your site by enabling users to comment on blog posts and articles on the site.

Mosets Tree

Finally, you need to have a directory of local vendors so that brides and grooms can have a one-stop location for finding information about local wedding vendors without having to dig through the phone book or query search engines. Mosets Tree will work well for this need because it not only gives you a directory, but it also enables brides and grooms to rate and comment on vendors listed in the directory and it enables vendors to "own" their listing, so they can modify it however they choose. As you learned earlier, Mosets is commercially supported, which means it is not a free component. Free directory components are available such as SOBI2, which you can find at www.sigsiu.net. You need to consider available features and ease of use before deciding which component to use, and price should not be the only determining factor in your decision unless you have philosophical disagreements with developing commercially supported components for a free and open source system like Joomla!. You can purchase and download Mosets Tree from Mosets.com.

Try It Out   Setting Up Mosets Tree

To set up Mosets Tree:

1. Download and install Mosets Tree.
2. Create a menu item to point to Mosets Tree, and set its title to **Directory** and its alias to **directory**.
3. Navigate to the Mosets Tree Control Panel, as shown in Figure 6-12, at Components ⇨ Mosets Tree.

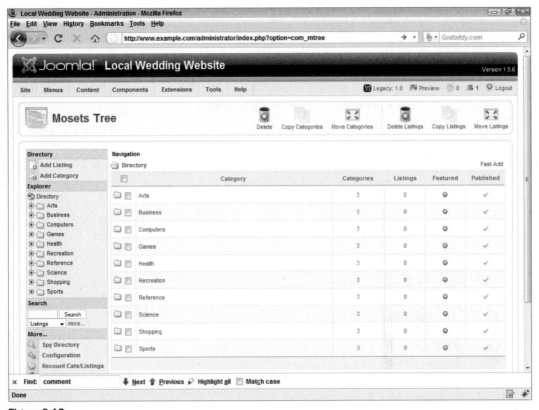

Figure 6-12

4. Delete all of the categories that are set up in Mosets Tree by default so that you can create categories that are specific to the site.
5. Click Configuration in the left side of the screen to edit Mosets Tree's configuration.
6. Add the following categories and sub-categories:
   ❑ Ceremony
   ❑ Ceremony ⇨ Music

- ❑   Ceremony ⇨ Flowers
- ❑   Ceremony ⇨ Venues
- ❑   Fashion
- ❑   Fashion ⇨ Bridal Gowns
- ❑   Fashion ⇨ Bridesmaids Dresses
- ❑   Fashion ⇨ Tuxedos
- ❑   Reception
- ❑   Reception ⇨ Music
- ❑   Reception ⇨ Caterers
- ❑   Reception ⇨ Venues

7.   Add listings to the categories.

How It Works

Mosets Tree is essentially a content management system within a content management system. The content managed by Mosets Tree is a set of directory listings organized into nested categories. The categories are laid out in a web directory format, as shown in Figure 6-13.

Figure 6-13

Summary

Joomla! is a powerful, feature-rich CMS with enough functionality built-in to enable you to build a high-quality, professional website, but sometimes you need more functionality than Joomla! can logistically provide out of the box. For that reason, Joomla! has a solid framework upon which developers can build extensions to extend the functionality of the core system.

Joomla! has five types of extensions: components, modules, plugins, templates, and languages. In this chapter you learned about each of the five types of extensions and how to manage them on your site. You also learned how to install extensions and where to go on the web to find extensions for Joomla!. This chapter also listed some of the most popular extensions, and discussed how extensions were selected for the book's sample site. Now that you know how to extend Joomla!, it's time to take a look at syndication in Joomla! 1.5. But first, take a few moments and complete the following exercises. You can find the solutions to these exercises in Appendix A.

Exercises

1.   What are the five types of extensions?

2.   Name two methods for installing extensions.

3.   Describe two methods for reordering modules.

4.   Go to the JED and find how many extensions are listed in the directory.

5.   Go to JoomlaCode.org and find out how many times Joomla! has been downloaded.

Syndication in Joomla! 1.5

Syndication is the process of automatically making your content viewable by third-party websites and/or applications. Many modern websites, weblogs, and web services syndicate their content by making it available in the form of a machine-readable text file in a standard XML format. Several format standards are used, but the most common is known as Really Simple Syndication (RSS).

Like with e-mail newsletters, the main purpose of RSS feeds is to increase traffic to your website by putting your site's content in front of as many people as possible. The benefits of syndication are numerous for both publishers (that's you) and consumers (that's visitors to your site). Using syndication, publishers can make their content available to a wider audience by giving their visitors options for how they consume the content available at the publishers' sites. As RSS readers grow in popularity, more and more of your site's visitors will want to have the ability to access your content from their RSS readers of choice. More than 2000 feed readers are currently available both as online services such as Google Reader, Netvibes, and Pageflakes, and as desktop applications like NewsGator and Firefox Live Bookmarks. Another advantage of syndication is that you also make it possible for other websites to spread your content by displaying your headlines on their site with links back to your site. Joomla! offers another benefit because it not only generates RSS feeds, but it can also parse RSS feeds and display their data, so if you have more than one site powered by Joomla!, you could syndicate content from one site to the other in order to help drive traffic between the sites.

Joomla! makes it not only possible, but also easy to syndicate your site's content so that your visitors can access your content from their favorite RSS readers and that other websites can display your headlines and help spread your content. In this chapter, you learn what can be syndicated in Joomla!. You also learn about some of the changes between syndication in Joomla! 1.0 and Joomla! 1.5. Then you learn how to set up syndication in your site. Finally, you take a look at a possible approach to syndication in our sample site.

What Can Be Syndicated in Joomla! 1.5?

For component developers, the Joomla! 1.5 framework provides tools for easily generating RSS feeds from the data generated through their components. Because these tools are available in the framework, literally any data can be syndicated in Joomla! 1.5, especially data that might be regularly updated like a blog. Imagine, for example, you run a site with classified ads. You could build a component that takes the key information from each classified ad and syndicates those details so that visitors are automatically updated whenever a new ad is submitted. This not only keeps your visitors informed, but it also drives traffic to your site as your visitors click the syndicated links to get more information about ads that might interest them. Although Joomla! makes it easy for third-party component developers to syndicate their components' data, it is up to the developers to take advantage of the tools available in Joomla! and offer an RSS feed. Joomla! does not automatically create a feed for them.

In Joomla! 1.5, three components offer syndicated feeds: content, contacts, and web links. Each component manages different types of data, so each component provides different types of data feeds. However, because Joomla! uses standard syndication formats like RSS, these feeds with different types of data can all be read with the same feed readers. In this section, you learn about how each of these components is syndicated and what data is part of the syndication feed.

Content

The content component syndicates articles within a section, a category, from the front page view, or all of the above, depending on how you set it up. The most common use of syndication for websites happens with the content component. For example, if you have a news or a blog section, you could syndicate those sections so that your readers can access them from their favorite feed readers.

Joomla! syndication classes generate a content feed with the following data:

- ❑ **Title:** The title of the page on which the section, category, or front page view is displayed.
- ❑ **Description:** The metadata description for the section, category, or front page view of the feed.
- ❑ **Link:** A link to the section, category, or front page view of the feed.
- ❑ **Last Build Date:** The last time the feed was generated by Joomla!. If you are not using caching for your feeds, the last build date will be the moment the user accessed the feed.
- ❑ **Generator:** The system that generated the feed, which is Joomla! 1.5.
- ❑ **Language:** The language in which the content in the feed is written.
- ❑ **Item(s):** The actual syndicated articles. Each item has the following data:
  - ❑ **Title:** The title of the article.
  - ❑ **Link:** A link to the article.
  - ❑ **Description:** The introductory text or the full text of the article depending on how you have it set up.
  - ❑ **Category:** This is one of three things: the word "frontpage" if the feed is from the front page view, the name of the section if the feed is from the section view, or the name of the category if the feed is from the category view.
  - ❑ **Pub Date:** The date the item was published.

Contacts

The contacts component organizes contacts into categories, much like the content component. With Joomla! 1.5, you can syndicate the contacts for each category, so every time a new contact is added to a category, those who are subscribed to the RSS feed for that category will get a notification in their feed readers.

Joomla! syndication classes generate a contacts feed with the following data:

- ❑ **Title:** The title of the page on which the contact category view is displayed.

- ❑ **Description:** The metadata description for the contact category page.

- ❑ **Link:** A link to the contact category page.

- ❑ **Last Build Date:** The last time the feed was generated by Joomla!. If you are not using caching for your feeds, the last build date will be the moment the user accessed the feed.

- ❑ **Generator:** The system that generated the feed, which is Joomla! 1.5.

- ❑ **Language:** The language in which the content in the feed is written.

- ❑ **Item(s):** The actual syndicated contacts from the category. Each item has the following data:

    - ❑ **Title:** The name of the contact.

    - ❑ **Link:** A link to the page with the contact's information.

    - ❑ **Description:** For each contact, there is an optional field called ''Miscellaneous Information.'' If you have entered data for this field, it will be included as the feed item's description.

    - ❑ **Category:** The name of the contacts category for which the feed is generated.

Unfortunately, the contacts feed does not give more specific contact information, so it is really only useful for presenting a name and miscellaneous information for each contact.

Web Links

The web links component organizes web links into categories like the content and contacts components. If you regularly add web links, and this is a feature that interests your visitors, you can syndicate links from a specific category so that your visitors can keep up with the links that you post to your site in their feed readers.

Joomla! syndication classes generate a web links feed with the following data:

- ❑ **Title:** The title of the page on which the web links category view is displayed.

- ❑ **Description:** The metadata description for the web links category page.

- ❑ **Link:** A link to the web links category page.

❑ **Last Build Date:** The last time the feed was generated by Joomla!. If you are not using caching for your feeds, the last build date will be the moment the user accessed the feed.

❑ **Generator:** The system that generated the feed, which is Joomla! 1.5.

❑ **Language:** The language in which the content in the feed is written.

❑ **Item(s):** The actual syndicated web links from the category. Each item has the following data:

   ❑ **Title:** The name of the web link.

   ❑ **Link:** A link to the web link, which redirects the visitor to the location to which the link points.

   ❑ **Description:** Each web link has an optional description field. If you enter a description for the link, it will be presented as the feed item's description.

   ❑ **Category:** The name of the page title from the menu item that links to the web links category or categories. It is not necessarily the name of the actual web link category.

The biggest drawback of web links syndication in Joomla! is that it does not drive traffic to your site, per se. It actually drives traffic to the sites to which you are linking via the web links component. The problem with this is that it defeats part of the purpose of syndicating your content, which is ultimately to drive traffic to your site.

Changes from Joomla! 1.0

Joomla! has always offered some level of syndication, even in version 1.0. However, Joomla! 1.0's syndication was extremely limited compared to that of Joomla! 1.5. Joomla! 1.0 only syndicated articles published to the front page of the site. If you wanted any other type of syndication, you had to use a third-party syndication tool to build custom feeds.

Joomla! 1.5 still offers syndication of articles published to the front page component, but it goes much further than version 1.0. For starters, Joomla! 1.5 introduces a syndication framework that makes it easier for core and third-party developers to incorporate syndication into their components in a standard way. Not only that, but it also offers section and category syndication in the content component as well as syndication for the contacts and web links components, which you learned about in the previous section.

Content Section Syndication

Content section syndication is simply syndication of all published articles from a specific content section. This is particularly useful because if you want to have a separate feed for separate sections, you can now do that in Joomla! 1.5. For example, if you have a news section and a blog section on your site, you might want to segregate the feeds for those sections because the content in each might be unrelated to each other. In version 1.0, you were limited to only one feed for articles published to the front page of the site.

Content Category Syndication

Content category syndication is just like content section syndication except that instead of generating feeds for specific sections, you can go one step further and create feeds for specific categories. Let's say, for example, that you have a newspaper site with several news categories like sports, local news, politics, and so on. Your visitors who are interested in the sports news might not necessarily be interested in subscribing to a news feed that contains sports and political news. They might want to subscribe to a feed with only sports news. With Joomla! 1.0, you could not have that level of granularity in your news feeds because the only feed available was the front page feed.

Component Syndication

With Joomla!'s new framework in version 1.5, component data syndication becomes very easy for core and third-party developers to implement. Because of this new framework, the core developers who built the contacts and web links components have included syndication of the data from those components. These components, although available in version 1.0, did not have the option to generate data feeds, and the framework making it easier for third-party developers to syndicate the data from their components was not available.

Setting Up Syndication

Now that you know about some of the benefits of syndication and how Joomla! 1.5 implements syndication in its framework and its components, it's time to take a look at how to set up syndication in your own site. You have basically two ways to set up syndication in Joomla!: set the display feed links for the menu item of the component for which you want to generate a news feed, or publish a "syndicate" module on the pages of the components for which you want to generate a feed. In this section, you learn how to use both of these methods for setting up syndication in your site.

Once you know how to set up feeds in your site, a common practice is to use a service like FeedBurner to manage and distribute your feeds. In this section, you also learn how to use FeedBurner for your news feeds and the benefits of using a service like FeedBurner.

Feed Links

Most of the newer web browsers can detect if a feed is available on a particular page based on a line of HTML markup entered into the header of the HTML document. That line of code would look something like this:

```
<link href="index.php?format=feed&amp; type=rss" rel="alternate"
type="application/rss+xml" title="RSS 2.0" />
```

After detecting that a page has a feed link in its header, the browser then displays a feed icon. For example, Firefox displays a feed icon in the address bar as shown in Figure 7-1. By clicking this icon, your visitors gain access to the feed and have the option to subscribe to that feed either through the browser or through their feed reader of choice.

Figure 7-1

Fortunately, you do not have to worry about the details of the specific HTML markup, because Joomla! handles that for you. All you have to do is enable it.

Setting Up Feed Links for the Front Page Blog Layout

To set up feed links for the front page blog layout:

1. Navigate to the menu item manager for the Main Menu as shown in Figure 7-2. As you learned in Chapter 5, you can access the menu in the administrator under Menus ⇨ Main Menu.

2. Click the default menu item to open the Menu Item form for that item.

3. In the right column under Parameters (Advanced), make sure Show a Feed Link is set to Yes.

How It Works

The Show a Feed Link parameter is set to Yes by default, so you really do not have to do anything to turn on the feed link. All you have to do is create a menu item to point to the front page blog layout, a category blog or list layout, a section blog or list layout, a contact category layout, or a web links category or category list layout. If you do not wish to have a feed for one of those particular items, you simply set Show a Feed Link to No.

Figure 7-2

The Syndicate Module

The second option for setting up syndication is to use the syndicate module to display links to your feeds in a module position. The syndicate module is automated, meaning very little configuration is necessary.

Try It Out   **Adding the Syndicate Module to Your Site**

To publish the syndicate module:

1. Access the module manager at Extensions ➪ Module Manager, which you learned how to do in Chapter 6.

2. Then, in the module manager, click the New button in the toolbar, which you can see in Figure 6-2.

3. Then, on the new module screen, as shown in Figure 7-3, you select the syndicate module from the list to create a new syndicate module. Once you have selected to create a syndicate module, the module editor for your new module is displayed, as shown in Figure 7-3.

4. Enter a title for the module. For this example, you can just enter **Syndication** as the title.

5. Set Show Title to No and set Enabled to Yes.

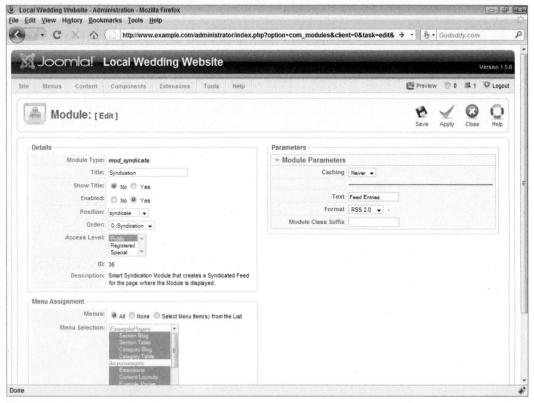

Figure 7-3

6. Select a module position in which to display this module.

7. Under Menu Assignment, select the option labeled Select Menu Item(s) from the List, and then choose the menu items on which you wish to publish the module. For now, just publish it to the front page, which currently is the Home menu item in the Main Menu.

8. In the parameters in the right column, set Text to Feed Entries, and set Format to RSS 2.0.

9. Click Save in the toolbar to save the module and return to the module manager.

How It Works

For this module, you need to pay careful attention to the Menu Assignment, which, as you learned in Chapter 6, is where you choose which pages (menu items) have this module published. The most important step in the configuration is making sure that you publish the module only on pages where you want a link to the pages' feeds to be generated. For example, if you want a feed to the front page view, you would publish the module to a module position on the front page. The module then automatically detects the fact that it is on the front page blog layout, and it generates a link to the feed for articles published to the front page. Whenever a visitor hits the front page, the syndicate module will display a feed icon and some text indicating that it is a link to a news feed.

If the syndicate module does not appear on the page where you want to see the feed link, you need to make sure that you have assigned it to the appropriate menu item. If you assign it to a menu item for a component view that does not have a data feed, the module title will appear on that page, but not the feed links.

The two important parameters in terms of displaying your feed are Text and Format. Text is what is displayed along with the feed icon in the module. You can see an example of this in Figure 7-4. Format is the feed's XML format standard that is used for the feed itself. The two options are RSS 2.0 and Atom 1.0. As you learned at the beginning of this chapter, RSS stands for Really Simple Syndication, and it is just one of the possible news/data feed formats available. Atom is simply an alternative to RSS, but it basically performs the same function of providing a standard method for sharing data feeds.

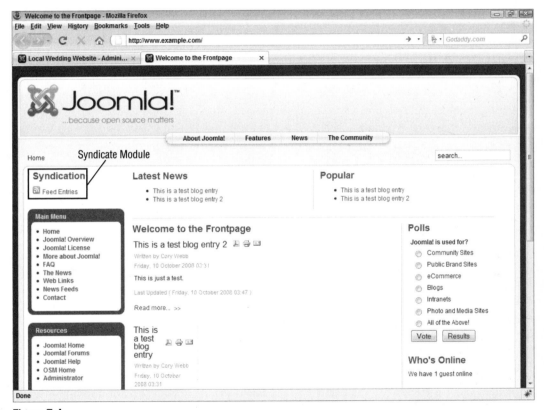

Figure 7-4

You now have a working RSS feed for the articles listed in your front page blog layout. In Figure 7-4, the phrase "Feed Entries" is a hyperlink to your RSS feed, and you can copy that link and use it as you integrate your RSS feed with the third-party service, FeedBurner.

Further Configuration

If you navigate in your administrator to the article manager and click the Parameters button as shown in Figure 7-7, you will pull up the content component parameters as seen in Figure 7-8. One of the parameters is "For each feed item show," and the options are Intro Text and Full Text. If you select Intro Text, only the introductory text of each article will be displayed in the news feed. If you select Full Text, the complete text from each article will be displayed in the news feed. Some feed readers can also shorten the amount of text that is actually displayed from each item. A good practice is to test your feed in a couple of different readers to determine the best settings to use for your feed. There are good arguments for and against each option, so my only recommendation is that you select the option that best fits with what you want to accomplish with your website. See Figure 7-5 for an example of a feed syndicated from a Joomla!-powered website being read in Google Reader.

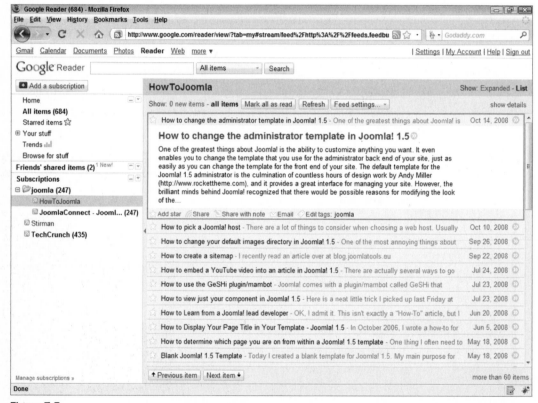

Figure 7-5

Integrating with FeedBurner

Now that you have a link to the news feed for the front page blog layout, you can use that link to integrate your feed with a third-party feed management and distribution service. Several services are available for managing and distributing data feeds, and one of the most popular services is called FeedBurner, which you can find at www.feedburner.com. FeedBurner takes a simple data feed and adds a number of services to it that make it a more feature-rich feed both in terms of subscription options and tools for managing your feeds and measuring their success.

Some of the tools offered by FeedBurner include subscriber statistics, e-mail subscriptions, update notifications to major blog portals and search engines, and many more features. Best of all, these features are absolutely free. FeedBurner has many more features, too numerous to be listed here because that is outside of the scope of this book. Whenever I build a site that has news feeds, I always use FeedBurner because it gives me so many more tools than a simple feed generated by Joomla!.

Setting Up FeedBurner

FeedBurner gives you a new feed URL for sharing your feed with your visitors. This URL will replace the URL automatically generated by Joomla!, but you still need Joomla!'s feed URL in order to tell Feed-Burner where your feed is generated and the contents of the feed.

Try It Out   **Setting Up FeedBurner**

To set up FeedBurner:

1. The first step is to set up your feed in Joomla! like you learned to do earlier in this chapter.

2. Next, set up an account at `www.feedburner.com`. You will be taken to your new account screen as shown in Figure 7-6.

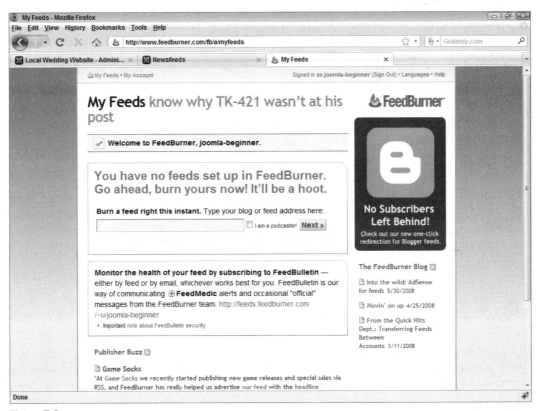

Figure 7-6

3. Go back to your site, and copy the Joomla! feed URL. This URL can be copied from the Feed Entries link shown in Figure 7-4. Your Joomla! feed URL might look something like this:

```
http://www.yoursite.com/index.php?format=feed&type=rss
```

4. Then, return to your FeedBurner account screen and paste your URL in the box where it says "Burn a feed right this instant. Type your blog or feed address here:."

5. Click the Next button.

   Once you have clicked the Next button, your feed is instantly added to the FeedBurner system.

6. On the next screen, you need to activate your feed.

How It Works

Once you have gone through these steps, FeedBurner gives you a new Feed URL that will look something like this:

```
http://feeds.feedburner.com/myfeedtitle
```

This URL is all you need to integrate FeedBurner into your site. This is as far as we will go with explaining the tools available in FeedBurner, and I encourage you to take a look for yourself and see what tools would be beneficial for your site.

Replacing the Joomla! Feed Link with the FeedBurner Link

Now that you have a FeedBurner URL, it's time to replace the Joomla! feed link, which you set up previously in this chapter, with the FeedBurner link as what your visitors see. The Joomla! feed link is still active so that it can share that information with FeedBurner, but you only want your visitors to see the FeedBurner link. You only want them subscribing to your feed through FeedBurner so that you can get accurate statistics for the number of subscribers to your feed.

Try It Out   Replacing the Joomla! Feed Link with the FeedBurner Link

To replace the Joomla! feed link with the FeedBurner link:

1. The first step is to remove any Joomla! feed link front-end display on your site. You will recall from the beginning of this chapter that you displayed the feed URL in your site in two ways: feed links and the syndicate module.

2. To remove the feed links, first you need to go to each menu item where you set Show a Feed Link to Yes, and set it to No so that the feed links will not automatically be displayed.

3. To remove the syndicate module(s), go to the module manager and locate all instances of the syndicate module. Check the box next to each syndicate module to select the module(s), and click either Disable to keep the module(s) but disable it from displaying, or Delete to simply remove the module(s).

4. The next step is to add the FeedBurner link in the locations where you removed the Joomla! feed URL. It is best to add both a feed link and a module to display a link to the feed.

5. You have several ways to add a feed link, but the simplest way is to hard code it into the template. To do this, you need to make a slight modification to the template's `index.php` file, which you can find at `www.yoursite.com/templates/your-template/index.php`. In between the `<head>` and `</head>` tags, you need to add the following line:

```
<link href="http://feeds.feedburner.com/myfeedtitle" rel="alternate"
 type="application/rss+xml" title="Your Feed Title" />
```

Remember to use your FeedBurner URL, not `http://feeds.feedburner.com/myfeedtitle`. Otherwise, you will be very disappointed with the results.

6. Several ways also exist to display a link to the feed in a module, but the easiest way is through a Custom HTML module. In the module, you simply add a link like this:

```
<a href="http://feeds.feedburner.com/myfeedtitle"><img
 src="images/M_images/livemarks.png" alt="RSS Feed" border="0" /> Feed Entries</a>
```

If you are using a WYSIWYG editor, you don't actually have to enter the HTML code. You can add the feed icon and link using the WYSIWYG editor, which makes it easier.

How It Works

If you decide to use FeedBurner to manage and distribute your RSS feeds, it is important to ensure that your visitors only have access to the link to the FeedBurner feed and not to the link generated by Joomla!. The data in both the Joomla!-generated link and the FeedBurner link are the same, but FeedBurner gives you more tools for distributing the feed and tracking the number of subscribers to your feed. To ensure that your visitors subscribe to your feed using only the FeedBurner feed, you must remove all references to the Joomla!-generated feed link.

Syndication for the Sample Site

For the local wedding community site, you need to carefully consider what information you want to syndicate to help drive traffic to the site. For starters, the site will not have regularly updated contacts or web links, so there is no need to syndicate data from those components. That leaves content syndication.

You will recall from Chapter 4 that the sample site has two categorized sections: Expert Tips and News. The Expert Tips sections will work much like a blog, where a local wedding expert will regularly share wedding tips for people planning weddings. Because this information is regularly updated, syndicating the articles from this section makes sense. The News section will also be regularly updated with news about recent weddings and wedding vendors, so it also makes sense to syndicate this information.

The content for this site has the following structure:

❑ Expert Tips
   ❑ Ceremony
   ❑ Fashion
   ❑ Reception

- ❏ News
  - ❏ Recent Weddings
  - ❏ Vendor News

You need at least two feeds, one for Expert Tips and one for News. However, you need to consider whether to use one feed for all Expert Tips and one feed for all News, or if a separate feed for each category within those sections is better.

For example, let's consider Expert Tips. This section has three categories: Ceremony, Fashion, and Reception. Should you just have one feed for the entire section, or a separate feed for each category, or do all of the above? You can approach this decision a couple of ways. One way to approach it is to consider what your customers would want either by asking them or by making a best guess. Would a bride really care to have separate feed for each category, or would she just want one feed for the entire section? The other approach is to do all of the above and then measure the results in FeedBurner a few months later so that you have solid data to support a decision. I prefer the latter approach because it's easy to set up feeds in FeedBurner, and whenever possible I like to see how people are actually using a feature before I make a decision to remove part of it.

In Chapter 5, you set up menu items for the Expert Tips and News sections in the Main Menu, and you created an Expert Tips menu with links to the Ceremony, Fashion, and Reception categories and a News menu with links to the Recent Weddings and Vendor News categories. As you learned earlier in this chapter, Show a Feed Link is set to Yes by default, so you already have feeds set up for both sections and for each category within each section. The next thing you need to do is set up your feeds in FeedBurner.

Try It Out   Setting Up the Wedding Site Feeds in FeedBurner

To set up your feeds in FeedBurner:

1. Visit each page on the site that has a feed in a browser that displays feed links: Expert Tips, Expert Tips – Ceremony, Expert Tips – Fashion, Expert Tips – Reception, News, News – Recent Weddings, and News – Vendor News. Firefox is a good browser to use for this purpose. Perform the following steps for each of these pages.

2. In the Firefox address bar, click the feed icon as shown in Figure 7-1. You will be given two choices: RSS 2.0 or Atom 1.0. Select the RSS 2.0 option, which will take you to the RSS feed for that page.

3. Copy the URL of the feed, and use the URL to set up a FeedBurner feed, as you learned to do earlier in this chapter. Create an account at www.feedburner.com if you do not already have one. Create a new FeedBurner feed by pasting your Joomla! feed link in the box where it says "Burn a feed right this instant. Type your blog or feed address here:." Click the Next button, and then activate your feed.

4. Navigate to the menu item manager at Menus ⇨ Menu Title where Menu Title is the title of the menu that contains the menu item you need to modify, and open the menu item. Set Show Feed Links to No to disable the feed links.

5. Navigate to the module manager at Extensions ⇨ Module Manager and disable or delete all syndicate modules.

6. Make a slight modification to the template's index.php file, which you can find at www.yoursite.com/templates/your-template/index.php. In between the <head> and </head> tags, you need to add the following line:

```
<link href="http://feeds.feedburner.com/myfeedtitle" rel="alternate"
type="application/rss+xml" title="Your Feed Title" />
```

7. Set up a "Custom HTML" module to display your list of FeedBurner feeds on the site. In the module, you simply add a link like this:

```
<a href="http://feeds.feedburner.com/myfeedtitle"><img
src="images/M_images/livemarks.png" alt="RSS Feed" border="0" /> Feed Entries</a>
```

How It Works

Setting up syndication in FeedBurner can be a tedious and monotonous process, but having the tools available in FeedBurner make the effort worthwhile. This process basically involves setting up feeds in Joomla! for each section and category for which you want to syndicate the content, then copying the links to those feeds into FeedBurner to create new FeedBurner feeds, and then replacing all of the Joomla! feed links on your site with the FeedBurner feed links.

Summary

Syndication is a powerful tool for giving your visitors options for how they consume your content and for driving traffic to your site. Joomla! 1.0 only enabled one feed for the front page component and nothing for content sections and categories and for other components, but Joomla! 1.5 makes it easier than ever before to set up and manage multiple feeds for your content.

You can enable feeds in your site through the "Show a Feed Link" parameter in your menu items, or by enabling the syndicate module. A great way to manage your feeds so that you get added features like subscriber statistics is to use a service like FeedBurner, which you learned how to do in this chapter.

Now that you know how to syndicate your content, it's time to learn how to build a template in Joomla! 1.5 and take advantage of all of the new template features the new framework has to offer. First, take a few moments to complete the following exercises to test your knowledge of syndication in Joomla! 1.5. You can find the answers to these exercises in Appendix A.

Exercises

1. Name four things that can be syndicated in Joomla! 1.5.

2. What choices do you have for data that you can show for each feed item in a content feed?

3. What does the "Show a Feed Link" parameter do?

Building a Custom Template

You've installed Joomla! and all the extensions you need, and you've created your content and menu structure. Now that your site's structure is in place, it is time to consider the look and feel of the site. As you learned in Chapter 1, templates are used for providing a layout and design within which all of the pieces of your Joomla! site come together.

To get the look you want for your site, you have several options for finding prebuilt templates. One option is to use one of the three templates that come pre-installed with Joomla!: Beez, Rhuk_Milkyway, or JA_Purity. Another option is to find a free template from one of the many places on the web that offer free Joomla! templates. If you intend to use a prebuilt template, the best option is to pay a small fee to purchase a template from one of the many companies that sell high-quality, professional, prebuilt Joomla! templates. Although there is a cost associated with professional prebuilt templates, many of the companies that provide these templates provide excellent support, regular updates, and source graphic files to help you customize your template, so they are well worth the price. You can find a list of some of the top companies that provide professional templates in Appendix D.

Many high-quality, prebuilt templates are available, and they are great options if you do not have the time or the money to build a custom template. With a custom template, you can create the exact look and feel you want to achieve with your site, matching not only your brand image, but also the structure that you have worked so hard to build.

With Joomla! 1.5, the core team has taken huge strides forward in giving web designers the ability to create unique, attractive, and flexible designs for their websites by greatly enhancing the template framework. The new framework gives you unprecedented control over what is output from the system by enabling you to override the default HTML that is generated by the core components and modules.

In this chapter, you learn how to build a custom Joomla! template from scratch. You go through the steps involved in first building what's known as a comp design, and then taking that design and converting it to a fully functioning Joomla! template. To get the most out of this chapter, you should have a working knowledge of XHTML, CSS, and PHP. If you intend to build a template from scratch, web and graphic design and layout skills will also come in handy. Even if you do not intend to build your own template from scratch, the concepts in this chapter will help you as you customize your template.

Creating a Comp Design

The first step in building any template is to create a comp design (or mock-up). In general terms, a comp design is basically a sketch of what the site will look like, either on paper or in a graphics program like Adobe Photoshop or Fireworks. It is important to go through this process so that you know where things go and how they will look on your site before you start writing code to put things in their proper place.

Creating a comp design is a process rather than a one-time event. You could go through several iterations of your design before you come up with the design that is right for your site. One of the main reasons you sketch out your design before coding is that it is much easier to fix a picture than to go through and recode parts of your template when you are not happy with it.

In this section, you go through the process of creating a comp design. You learn about some of the things you need to consider when building a comp design. You look at some of the pros and cons of the top graphics programs and how to slice up the graphic elements of your comp design for use in your template.

Fireworks Versus Photoshop

Several graphics applications are available for designing websites, but the two most popular applications are Adobe Fireworks and Adobe Photoshop. Both programs are excellent choices for creating a comp design and generating graphics for your site, and it can be difficult to decide which one is right for you. The following table is a side-by-side comparison of each application with criteria you should consider when choosing a graphics program.

Criteria	Fireworks	Photoshop
Ease of use	Fireworks makes it easy to create custom layouts with vector tools and shapes, and it makes it easy to export parts of your design for use as graphics in your template.	For a beginning web designer, Photoshop can be a nightmare to learn. The interface is difficult to navigate, and making simple adjustments can be quite difficult for those not familiar with the software. Designers who have experience working with Photoshop might tend to disagree, but if you have never used a graphics application, Photoshop is probably not where you want to get started.

Criteria	Fireworks	Photoshop
Features & Power	Fireworks is presented as a "rapid prototyping" application, which makes it perfect for building quick mock-ups of your sites. However, a lot of features in Fireworks make it possible to build high-end, sophisticated designs for your website.	Photoshop offers the largest feature set in terms of the types of functions you can perform with the software. It offers a large variety of filters, brushes, and other options to enable designers to build high-end graphics for any medium.
Support	Both applications are supported by Adobe, so you will likely get the same level of support for each product.	

The choice of whether to use Fireworks or Photoshop for creating your comp design really comes down to your level of experience and personal preference. If you are a beginner who has never used a graphics application, Fireworks is probably the right choice for you. If you are a seasoned veteran who has been working with Photoshop for years, you will probably want to use Photoshop unless you prefer working with Fireworks. Personally, I prefer to work with Fireworks because it gives me enough functionality and performance while being easier to use for building quick mock-ups. Many professional template providers work in Fireworks and offer their source files in a format that is easily editable in Fireworks.

Once you have selected a graphics program, it is time to design the look and feel of your site. For the sample site, you use the comp design shown in Figure 8-1. The source files in Fireworks PNG format are available for download at wrox.com. You'll notice that the comp design has some strange text that seems to be written in some unknown language. That text is often referred to as "Lorem Ipsum" or "Lipsum" text, and it is commonly used as filler text for the purposes of creating a layout. You can find out more about this at http://www.lipsum.org.

Slicing Your Design

Now that you have a design, it is time to decide how best to split up the graphics for use in your template. Both Fireworks and Photoshop have slicing tools to help you literally cut out the parts of your design mock-up that you want to use as graphics in your template, and export them in any web-safe graphics format you choose.

In Figure 8-1, you will notice that the design mostly consists of plain text, borders, and a background color for a module in the left column. All of these items can be rendered with a combination of HTML and CSS, so there is no need to cut them out and use them as graphics for the site. For the sake of simplicity, the only graphic used in this template is the logo. Your template will likely have more graphics than this, so be prepared to do a lot of slicing. Full-blown templates usually have background images, icons, and other images that need to be sliced. For the sample template, export the logo as a GIF and call it logo.gif.

Figure 8-1

XHTML/CSS

Now that you have all of the graphics you need for your template, it is time to start building the XHTML and CSS that will be used to render the layout of the site. The XHTML and CSS files will take the following structure:

- ❑   `/templatename/index.php`
- ❑   `/templatename/images/logo.gif`
- ❑   `/templatename/css/template.css`

For this step in the process, you don't add any Joomla!-specific PHP or HTML. This step is merely for building the XHTML and CSS layout so that you can easily add in Joomla! code later. The file structure is important because it follows along with the overall file structure that you learn about in the next section.

XHTML

For starters, you write all of your XHTML in the index.php file. You could use a program like Adobe Dreamweaver to generate your XHTML and CSS, but for the sake of gaining a better understanding of the code, this example shows you how to go through and build it all the old-fashioned way, by hand. It's a good idea to build the XHTML as a stand-alone document before adding any Joomla! tags. Take a look at the markup:

```
<?xml version="1.0" encoding="utf-8"?>
<!DOCTYPE html PUBLIC "-//W3C//DTD XHTML 1.0 Transitional//EN"
"http://www.w3.org/TR/xhtml1/DTD/xhtml1-transitional.dtd">
<html xmlns="http://www.w3.org/1999/xhtml"
xml:lang="en-gb" lang="en-gb" dir="ltr" >
<head>
  <link rel="stylesheet" href="css/template.css" type="text/css" />
</head>
<body>

<div id="container">
    <div id="header">
        <div id="logo"><a href=""><img src="images/logo.gif" width="407"
height="69" alt="Local Wedding Site" border="0" /></a></div><!-- /logo -->
        <div id="advert">Advert1 Module</div><!-- /advert -->
    </div><!-- /header -->
    <div id="nav">
        <ul>
            <li><a href="#">Home</a></li>
            <li><a href="#">About Us</a></li>
            <li><a href="#">Contact Us</a></li>
        </ul>
    </div><!-- /nav -->
    <div id="maincontent">
        <div id="banner">
            <div class="moduletable">
                Banner Module
            </div><!-- /moduletable -->
        </div><!-- /banner -->
        <div id="mainbody">
            <h1>Component Area</h1>
            <p>Lorem ipsum dolor sit amet, consectetuer adipiscing elit. Integer eu
            justo. Aliquam pharetra, leo nec vestibulum feugiat, felis massa
            imperdiet neque, eget porttitor lectus est sit amet mi. Aliquam erat
            volutpat. Vivamus ornare mattis sem. Cras quis urna vel urna scelerisque
            fringilla. Proin at velit. Mauris interdum adipiscing nisi. Nullam erat
            quam, feugiat non, lacinia eu, feugiat ac, nulla. Sed purus. Quisque in
            arcu ut turpis fringilla vulputate. Vestibulum eget tortor non nisl
            tincidunt luctus. Ut vehicula erat ut urna. Maecenas fermentum augue.
            Proin eu felis eu risus faucibus consequat.</p>
            <p>In aliquet elit sit amet velit. Etiam id mauris. In at enim. Sed et
            velit eu orci fermentum imperdiet. Praesent tempor augue at nunc. Vivamus
```

145

```
      nec dui in enim tempus fringilla. Donec ac tortor. Sed vitae justo
      eleifend tortor consectetuer tincidunt. Integer a lorem. Morbi varius sem
      sed magna.</p>
      <p>Curabitur pellentesque, erat vitae iaculis viverra, quam dolor
      venenatis magna, ut varius dui nibh ultricies neque. Suspendisse
      condimentum viverra risus. Praesent tincidunt orci ut erat. Praesent nec
      arcu. Sed leo arcu, porta eu, faucibus a, sollicitudin ac, quam.
      Vestibulum tincidunt convallis mi. Nam pretium interdum libero. Nulla in
      nulla id augue vulputate commodo. Aliquam fringilla, augue id fermentum
      aliquam, ante arcu porta magna, et fermentum leo metus a felis. Etiam
      adipiscing cursus neque. Mauris nec libero at purus euismod dapibus.
      Donec sed diam nec augue sodales pulvinar. Fusce mi. In in dolor.
      Suspendisse sollicitudin nisi et nisl.</p>
       <p>Curabitur quis mauris. Duis volutpat felis vel mi. Lorem ipsum dolor
      sit amet, consectetuer adipiscing elit. Proin purus libero, faucibus sit
      amet, malesuada nec, mollis id, odio. Maecenas porta, tellus a fermentum
      fermentum, metus lectus varius magna, sed venenatis libero felis et
      felis. Curabitur iaculis risus ut orci. Donec eget elit sit amet ligula
      auctor egestas. Sed vitae est id turpis ultrices posuere. Nulla
      vulputate. Etiam tempus. Vivamus libero. Quisque nec dui. In egestas pede
      sed justo.</p>
  </div><!-- /mainbody -->
  <div id="bottom">
      <div class="moduletable">
          <h3>Bottom Module</h3>
          <p>Lorem ipsum dolor sit amet, consectetuer adipiscing elit. Integer
          eu justo. Aliquam pharetra, leo nec vestibulum feugiat, felis massa
          imperdiet neque, eget porttitor lectus est sit amet mi. Aliquam erat
          volutpat. Vivamus ornare mattis sem. Cras quis urna vel urna
          scelerisque fringilla. Proin at velit. Mauris interdum adipiscing
          nisi. Nullam erat quam, feugiat non, lacinia eu, feugiat ac, nulla.
          Sed purus. Quisque in arcu ut turpis fringilla vulputate. Vestibulum
          eget tortor non nisl tincidunt luctus. Ut vehicula erat ut urna.
          Maecenas fermentum augue. Proin eu felis eu risus faucibus
          consequat.</p>
      </div><!-- /module -->
  </div><!-- /bottom -->
</div><!-- /maincontent -->
<div id="sidebar">
  <div class="moduletable">
      <h3>Left Module</h3>
      <p>Lorem ipsum dolor sit amet, consectetuer adipiscing elit. Integer eu
      justo. Aliquam pharetra, leo nec vestibulum feugiat, felis massa
      imperdiet neque, eget porttitor lectus est sit amet mi. Aliquam erat
      volutpat. Vivamus ornare mattis sem. Cras quis urna vel urna scelerisque
      fringilla. Proin at velit. Mauris interdum adipiscing nisi. Nullam erat
      quam, feugiat non, lacinia eu, feugiat ac, nulla. Sed purus. Quisque in
      arcu ut turpis fringilla vulputate. Vestibulum eget tortor non nisl
      tincidunt luctus. Ut vehicula erat ut urna. Maecenas fermentum augue.
      Proin eu felis eu risus faucibus consequat.</p>
  </div>
  <div class="moduletable-background">
      <h3>Left Module -background</h3>
      <p>Lorem ipsum dolor sit amet, consectetuer adipiscing elit. Integer eu
      justo. Aliquam pharetra, leo nec vestibulum feugiat, felis massa
      imperdiet neque, eget porttitor lectus est sit amet mi. Aliquam erat
```

```
        volutpat. Vivamus ornare mattis sem. Cras quis urna vel urna scelerisque
        fringilla. Proin at velit. Mauris interdum adipiscing nisi. Nullam erat
        quam, feugiat non, lacinia eu, feugiat ac, nulla.</p>
    </div>
  </div><!-- /sidebar -->
  <div id="footer">
      <p>Copyright 2008, Local Weddings Site | <a href="#">Privacy Policy</a> |
      <a href="#">Terms and Conditions</a></p>
  </div><!-- /footer -->
</div><!-- /container -->
</body>
</html>
```

This markup is written just like any other XHTML document. It has the XML and DOCTYPE declarations, the `<head>` and CSS `<link>` references, and the `<body>`, complete with normal HTML tags. Within this markup, there is now space for six module positions and the main content or component area. The logo will be hard-coded into the template, but you could just as easily create a "logo" module position. This markup also contains the filler "Lipsum" text, which will be replaced in the template with either module position declarations or the component declaration.

The module positions used in this template are advert1, nav, banner, bottom, left, and footer. These positions will be contained within the `<div>` tags with the IDs advert, nav, banner, bottom, sidebar, and footer, respectively. Notice that the `<div>` IDs do not necessarily match up with the module position names because they do not have to.

Although each position in the mock-up contains only one module except for the left position, each module position can contain almost infinitely many modules. All modules within a given position have a style associated with them, which you learn more about later in this chapter. Knowing a little about how each possible style renders modules will help with the process of creating your XHTML. One such style is the xhtml style, which renders modules like this:

```
<div class="moduletable[module class suffix]">
    <h3>Module Title</h3>
    Module Content

</div>
```

The banner, bottom, and left positions will be using the xhtml module style, so the sample markup contains this pattern in those positions. The module title is optional depending on whether or not you set it to display, as you learned in Chapter 6. The module class suffix is a parameter that you can set in the module so that it adds a unique identifying suffix to the module class. This is used to give modules different styles within the same position.

CSS

Now that the basic XHTML structure is in place, take a look at the CSS that will define the styles and colors of the template. There are no Joomla!-specific selectors in the CSS yet except for the moduletable selector. You add some more Joomla!-specific selectors later when you need them.

```
body {
    background-color: #fff;
    color: #000;
```

```
        font-family: Arial, Helvetica, Sans-Serif;
        font-size: 12px;
        text-align: center;
        margin: 0;
        padding: 0;
}
h1, h2, h3, h4 {
        font-weight: normal;
        line-height: 1.2em;
        color: #000;
        margin: 0 0 1em;
}
h1 {
        font-size: 28px;
}
h2 {
        font-size: 24px;
}
h3 {
        font-size: 20px;
}
h4 {
        font-size: 16px;
}
p {
        margin: 0 0 1em;
        line-height: 1.35em;
}
div#container {
        width: 960px;
        margin: 0 auto;
        text-align: left;
}
div#header {
        width: 960px;
        height: 100px !important;
        height: 101px;
        border-bottom: 1px solid #000;
        position: relative;
}
div#logo {
        width: 407px;
        height: 69px;
        position: absolute;
        left: 6px;
        top: 23px;
}
div#advert {
        width: 468px !important;
        height: 60px !important;
        width: 470px;
        height: 62px;
        border: 1px solid #000;
        position: absolute;
```

```
        right: 0;
        top: 20px;
}
div#nav {
        width: 960px;
        height: 30px !important;
        height: 31px;
        border-bottom: 1px solid #000;
        margin-bottom: 30px;
}
div#nav ul {
        width: 960px;
        height: 30px;
        margin: 0;
        padding: 0;
}
div#nav ul li {
        float: left;
        height: 30px;
        list-style-type: none;
        margin: 0;
        padding: 0;
}
div#nav a {
        display: block;
        float: left;
        height: 30px;
        line-height: 30px;
        padding: 0 10px;
        color: #000;
        background-color: #fff;
        text-decoration: none;
}
div#nav a:hover {
        background-color: #000;
        color: #fff;
}
div#maincontent {
        width: 690px !important;
        width: 711px;
        float: right;
        padding-left: 20px;
        border-left: 1px solid #000;
        margin-left: 20px;
        margin-bottom: 30px;
}
div#banner {
        width: 648px !important;
        width: 690px;
        border: 1px solid #000;
        padding: 20px;
        margin-bottom: 20px;
}
div#mainbody {
```

```
        width: 690px;
        padding-bottom: 30px;
        border-bottom: 1px solid #000;
        margin-bottom: 20px;
    }
    div#sidebar {
        width: 229px;
        float: left;
        margin-bottom: 30px;
    }
    div.moduletable {
        margin-bottom: 20px;
    }
    div.moduletable-background {
        background-color: #000;
        color: #fff;
        padding: 20px;
        margin-bottom: 20px;
    }
    div.moduletable-background h3 {
        font-size: 16px;
        color: #fff;
    }
    div#footer {
        width: 960px;
        clear: both;
        padding-top: 10px;
        border-top: 1px solid #000;
        text-align: center;
    }
    div#footer a {
        color: #000;
    }
    div#footer a:hover {
        text-decoration: none;
    }
}
```

Now that the basic XHTML and CSS structures are in place, it's time to take a look at the actual files that make up the template.

Template File Structure

A Joomla! template is nothing more than a combination of PHP, CSS, JavaScript, XML, and image (GIF, JPG, PNG) files. Only two files are required for building an installable Joomla! template: the `index.php` file and the template manifest file, called `templateDetails.xml`. However, that would be quite a boring template without styles and graphics, and you miss out on a lot of the important template features available in Joomla! 1.5 templates. In this section, you learn about the various files that make up a full-featured Joomla! template.

Files

In the root of your template folder, found at `yoursite.com/templates/yourtemplate/`, you can have a virtually infinite number of files, but Joomla! looks for a number of standard files by default. These files are `index.php`, `templateDetails.xml`, `component.php`, `error.php`, `offline.php`, and other ancillary files that serve various purposes.

index.php

The `index.php` file is Joomla!'s main entry point into your template. This file is used to layout your site's XHTML, reference your style sheets, and position Joomla!'s components and modules on the screen. Because this is just a PHP file, you can do a lot of things with it, like query the database, perform various functions, or even write a mini web app. However, you should avoid the temptation to do too much with your template `index.php` file and only use it for presentation-related code and markup. Let's take a look at the `index.php` file one piece at a time with Joomla! code added in and filler text removed. For starters, we'll look at the header of the file:

```
<?php
defined('_JEXEC') or die('Restricted access');
$url = clone(JURI::getInstance());
?>
<?xml version="1.0" encoding="utf-8"?>
<!DOCTYPE html PUBLIC "-//W3C//DTD XHTML 1.0 Transitional//EN"
  "http://www.w3.org/TR/xhtml1/DTD/xhtml1-transitional.dtd">
<html xmlns="http://www.w3.org/1999/xhtml" xml:lang="<?php echo $this->language;
 ?>" lang="<?php echo $this->language; ?>" dir="<?php echo $this->direction; ?>" >
<head>
  <link rel="stylesheet" href="<?php echo $url->base();
 ?>templates/weddingsite/css/template.css" type="text/css" />
</head>
```

The first four lines of the template header include the PHP open and close tags along with two lines of PHP code. The first line of code, `defined('_JEXEC') or die('Restricted access')`, is simply a test to make sure that Joomla! is calling this template file, which prevents people from accessing this file directly. The second line of code, `$url = clone(JURI::getInstance())`, creates a clone of the JURI object in the variable `$url`. This will be used later in the template to reference the site's URL. You could just as easily hard-code the site's URL, but it is good practice to use the JRUI object so that you can easily reuse your template on other domains.

In the `<html>` tag, you can see that the site's language and direction are set dynamically using Joomla! parameters, `$this->language` and `$this->direction`. In programming terms, `$this` is the JDocumentHTML object used to render the template, but you can just think of `$this` as the template, and it has a number of useful parameters and functions that you use throughout your template. In this case, the `language` parameter is the language used by your Joomla! installation or selected by a particular user, and the `direction` parameter is the direction in which the text is rendered (right-to-left or left-to-right).

The style sheet reference now includes the path to the file. In the XHTML mock-up, the path was simply `css/template.css`. This path will not suffice for the template, because the CSS file is located in the css folder inside the `templates/weddingsite` folder. For that reason, you need to add this information to the path. You'll also notice that $url->base() is used in the path. This is the base URL of the site, which lets you know you have an exact reference to the CSS file.

Next, examine the first part of the body of the template:

```
<body>
<div id="container">
    <div id="header">
        <div id="logo"><a href="<?php echo $url->base(); ?>">
        <img src="<?php echo $url->base(); ?>templates/weddingsite/images/logo.gif"
        width="407" height="69" alt="Local Wedding Site" border="0" /></a></div>
        <!-- /logo -->
            <?php if ($this->countModules('advert1')) : ?>
            <div id="advert"><jdoc:include type="modules" name="advert1" /></div>
            <!-- /advert -->
        <?php endif; ?>
    </div><!-- /header -->
    <div id="nav">
        <jdoc:include type="modules" name="nav" />
    </div><!-- /nav -->
```

The first a href uses $url->base() to link the logo to the home page of the site, and the src parameter of the logo's img tag also uses $url->base() and /templates/weddingsite to reference the logo file directly from its location in the images folder in the template. After the logo, you come to the first module position declaration for the advert1 position.

Module positions are loaded with the following markup, which is specific to Joomla! templates:

```
<jdoc:include type="modules" name="position_name" style="some_style" />
```

where position_name is the name of the module position you wish to load and some_style is the name of the style with which the module position is loaded. The position name can be anything you want it to be, like advert1, banner, myposition, monkey, icecream, and so on, as long as you declare the position name in your template manifest file, which you learn about in the next section. Five default module position styles are available: none, table, horz, xhtml, and rounded. If you do not add a style parameter, it defaults to none. You can also create your own module position style, which you learn about in the "Overriding Default Layouts" section later in this chapter.

In the sample template, the advert1 position is loaded without a style, so it defaults to style="none". Before the position is loaded, there is a bit of PHP code that tells the template to first count the number of modules that are published to the advert1 position for a given page before loading the advert1 position along with its accompanying markup in the template. The code used is:

```
<?php if ($this->countModules('advert1')) : ?>
<div id="advert1">

    <jdoc:include type="modules" name="advert1" />
</div>
<?php endif; ?>
```

This uses the function countModules in the JDocumentHTML object. This function can be used to count the modules in a single position, multiple positions, or with Boolean logic, to determine if multiple positions have at least one module. The following table shows some examples.

Example	Description
`$this->countModules('position1 + position2')`	This will return the total number of modules in `position1` and `position2` combined.
`$this->countModules('position1 AND position2')`	This will return `true` if both `position1` and `position2` have modules, and `false` if neither has modules.
`$this->countModules('(position1 + position2) AND position3')`	This will return `true` if `position1` or `position2` has modules and `position3` has modules, otherwise it will return `false`.

You may also notice that the `nav` position is loaded without using the `countModules` function to determine whether there are modules in this position. That is because we are assuming there will always be modules in the `nav` position because this is where the main menu will be. It is not necessary to use `countModules` before loading a module position. You only need to use it when you do not want to load the position if it contains no modules.

The next section of markup and code contains two more module positions and the location where the main component is loaded on the page:

```
<div id="maincontent">
    <?php if ($this->countModules('banner')) : ?>
    <div id="banner">
       <div class="moduletable">
           <jdoc:include type="modules" name="banner" />
       </div><!-- /moduletable -->
    </div><!-- /banner -->
    <?php endif; ?>
    <div id="mainbody">
       <?php if ($this->getBuffer('message')) : ?>
       <div class="message">
           <jdoc:include type="message" />
       </div>
       <?php endif; ?>
       <jdoc:include type="component" />
    </div><!-- /mainbody -->
    <?php if ($this->countModules('bottom')) : ?>
    <div id="bottom">
       <jdoc:include type="modules" name="bottom" style="xhtml" />
    </div><!-- /bottom -->
    <?php endif; ?>
</div><!-- /maincontent-->
```

The `banner` and `bottom` module positions are loaded in the same way as the `advert1` module position. Let's focus our attention on the middle portion of this section of markup. This portion contains the code and markup that presents a system message if one exists and presents the component.

Before the system message is loaded using `<jdoc:include type="message" />`, there is a bit of code, `$this->getBuffer('message')`, that checks the system buffer to see if it contains a message. If it does, the message is displayed. If not, the message is not displayed.

Usually there is no test to determine whether to load the component with `<jdoc:include type="component" />` because it is assumed that you always want to load the component since, as you learned in Chapter 1, the component performs the main functionality on a given page in your Joomla! site. That doesn't mean that you couldn't set up your own test to determine when and where to load the component, and you learn some ways to do that in Chapter 10.

The final section of the `index.php` file simply loads the `left` and `footer` module positions, and it closes out any open HTML tags:

```php
<?php if ($this->countModules('left')) : ?>
<div id="sidebar">
    <jdoc:include type="modules" name="left" style="xhtml" />
</div><!-- /sidebar -->
<?php endif; ?>

<div id="footer">
    <jdoc:include type="modules" name="footer" />
</div><!-- /footer -->
</div><!-- /container -->

</body>
</html>
```

With the code in the `index.php` file, the module positions and the main component area have been loaded into the template's layout, and will appear in the template as shown in Figure 8-2.

Try It Out   **Building a Comp Design and Template index.php File**

Building a comp design and `index.php` file involves the following steps:

1. Create a comp design in your graphics design program of choice. For this step, you can download the mock-up from Figure 8-1 from `wrox.com` and either use that as your comp design or use it as a starting point for creating your own comp design.

2. Create a file called `index.html` and build your XHTML and CSS to match the look of your comp design using filler text from `http://www.lipsum.org`. You can code this file from scratch using the example from this chapter, or you can use an application like Dreamweaver to develop the HTML for your template. To follow the most commonly used naming convention, name your CSS file `template.css` and place it in a folder called `css` rather than in the same folder as the `index.html` file.

3. After you have finished getting your HTML file and CSS to match the look of your comp design in a browser, rename `index.html` to `index.php`.

4. Convert all relative paths to paths to your template folder using the JURI object. Get access to the JURI object with the following line of code:

```php
<?php $url = clone(JURI::getInstance()); ?>
```

Then, change any relative paths from something like this:

```html
<link rel="stylesheet" href="css/template.css" type="text/css" />
```

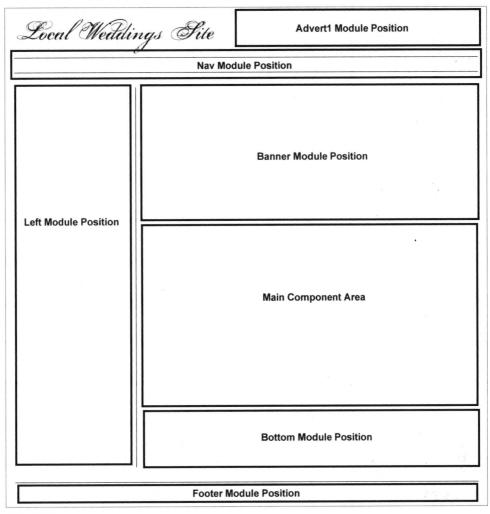

Figure 8-2

to this:

```
<link rel="stylesheet" href="<?php echo $url->base();
    ?>templates/yourtemplatename/css/template.css" type="text/css" />
```

5. Replace filler text with module positions and code to load the component. To load a module position, add code like this for each position:

```
<jdoc:include type="modules" position="position_name" style="style_name" />
```

where `position_name` is the name of the module position you are loading and `style_name` is the name of the style you want to use for the position. For the style name, you can choose one of the following styles: none, table, horz, xhtml, or rounded. To load the component, add the following code:

```
<jdoc:include type="component" />
```

How It Works

Building a template from scratch starts with a comp design, followed by the development of XHTML and CSS. After you are satisfied with your markup and style sheets, you go through the process of converting your markup into Joomla! template code. Now that you've seen how the index.php file is constructed, it's time to look at the template manifest file, templateDetails.xml.

templateDetails.xml

The template manifest file, templateDetails.xml, is an XML file that is used by the extension installer to determine which files are included in the template installation package and where they should go. It also contains information about the template, like the name of the template, the author of the template, and so on. As a new feature in Joomla! 1.5, this file can also contain a set of parameters for the template. These parameters can be set in the template manager, which uses the template manifest file to determine the name and types of parameters available, and writes the values to a file called params.ini. Figure 8-3 shows the parameters in the template editor for the JA Purity template that comes with Joomla!.

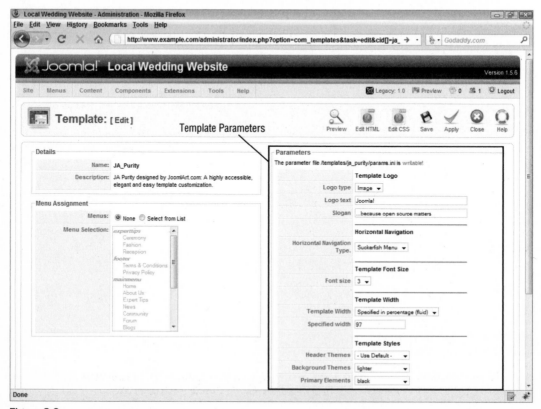

Figure 8-3

rf3 bodyp

The template manifest file also lists the module positions used in the template, so you can use any name you wish for a module position as long as you list it in the template manifest file. This is what the file's contents look like:

```xml
<?xml version="1.0" encoding="utf-8"?>
<!DOCTYPE install PUBLIC "-//Joomla! 1.5//DTD template 1.0//EN"
"http://dev.joomla.org/xml/1.5/template-install.dtd">
<install version="1.5" type="template">
    <name>weddingsite</name>
    <creationDate>16 October 2008</creationDate>
    <author>Cory Webb</author>
    <authorEmail>cory@corywebbmedia.com.com</authorEmail>
    <authorUrl>http://www.corywebbmedia.com</authorUrl>
    <copyright>Copyright 2008 Cory Webb</copyright>
    <license>GNU/GPL</license>
    <version>1.0.0</version>
    <description>Template for Joomla! 1.5. Developed for Beginning Joomla!
        book.</description>
    <files>
        <filename>component.php</filename>
        <filename>en-GB.tpl_weddingsite.ini</filename>
        <filename>error.php</filename>
        <filename>favicon.ico</filename>
        <filename>index.html</filename>
        <filename>index.php</filename>
        <filename>offline.php</filename>
        <filename>params.ini</filename>
        <filename>template_thumbnail.png</filename>
        <filename>templateDetails.xml</filename>
        <folder>admin</folder>
        <folder>css</folder>
        <folder>html</folder>
        <folder>images</folder>
    </files>
    <languages>
        <language tag="en-GB">en-GB.tpl_weddingsite.ini</language>
    </languages>
    <administration>
        <languages folder="admin">
            <language tag="en-GB">en-
GB.tpl_weddingsite.ini</language>
        </languages>
    </administration>
    <positions>
        <position>advert1</position>
        <position>banner</position>
        <position>bottom</position>
        <position>footer</position>
        <position>left</position>
        <position>nav</position>
    </positions>
    <params>
        <param name="someParameter" type="text" default="" size="50"
label="Some Parameter" description="SOME PARAMETER DESCRIPTION" />
    </params>
</install>
```

The first line, `<install version="1.5" type="template">`, tells the Joomla! extension installer that this extension installation package is built for Joomla! 1.5, and that it is a template. The following elements contain the name, creation date, and the name of the author of the template along with the author's e-mail address and web address, the template copyright, license, and version information, and a description of the template.

The next part of the XML contains a list of files in the template installation package. Each file in the root of the template is listed within `<filename></filename>` tags. A great new feature in Joomla! 1.5 is that you no longer need to list all the files in the subfolders of the template. You simply list the subfolders each within `<folder></folder>` tags, and Joomla! searches those folders for each file within them saving you the time and hassle of listing each filename.

After the files are listed, the template's language files are listed. These files are necessary only if you are displaying words directly in the template to the end user that need to be translated into multiple languages. Otherwise, you can leave this off.

Next, the module position names are listed, each within the `<position></position>` tags. Technically, this isn't necessary, but it sure makes life a lot easier when you are managing your modules in the module manager. By listing the module positions used in your template, you are letting Joomla! know that these module position names are being used, and Joomla! will automatically populate a drop-down list of module positions in the module manager using this list. You can see an example of this in Figure 8-4.

Figure 8-4

Finally, the template's parameters are listed. Parameters are not necessary, but if you intend to use the same template on multiple sites, they can be useful for giving the template different settings for each site. Although the sample template does not actually use any parameters, the sample template manifest file lists a parameter so that you can see what it looks like. You can see an example of where you set template parameters in Figure 8-3. Several predefined types of parameters are available, although most people would only need to use list, radio, spacer, text, and textarea. The list parameter type provides a predefined list of items from which to choose. The radio parameter type provides a list in the form of radio buttons. The spacer type is a way to set apart groups of parameters. The text type is just a short text box for typing short bits of text, like the site title. The textarea type is for entering longer text. The complete list of parameter types is shown here:

- category
- editors
- filelist
- folderlist
- helpsites
- hidden
- imagelist
- languages
- list
- menu
- menuitem
- password
- radio
- section
- spacer
- sql
- text
- textarea
- timezones

The index.php and templateDetails.xml files are the only two files that are required to build a Joomla! template, but other files can be used to customize the look and feel of different aspects of the site. Now that you know more about the required files, it's time to learn about the other files that can be used in your template.

component.php

Joomla! has a feature with which you can view a component without all of the modules on the page by adding &tmpl=component to the URL. Doing this loads the component.php file. If your template does not have a component.php file, it loads the system component.php file, which is located at yoursite.com/templates/system/component.php. This file is similar to the index.php file, except that it only loads the component. Here is what the file might look like, although you can modify this to suit the needs of your template:

```php
<?php
// no direct access
defined( '_JEXEC' ) or die( 'Restricted access' );
?>
<!DOCTYPE html PUBLIC "-//W3C//DTD XHTML 1.0 Transitional//EN"
"http://www.w3.org/TR/xhtml1/DTD/xhtml1-transitional.dtd">
<html xmlns="http://www.w3.org/1999/xhtml"
xml:lang="<?php echo $this->language; ?>" lang="<?php echo $this->language; ?>"
dir="<?php echo $this->direction; ?>">
<head>
    <jdoc:include type="head" />
    <link rel="stylesheet"
href="<?php echo $this->baseurl ?>/templates/weddingsite/css/template.css"
type="text/css" />
</head>
<body>
    <jdoc:include type="message" />
    <jdoc:include type="component" />
</body>

</html>
```

error.php

In Joomla!, if you type an incorrect URL or if some other error occurs within the system, an error page is displayed. You can see an example of an error page using Joomla!'s default `error.php` template in Figure 8-5.

As you can see, this error message is complete departure from the look and feel of your own site, and it can be quite a jarring experience for your user to see such an error. For that reason, Joomla! makes it possible to customize this error page using a file called `error.php` in your template. On the rare occasion that one of your visitors encounters an error like this, you want to give that error the same look and feel of the rest of your site, so visitors do not feel like they've just broken your site and feel comfortable enough to continue browsing your site.

The default `error.php` file is located at `yoursite.com/templates/system/error.php`. You can copy this file to your template folder and easily customize it by changing out the CSS reference and any HTML in the file. The default CSS reference in the `error.php` file is as follows:

```
<link rel="stylesheet" href="<?php echo $this->baseurl; ?>
    /templates/system/css/error.css" type="text/css" />
```

To change this reference, you would simply change `system/css/error.css` to `yourtemplatename/css/template.css`. You could also keep the system error CSS file and add a reference to your own CSS file. You would then want to add your own layout HTML to match that of your template, so that the error page has a look and feel consistent with the rest of the site.

The important thing to remember is that if you want to display Joomla!'s error information, you need to keep the PHP code in the file that contains this information. This is not necessary, and you could simply create an error template that says something like "Oops! Looks like there was a bit of a problem." The problem with such a simple error message is that it's not very informative and it's difficult as a developer to figure out what caused the problem.

Figure 8-5

offline.php

In Joomla!'s global configuration, you have the option to set the site off-line as you learned in Chapter 3. One possible reason to do this is when the site is being built, you can set it off-line so that someone who happens across the site doesn't see the construction site going on inside. Joomla! has a default off-line template located at `yoursite.com/templates/system/offline.php`. You can see what the off-line page looks like with the default template in Figure 8-6.

The default off-line template is fine if you don't mind people thinking that your company name is Joomla!, but for those companies that want to include their own logo on this page, it makes sense to customize this page. To do this, simply copy `offline.php` to your template folder and make any necessary modifications to the HTML and PHP. You can add your own style sheets or use the system style sheets and simply change out the logo. It is a good idea to keep the code that allows you to log in, because as an administrator you want to be able to log in and see the site even when it is off-line. However, you can use any code you want to use in `offline.php`, and it is not necessary to keep any of the code that is in the default system off-line template.

Figure 8-6

Other Files

A Joomla! template has other ancillary files in the root folder of the template that perform a particular function. These files are index.html, params.ini, template_thumbnail.png, and favicon.ico. The following table contains a brief description of each of these files and the purpose that they serve.

File	Purpose
index.html	This file is an empty HTML file that serves to keep people from directly accessing the template folder. This is not necessary because index.php serves the same purpose, although some people still prefer to have this in their template.
params.ini	You learned earlier that parameters are defined in the template manifest file, and administrators can assign values to parameters in the template manager. This file is used to store those parameter values.
template_thumbail.png	In the template manager, Joomla! displays a thumbnail of your template if you include this file in your template. It is typically a smaller image file, around 200 pixels wide by 150 pixels tall.

File	Purpose
favicon.ico	The favicon is a little icon that typically sits in the browser address bar and is associated with your site. Usually, companies will just shrink their logo to 16x16 pixels and convert it to an .ico file called favicon.ico. This file is then embedded into the HTML of the site, and browsers then use the icon for the site in the browser bar and in the bookmarks. By including this file in your template, Joomla! automatically embeds it into your HTML. To create a favicon, you need to have the proper icon creation software. Fortunately, websites are available that enable you to upload a regular image file, and they will convert the image to an .ico file for you. You can find one such website at http://favicon.cc.

Folders

A typical Joomla! template contains more than just the files in the root folder. Usually, template files contain style sheets and images as well as HTML overrides, which you learn more about in a later section, "Overriding Default Layouts."

css

Style sheets are normally kept in a folder called css, although they do not have to be in that folder. For the sake of following convention, you can have as many or as few style sheets as you feel your template needs. The most common practice is to name your main style sheet template.css, but you can name your style sheets whatever you want to name them, as long as you reference them correctly in your template's HTML. Many people like to include a blank index.html file in this folder to prevent direct access to the folder, but it is not necessary.

images

Most templates use images to create the look and feel of a site. Whether it's a background image, a logo, an icon, or some other image, it will usually be stored in a folder named images. You could call this folder anything you want to call it, or you could just store your images in the template's root folder, but most people call this folder "images." Many people like to include a blank index.html file in this folder to prevent direct access to the folder, but it is not necessary.

html

The Joomla! 1.5 framework enables any template to override the HTML output from core components and other components that adhere to core framework coding practices. The files and folders that perform these overrides are stored in a folder named html. Unlike the css and images folders, this folder and all of its files and subfolders must follow a strict naming convention, because that is how the framework knows where to look for them. You learn more about HTML overrides in the section "Overriding Default Layouts."

Languages

Language files are used in various parts of Joomla! to facilitate translating the interface into multiple languages. In Joomla! 1.5, you now have the ability to use language files in templates. If you are using text anywhere in your template, and you intend to have visitors who speak a different language than the default language of your site, it is a good idea to incorporate language files into your template.

Like HTML overrides, language files also follow a strict naming convention. The language file for the sample template is named `en-GB.tpl_weddingsite.ini`. The first part of the filename is the language code. In this case it is `en-GB` for English. That way, if you have two or three language files, Joomla! can tell them apart by their language code. The second part of the name, `tpl_`, indicates that this language file is for a template. The next part, `weddingsite`, indicates that the language file is for the template named `weddingsite`, and the file extension is `.ini`.

A language file contains a list of keys and values, and looks like this:

```
SOME LANGUAGE KEY=Some language value
ANOTHER LANGUAGE KEY=Another language value
```

To use the language file in your template, all you do is use the `JText` object to add text rather than simply typing the text directly into the template. For example, if you wanted to write "Some language value" from the preceding sample, you would add it to the template like this:

```
<?php echo Jtext::_('SOME LANGUAGE KEY'); ?>
```

That way, if there are other language files and the user's language is one of those files, the text will display according to their language file instead of the English version.

Overriding Default Layouts

Perhaps my favorite feature in Joomla! 1.5 is the ability to override the default HTML layout presented by the core components. The core content component and other components have had notoriously bad HTML output, so designers have welcomed the opportunity to build a truly table-free Joomla! template with layout overrides. The overridden layouts may not always look any different than the default layouts to the end user. The real value in the layouts comes in the ability for developers to create standards-compliant markup for their websites, because they can have complete control over the HTML that is generated.

The Beez template that comes pre-installed with Joomla! 1.5 uses all of the possible core layout overrides, and the best way to learn about overrides is to copy the `html` folder from the Beez template and modify them to suit your needs. It contains overrides for seven components and five modules, and it contains custom module styles and pagination overrides as well as a style sheet specifically for WYSIWYG editor content.

Component and module layout overrides are contained in folders with the name of the component or module. For example, the core content component overrides are contained in a folder called `com_content`, which is divided into four folders corresponding to the four views in the content component: `article`, `category`, `frontpage`, and `section`. Custom module styles are contained in the file `modules.php`. The pagination layout override is contained in the file `pagination.php`. The WYSIWYG editor style sheet is called `editor_content.css`.

In this section, you learn how a layout override for the article view of the core content component is structured. You also learn how to create a custom module position style, also known as module chrome.

Content Article Override

The content article layout override goes in `html/com_content/article/default.php` in your template folder. The following is the code from the sample template's article layout override. It is slightly modified from the article layout override from the Beez template.

```php
<?php defined('_JEXEC') or die('Restricted access'); ?>

<?php if ($this->params->get('show_page_title',1) &&
$this->params->get('page_title') != $this->article->title) : ?>
<h2 class="pagetitle<?php echo $this->params->get('pageclass_sfx'); ?>">
        <?php echo $this->escape($this->params->get('page_title')); ?>
</h2>
<?php endif; ?>

<div id="article">

<?php if ($this->params->get('show_title')) : ?>
<h2 class="articletitle<?php echo $this->params->get('pageclass_sfx'); ?>">
    <?php if ($this->params->get('link_titles') &&
        $this->article->readmore_link != '') : ?>
    <a href="<?php echo $this->article->readmore_link; ?>"
        class="contentpagetitle<?php echo $this->params->get('pageclass_sfx'); ?>">
        <?php echo $this->article->title; ?></a>
    <?php else :
        echo $this->escape($this->article->title);
    endif; ?>
</h2>
<?php endif; ?>

<?php if (($this->user->authorize('com_content', 'edit', 'content', 'all') ||
    $this->user->authorize('com_content', 'edit', 'content', 'own')) &&
    !($this->print)) : ?>
<div class="edit<?php echo $this->escape($this->params->get('pageclass_sfx')); ?>">
    <?php echo JHTML::_('icon.edit', $this->article,
    $this->params, $this->access); ?>
</div>
<?php endif; ?>

<?php if ((!empty ($this->article->modified) &&
    $this->params->get('show_modify_date')) ||
    ($this->params->get('show_author') && ($this->article->author != "")) ||
    ($this->params->get('show_create_date'))) : ?>
<div class="articleinfo">
    <?php if (!empty ($this->article->modified) &&
        $this->params->get('show_modify_date')) : ?>
    <span class="modifydate">
        <?php echo JText::_('Last Updated').' ('.
            JHTML::_('date', $this->article->modified,
            JText::_('DATE_FORMAT_LC2')).')'; ?>
    </span>
    <?php endif; ?>

    <?php if (($this->params->get('show_author')) &&
```

```php
        ($this->article->author != "")) : ?>
        <span class="createdby">
            <?php JText::printf('Written by',
                ($this->article->created_by_alias ?
                $this->article->created_by_alias : $this->article->author)); ?>
        </span>
        <?php endif; ?>

        <?php if ($this->params->get('show_create_date')) : ?>
        <span class="createdate">
            <?php echo JHTML::_('date', $this->article->created,
                JText::_('DATE_FORMAT_LC2')); ?>
        </span>
        <?php endif; ?>
</div>
<?php endif; ?>

<?php if (!$this->params->get('show_intro')) :
    echo $this->article->event->afterDisplayTitle;
endif; ?>

<?php if ($this->print || $this->params->get('show_pdf_icon') ||
    $this->params->get('show_print_icon') ||
    $this->params->get('show_email_icon')) : ?>
<div class="buttonheading">
    <?php if ($this->print) :
        echo JHTML::_('icon.print_screen', $this->article,
        $this->params, $this->access);
    elseif ($this->params->get('show_pdf_icon') ||
        $this->params->get('show_print_icon') ||
        $this->params->get('show_email_icon')) : ?>
        <img src="<?php echo $this->baseurl ?>/templates/beez/images/trans.gif"
            alt="<?php echo JText::_('attention open in a new window'); ?>" />
        <?php if ($this->params->get('show_pdf_icon')) :
            echo JHTML::_('icon.pdf', $this->article, $this->params,
                $this->access);
        endif;
        if ($this->params->get('show_print_icon')) :
            echo JHTML::_('icon.print_popup', $this->article,
            $this->params, $this->access);
        endif;
        if ($this->params->get('show_email_icon')) :
            echo JHTML::_('icon.email', $this->article,
                $this->params, $this->access);
        endif;
    endif; ?>
</div>
<?php endif; ?>

<?php if (($this->params->get('show_section') && $this->article->sectionid) ||
    ($this->params->get('show_category') && $this->article->catid)) : ?>
<div class="iteminfo">
    <?php if ($this->params->get('show_section') && $this->article->sectionid) : ?>
    <span>
        <?php if ($this->params->get('link_section')) : ?>
```

```php
        <?php echo
        '<a href="'.JRoute::_(ContentHelperRoute::getSectionRoute(
        $this->article->sectionid)).'">'; ?>
    <?php endif; ?>
    <?php echo $this->article->section; ?>
    <?php if ($this->params->get('link_section')) : ?>
        <?php echo '</a>'; ?>
    <?php endif; ?>
    <?php if ($this->params->get('show_category')) : ?>
        <?php echo ' - '; ?>
    <?php endif; ?>
    </span>
    <?php endif; ?>
    <?php if ($this->params->get('show_category') && $this->article->catid) : ?>
    <span>
        <?php if ($this->params->get('link_category')) : ?>
        <?php echo
        '<a href="'.JRoute::_(ContentHelperRoute::getCategoryRoute(
        $this->article->catslug, $this->article->sectionid)).'">'; ?>
    <?php endif; ?>
    <?php echo $this->article->category; ?>
    <?php if ($this->params->get('link_category')) : ?>
        <?php echo '</a>'; ?>
    <?php endif; ?>
    </span>
    <?php endif; ?>
</div>
<?php endif; ?>

<?php echo $this->article->event->beforeDisplayContent; ?>

<?php if (isset ($this->article->toc)) :
    echo $this->article->toc;
endif; ?>

<?php echo JFilterOutput::ampReplace($this->article->text); ?>

<?php echo $this->article->event->afterDisplayContent; ?>

</div>
```

The first line, `<?php defined('_JEXEC') or die('Restricted access'); ?>`, prevents direct access to this file. The second section of code is the page title. This value may be different from the article title. First, the code checks to determine whether the page title should be shown, if it exists, and if the page title is different from the article title. If all of these things are true, the page title is displayed.

The next section displays the article title. First, it checks if the title should be shown, then it starts the header tag that contains the title, and then checks if the title should contain a link to the article. If it should contain a link to the article, it displays the title as a link. Otherwise, it just displays the title.

The next section displays an icon that links to a form used to edit the article if the user is logged in and has the proper access to edit the article. After that, the code determines if the last date that the article was modified, the article's author's name, or the date the article was created should be displayed, and then it displays that information.

The next piece of code is a trigger for content plugins. It checks to see if the parameters are set to show the introductory text of the article. If not, it then sets a trigger to load plugins that are triggered after the article title is displayed. If that doesn't make sense, don't worry. It makes sense to the people who build plugins.

The next section determines if icons should be displayed to enable visitors to open the article as a PDF file, print the article, or e-mail the article to a friend. If one or more of these icons should be displayed, the article displays the icons with links to perform each of the functions.

The next section checks the article's parameters to determine whether the name of the article's section or category should be displayed, and if the names should link to the section or category. If so, it displays the name or names. If the names should be linked, it links them to their respective pages.

The next line of code is another plugin trigger. It triggers plugins that are set to run before content is displayed. After this plugin trigger, if the article has a table of contents, it is rendered. Finally, the article text is displayed. After the article is displayed, one more plugin trigger is needed to trigger plugins that are set to run after content is displayed.

Module Chrome

Another great feature of Joomla! 1.5 templates is the ability to create custom module styles by building what's often referred to as "module chrome." As you learned previously in this chapter, module positions are loaded in the template with the following code:

```
<jdoc:include type="modules" name="position_name" style="some_style" />
```

You also learned that five core styles are available to be used: none, table, horz, xhtml, and rounded. Applying the none style or just not adding a style parameter tells Joomla! just to load the module output without any added HTML, and it does not load the module title. The table style wraps each module's output in a table and loads the module title within a th tag in the table. The horz style wraps the each module's output in the table from the table style, and then wraps that in another table. The xhtml style is the most widely used style, and it wraps each module's output in a div and loads the module title within an h3 tag. Finally, the rounded style wraps each module's output in four divs, so that you can apply special CSS techniques to create a rounded corner effect on each module, and it loads the module title in an h3 tag.

With module chrome, you can create custom styles to customize the HTML markup that wraps a module's output in a specific module position.

To create a custom style, you create a file called modules.php in the html folder of your template, and add a PHP function to that file. The following is an example of what this file might look like:

```php
<?php
defined('_JEXEC') or die('Restricted access');

function modChrome_weddingsite($module, &$params, &$attribs)
```

```
    {
        if (!empty ($module->content)) : ?>
            <div class="weddingsitemodule<?php echo
                $params->get('moduleclass_sfx'); ?>">
            <?php if ($module->showtitle != 0) : ?>
                <h3><?php echo $module->title; ?></h3>
            <?php endif; ?>
                <div class="weddingsitemodulecontent<?php echo
                    $params->get('moduleclass_sfx'); ?>">
                    <?php echo $module->content; ?>
                </div>
            </div>
        <?php endif;
    }

    ?>
```

This example is very similar to the XHTML style, but it uses a different class, weddingsitemodule, for the div that wraps the module's output. You can customize the HTML however you want to customize it. For example, instead of an h3 tag for the module title, you could use an h2 tag, an h4 tag, a div, or any other HTML markup that suits your purposes. There are no limits to what you could do with module chrome.

You will likely recognize the first line of code in the previous example as the line that prevents direct access to this file. After this line, you can add as many module chrome functions as you would like to add. The functions must follow this pattern:

```
function modChrome_stylename($module, &$params, &$attribs)
{
    // Module Chrome PHP Code
}
```

The name of the function follows the pattern modChrome_stylename, where stylename is the value you use for the style parameter in the jdoc:include tag in your template's index.php file. You should not use one of the predefined style names, which are none, table, horz, xhtml, and rounded.

Module chrome serves as a template for all modules loaded in a given position. In the previous example, first the code checks to see if the module being loaded has content before loading the module. Then, it wraps the module in a <div> tag with the class weddingsitemodule followed by <?php echo $params->get('moduleclass_sfx'); ?>. That bit of PHP code added to the module class is the module class suffix, which is set as a parameter in each module.

Then, the module chrome checks the module's parameters to see if its title should be displayed. If so, it displays the title within <h3> tags. After the title is either displayed or not displayed, the module content is displayed.

None of the code within the function is required for the module chrome to work properly, so you can customize the function as much as you would like. However, you must be sure to include echo $module->content; somewhere in the function if you want to display the module's content.

Creating an Installation Package

Your template files should all be in a folder with the name of your template. For the sample template, the files are all in a folder named weddingsite. The file structure looks like this:

- ❑ weddingsite
    - ❑ /component.php
    - ❑ /en-GB.tp._weddingsite.ini
    - ❑ /error.php
    - ❑ /favicon.ico
    - ❑ /index.html
    - ❑ /index.php
    - ❑ /offline.php
    - ❑ /params.ini
    - ❑ /template_thumbnail.png
    - ❑ /templateDetails.xml
    - ❑ /admin
    - ❑ /css
    - ❑ /html
    - ❑ /images

In the template manifest file listed previously in this chapter, templateDetails.xml, all of these files are listed. For the sake of keeping the list short, all of the files in admin, css, html, and images are not listed.

With all of your files in the template folder, it is time to create the installation package. To do this, all you need to do is compress the files into a .zip, .tar.gz, or .tar.bz2 file. Several applications are available that enable you to zip up files, such as WinZip from WinZip.com, or ALZip from ALTools.net.

Summary

Joomla! 1.5 introduces many features to template building that Joomla! 1.0 did not have. Covering these features in full detail would take an entire book. It is important to get a basic understanding of the workings of the main template files, so you can begin to learn to develop your own custom templates. The only required files in a Joomla! template are index.php and templateDetails.xml. However, to truly take advantage of all of the template features available, you will need to incorporate more files. The following files perform a particular function in a Joomla! 1.5 template:

- ❑ component.php
- ❑ error.php
- ❑ index.php

- ❏   offline.php
- ❏   params.ini
- ❏   template_thumbnail.png
- ❏   templateDetails.xml
- ❏   favicon.ico
- ❏   en-GB.tpl_templatename.ini

One of the most exciting new features in Joomla! 1.5 template development is the ability to override HTML layouts from core components. The files used to generate these overrides are contained in a folder called html in the template.

Now that you know how a template works, it is time to look at how to troubleshoot your Joomla! site. Before you move on, please take a few moments to complete the following exercises. You can find the solutions to these exercises in Appendix A.

Exercises

1.   Where can you find an abundant source of filler text?

2.   What are the only two files required for building a functioning template?

3.   What purpose does offline.php serve?

4.   What pattern does a module chrome function follow?

Troubleshooting Your Site

You've just learned the language, installed Joomla!, picked out some great extensions from the JED, configured your site, managed your content and menus, set up those great extensions you found, set up RSS feeds, and built a shiny new template! Congratulations, you're . . . half-way there! Now that your site is assembled just the way you like it, you need to take some time to test and re-test everything on the site to make sure it is working properly.

My ninth-grade biology teacher used to always say, "I've only made one mistake in my life, but then it turned out not to be a mistake, so I was mistaken." I'm still not quite sure what he meant by that, but I think he was claiming to be perfect. He also used to say, "I'm not God, but I will be some day," so I think he might have been a little crazy, but that's beside the point. Unless you are my ninth-grade biology teacher, you are not perfect. Everyone makes mistakes, which is why it is so important to double-check your work.

Joomla! makes building websites easy. It performs many of the mundane tasks that used to be done by hand-coding every page in HTML, and it makes managing content simple. Because Joomla! makes things so easy, it is natural to get complacent and get unintended results on your site. Think of Joomla! as a piece of software or an operating system. You must keep your software up-to-date and monitor its performance to ensure that it continues to work consistently the way you need it to. This includes making security updates and managing the software (extensions) that is installed on your system in much the same way you would work with a personal computer.

In this chapter, you learn how to troubleshoot your Joomla! site. You get solutions to some common problems that people encounter, and you learn where to look for help when things go wrong and you can't seem to find the answers you need.

Common Problems

If you are having a problem with your site, chances are someone else has had the same problem at one point or another. Some problems happen to just about everyone at one point or another in their quest to build sites with Joomla!. In this section, you learn about some of these common problems, and you get some solutions to these problems.

Search Module Without the Component

Problem: You publish a search module on your site, and it works great, but you can't seem to control which modules are displayed on the search results page.

Cause: The search results page is part of the search component. If you do not have menu item for the search component, there is no Item ID for the component. As you learned in Chapter 5, the Item ID is needed to help set when and where modules are placed on a particular page. The search module can access the search results page without the site having a menu item for the search component, but without the Item ID, it is not possible to control which modules are displayed on the page.

Solution: The first step is to determine whether or not you have a menu item that points to the search component. Log in to your administrator control panel, which is located at `www.yoursite.com/administrator`, and check each menu to see if there is a search menu item. See Figure 9-1 to see a list of menu items and where to determine if the item is for the search component.

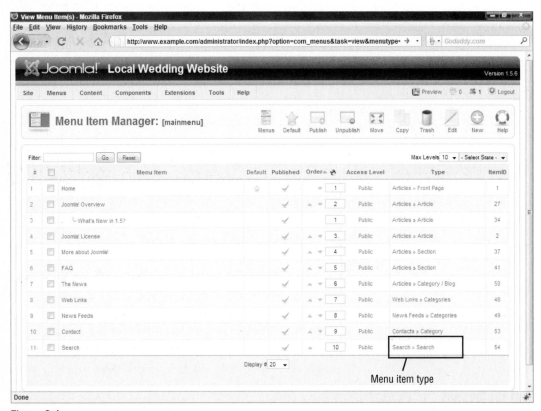

Figure 9-1

To determine if you have a search menu item, look at the type of each item and see if there is one labeled Search » Search. If there is not, add a new search menu item. This menu item does not have to be visible if you do not want it to be. One trick for adding a menu item that is not visible on the site is to create a menu called Hidden Menu that will never be published to the site, and add all menu items you wish to keep hidden to that menu.

SEF URLs Not Working Properly

Problem: Some of the most common problems people encounter in Joomla! involve SEF URLs. You go through the process of setting up SEF URLs, and for some reason they are not working the way you want them to.

Cause: Three possible causes exist for SEF URLs not working properly. The first cause is that you forgot to enable them properly in your global configuration. Because doing this is pretty obvious, this is the least likely cause of the problem, but it does happen.

The second, and probably most common cause, is that you forgot to rename htaccess.txt to .htaccess. This step is not necessary for having SEF URLs in Joomla! 1.5, but without it you still have index.php in the URL. With .htaccess, you get a nice, clean URL like this: www.yourdomain.com/some/sef/url/. Without .htaccess, you get something like this: www.yourdomain.com/index.php/some/sef/url/.

The third possible cause is that your web host does not support mod_rewrite, which is the Apache functionality that makes SEF URLs possible. Although this is quite rare, some hosts out there still do not support mod_rewrite.

Solutions: The first thing you need to do is check your global configuration to make sure that SEF URLs are enabled and you are using mod_rewrite. To access the global configuration, log in to your administrator panel at www.yoursite.com/administrator and click Site ⇨ Global Configuration. You can see these settings in Figure 9-2.

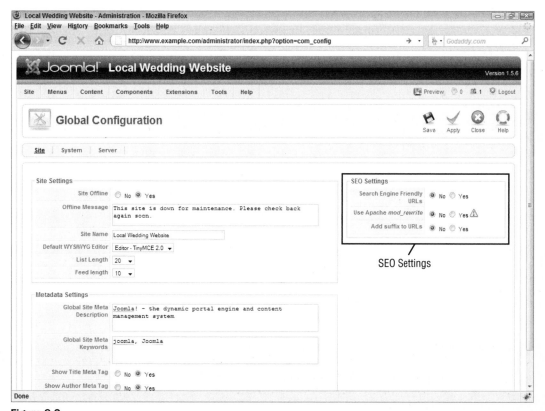

Figure 9-2

Once you have determined that Search Engine Friendly URLs is set to Yes and Use Apache `mod_rewrite` is also set to Yes, you then need to make sure that `htaccess.txt` has been renamed to `.htaccess`. If you intend to use `mod_rewrite`, this file must be named `.htaccess`.

If you have turned on SEF URLs in your global configuration and renamed `htaccess.txt` to `.htaccess` and your SEF URLs still aren't working, the only other possibility is that your web host does not support `mod_rewrite`. You have two possible solutions in this scenario. The first solution would be to try and request that that your host support this. If your host refuses to support this, the only other solution is to switch web hosts.

JavaScript Not Embedding in an Article

Problem: You are trying to embed JavaScript into an article, but the script isn't saved correctly as part of the article.

Cause: A couple of possible causes for this problem exist. One possible cause is the WYSIWYG editor stripping out part of the code you are trying to add to an article. Most WYSIWYG editors do not work well with adding code like JavaScript, and they will often strip out some or all of the script. Another possible cause is that Joomla! is removing JavaScript from your articles because the script tag is not allowed in articles based on your configuration of the content component.

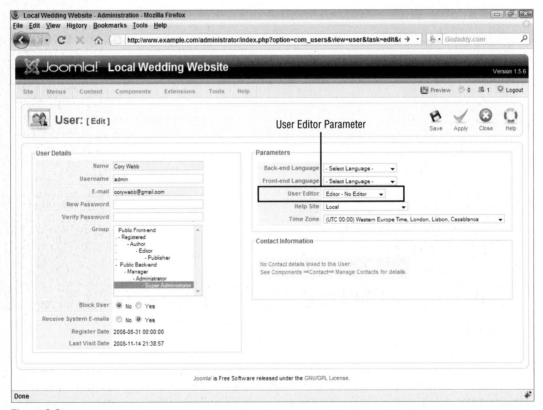

Figure 9-3

Solutions: For the first cause of this problem, there is a simple solution. Simply turn off the WYSIWYG editor and try pasting the script into the HTML of the article. In Figure 9-3, you can see where you set your editor to Editor – No Editor in your user account manager. To access the user account manager, log in to your administrator panel at `www.yoursite.com/administrator`, click Site ➪ User Manager, and click the name of the user account your want to manage.

After you have turned off the WYSIWYG editor, you can paste your code anywhere in the article without the editor stripping it out.

The other possible cause of this problem is that one of Joomla!'s security features strips out the code as the article is being saved. As you learned in Chapter 3, the core content component has a set of filtering options for filtering out or allowing certain HTML tags in articles. The `script` tag is part of the default "blacklist" of tags, meaning by default the `script` tag is not allowed. If you need to embed scripts into articles, you need to add the `script` tag to the whitelist. Figure 9-4 shows the filtering options parameters in the content component.

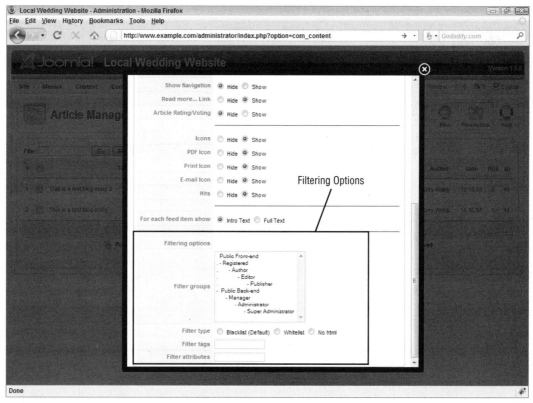

Figure 9-4

In the filtering options, the first thing you do is select the groups for which you want to add the `script` tag to the whitelist. It is probably best to limit this to administrators and super administrators, to prevent others from adding scripts to articles. Next, you select "Whitelist" as the filter type, and then type **script** into the filter tags parameter.

Adding JavaScript to an Article

Adding JavaScript to an article involves the following steps:

1. Log in to your administrator panel at `www.yoursite.com/administrator`.

2. Navigate to you user manager by clicking Site ⇨ User Manager.

3. Select your user account by clicking your name in the list of users.

4. Disable the WYSIWYG editor for your user account by setting the User Editor parameter to Editor – No Editor.

5. Navigate to the article manager by clicking Content ⇨ Article Manager.

6. Click the Parameters button in the toolbar.

7. Scroll down to the bottom of the parameters window and set Filter Type to Whitelist.

8. Set the value of Filter Tags to script.

9. Scroll back to the top of the parameters window and click Save.

10. Back in the article manager, click the New button in the toolbar to create a new article.

11. Give the article a title and an alias, and select a section and a category.

12. Add the following JavaScript into the article:

```
<script type="text/javascript">
    alert("Hooray! JavaScript in an article!");
</script>
```

13. Click Save in the toolbar.

How It Works

Adding JavaScript to an article is as easy as copying and pasting code. However, to ensure that the WYSIWYG editor and Joomla! do not strip out your code, you must disable the editor and add the script tag to the filter's whitelist.

If done correctly, this article will pop up an alert box that says, "Hooray! JavaScript in an article!" However, if you fail to add script to your whitelist, the `<script type="text/javascript">` and `</script>` tags are removed from the article, and the article just displays the text `alert("Hooray! JavaScript in an article!");` rather than popping up the alert box. If you try to add the script directly in the WYSIWYG editor, the article will display:

```
<script type="text/javascript">
    alert("Hooray! JavaScript in an Article!");
</script>
```

This happens because the WYSIWYG editor just assumes that the script tags are text, and it converts them to a format so that they can be displayed as text rather than function as actual JavaScript.

Can't get "Welcome to the Frontpage" off of the Front Page

Problem: The home page of your site says "Welcome to the Frontpage," and you can't seem to get rid of it.

Cause: When you first install Joomla!, the default menu item is a link to the front page view of the content component. For this menu item, the page title parameter, which you learned about in Chapter 3, is set to "Welcome to the Frontpage," and that is what is displaying on the front page of your site.

Solution: To remove this, you simply go to the menu manager for your main menu and select the Home menu item. Then, under Parameters (System), delete Welcome to the Frontpage from the page title parameter. Deleting the page title sets the menu item title as the new page title. If you want to get rid of the page title completely, you need to set the Show Page Title parameter to No. Figure 9-5 shows the location of these parameters in your menu item manager.

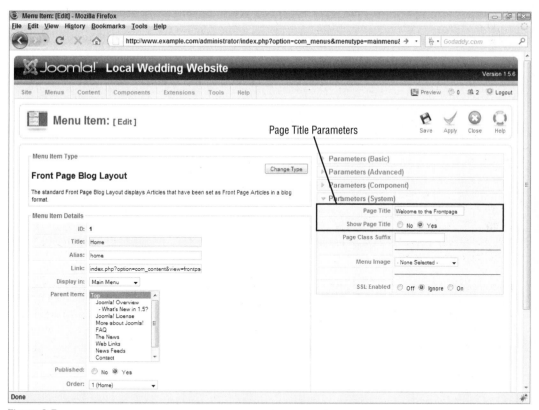

Figure 9-5

The page title parameter is available in all menu items, regardless of which type of menu item you are creating. However, not all components make use of the page title parameter in the same way that the core content component uses it, so changing this parameter may not have any effect on certain components.

Trial and Error

Trial and error is a method for solving problems. Oh, and the sky is blue, the Pope is Catholic, and bears poop in the woods. Trial and error can be thought of as randomly guessing a solution for a particular problem, trying that solution and seeing if it fixes the problem, and repeating those steps until you have found a satisfactory solution. It's not the best way to solve a problem in a complex system, but it is a great way to learn your way around the system.

With Joomla!, as with any system, the best way to learn is to do. My roommate in college always said the best way to learn your way around a new city is to get lost and try to find your own way home. If you find a problem, try to solve it without asking for help. If you can't figure it out right away, keep trying. You'll eventually figure it out, and you might learn some new tricks along the way. The following list contains some common items to check as you go through the process of eliminating potential causes of the problems you may be experiencing:

❏ Try viewing your site on a different browser. The problem may be a browser-related issue, because each browser tends to handle HTML, CSS, and JavaScript differently.

❏ Try viewing your site with a different computer. Check the version of your operating system, your browser, and Adobe Flash.

❏ Trace back over changes you have recently made to the site and undo the changes one by one, no matter how simple or unrelated they may seem.

❏ Disable any third-party plugins.

❏ Check with your hosting company to see if it has recently made any changes to the server software, PHP, MySQL, or any other server-side software.

❏ Get a second hosting company to compare the same site running in a different hosted environment. The problem could be related to different PHP settings that are outside of your control.

Over time, trial and error becomes a bit less random and a little more systematic. Before long, you will find yourself saying "I've seen this problem before, and this is how I fixed it." That's the point when you've shifted from "newbie" to seasoned veteran.

Where to Find Help

Sometimes you can't solve a problem yourself, and you need to get help. Fortunately, Joomla! is a huge community full of people and resources to help you get to the bottom of whatever problem you are experiencing. If you're like me, you probably hate asking for help and want to do it all yourself. Believe me, I understand, but sometimes you just have to swallow your pride and ask for help. Chances are, no matter what problem you are experiencing, someone has already been through it and found a solution.

In this section you find a list of useful resources in the Joomla! community and what they have to offer. You get some tips on how to effectively ask for help and get the results you want. The following table lists some useful resources.

Resource	Description
Joomla! Documentation	Location: `http://docs.joomla.org/` The first place you should always look for answers is in the Joomla! documentation. There is a wealth of information available. It has an FAQ section with loads of answers to frequently asked questions, and a helpful tips and tricks section.
Joomla! 1.5 API Reference	Location: `http://api.joomla.org/` If you really want to get a solid understanding of the classes and functions that work together to make Joomla! tick, this is the place to go. If you don't already have a good understanding of PHP, stay away from this section. It is mainly for the programmers out there who want to dive a little deeper.
Joomla! Community Forums	Location: `http://forum.joomla.org/` If you haven't already signed up for an account on the Joomla! forums, put the book down and go get yourself an account. The forums are perhaps the most valuable source of information available to you. Not only that, but many experts in the forums are ready to answer your questions and help you solve even the toughest problems.
Joomla! Community Portal	Location: `http://community.joomla.org/` The Joomla! team has put a lot of work into developing a new community portal. This portal contains a list of community events, team blogs, local user groups, and other resources. This is a great place to connect with other Joomla! users. Depending on where you live, you may be in close proximity to a local user group. These groups are a great way to meet people and get help from other users in person.
JoomlaTutorials.com	Location: `http://www.joomlatutorials.com/` Although not an official Joomla! site, this site offers a lot of great written and video tutorials covering a wide range of topics.
Alledia.com	Location: `http://www.alledia.com/` Alledia is a site about search engine optimization (SEO) in Joomla!. It offers a lot of great insights, tips, tricks, and tutorials.
CompassDesigns.net	Location: `http://www.compassdesigns.net` Compass Designs has a lot of great Joomla! tutorials.
HowToJoomla.net	Location: `http://www.howtojoomla.net` This is a site that I built in 2006 as a way to share tips and tricks with the Joomla! community. Dozens of tutorials are available with a wide range of information.

How to Ask for Help

The Joomla! community is full of people who genuinely want to help you. Many people volunteer count-less hours answering questions and helping people in the Joomla! forums, and they get little to nothing in return for their efforts. With this in mind, it is important to understand the good practices to use when asking for help:

❑ **Do some research before you ask your question.** The Joomla! forums have close to 1.5 million posts, and chances are your question has already been asked at least once. Before you ask your question, save everyone some time and do a quick search through the forums to see if your question has already been answered. If you do not find a satisfactory answer, at least you can say you made a good faith effort to find one.

❑ **Provide as much detail as possible.** It is extremely difficult to help someone who simply says, "My site is broken! What's wrong with it?" There could be any number of things wrong with a site, and this is not enough information to help you diagnose the problem. You will make the process of helping you much easier if you communicate the problem you are experiencing in great detail. Include things like which version of Joomla! you are using, a link to a specific page where the problem is occurring, a thorough description of the problem, and any other details that would help someone determine what is happening.

❑ **Be polite.** This should probably go without saying, but be polite. If someone offers you help, but their answer is less than satisfactory, kindly say thank you while informing them that the solution they offered does not solve your problem. You'd be surprised how many people resort to insults and name-calling when their problems are not solved by volunteers who offer their help for free.

❑ **Be patient.** It is understandable that you feel that your particular problem is the most important thing in the world, but other people are busy and not always able to answer your questions right away. If you don't get an answer immediately, don't worry. Someone will eventually come along and try to answer your question.

❑ **Spread the wealth.** Joomla! is a highly advanced system that would cost millions of dollars to develop from scratch, and you get to use it for free. Not only that, but people volunteer their time to try and help you in the forums. With that in mind, take some time and try to help other people with their issues.

You may have also purchased extensions or services from companies that specialize in Joomla!. If this is the case, you are most likely entitled to a certain level of tech support. Even though you have paid for this support, you may find that service and responsiveness varies from company to company, and the practices listed previously should still apply when asking for help from these companies.

Summary

Nobody's perfect. We all make little mistakes here and there. That is why it is so important to take the time to test and retest your site before you make it live to the world. In this chapter you learned about some common problems that people encounter, and you learned solutions for those problems. You also learned that it is important to take the time to do trial and error when you encounter problems. You may not solve the problem on your own, but you will certainly learn a lot about Joomla! in the process.

You also learned about some valuable resources in the Joomla! community for finding help, and you learned some basic tips for effectively asking for help. Now that you've learned a little bit about troubleshooting your Joomla! site, it's time to learn some advanced tips and tricks. First, take a few moments and complete the following exercises to test your understanding of this chapter. You can find the solutions to these exercises in Appendix A.

Exercises

1. What are two common problems encountered with Joomla! websites?

2. List three websites where you can go for help.

3. Why is it important to a) try to solve a problem yourself through trial and error, and b) do some research before asking for help in a forum?

Advanced Tips and Tricks

Now that you've built your site and tested and retested it, you're ready to start learning some advanced tips and tricks for customizing your site. Joomla! is a very open platform, meaning you can modify it and extend it far beyond what the core can do on its own. As you get more and more comfortable with the system, you want to poke around a little and try new things. Experimenting with the system like this is a great way to learn the possibilities and limitations of working with Joomla!.

In this chapter, you learn some useful advanced tips and tricks for customizing your site. These tips can help you as you work toward advancing beyond a Joomla! beginner and becoming a Joomla! professional. The purpose of this chapter is not to be an exhaustive list of possibilities. It examines only a handful of things that you can do with your site. The possibilities are virtually limitless with what you can do with Joomla!. The only real limitations are your own skill and creativity. By working through the examples in this chapter, you should start to get an idea of what is possible.

The tips and tricks you learn in this chapter are:

- ❏ Changing the HTML title from the template
- ❏ Advanced module position conditions
- ❏ Building a "split menu" with one menu and the main menu module
- ❏ Organizing content in more levels than just sections and categories
- ❏ Loading different components in different areas of the template
- ❏ Using different WYSIWYG editors for different users
- ❏ Using multiple templates
- ❏ Using page-specific CSS in a template

Changing the HTML Title from the Template

The HTML title is the title that is displayed in the title bar of your browser window, as shown in Figure 10-1. This title is contained within the `<title></title>` tags in the HTML of each page. As you learned in Chapter 8, Joomla! loads the title through the tag `<jdoc:include type="head" />`. Because you do not load the title directly in the template, you can't simply type a new title.

Figure 10-1

In Joomla! 1.5, the HTML title is simply the title of a given page. If you are on a page where an article is displayed, the HTML title will be the title. In other instances, the title is set by the component on a given page, and in other cases, the page title is set in the menu item for a page, as you learned in Chapter 5. For most sites, the standard title that Joomla! sets will suffice. However, you might want to modify the page title by adding the name of the site or some other keywords.

Try It Out   **Changing the HTML Title**

To change the HTML title:

1. Open your template's `index.php` file. You can either download the file to edit it on your computer before uploading it back to the server, or you can edit the file directly on the server. You can edit the file directly on the server through the template manager. Follow these steps to access the HTML editor for your template in the template manager:

    a. Log in to your Joomla! administrator.

    b. In the administrator main menu, click Extensions ⇨ Template Manager.

    c. Click the name of your template in the list of templates.

    d. On the template edit screen, shown in Figure 10-2, click the Edit HTML button to open the HTML editor.

2. Next, you need to access the default page title with PHP. The following code will access the page title and put it into a variable called `$mypagetitle`:

    ```php
    <?php
     $mypagetitle = $this->getTitle();
    ?>
    ```

3. Now that you have your page title, you can manipulate it any way you choose. One option would be to add the name of your site to the page title, like this:

    ```php
    <?php
    $mynewpagetitle = 'My Site Name - '.$mypagetitle;
    ?>
    ```

4. Next, you add the new value of your page title to the template header with the following code:

    ```php
    <?php
    $this->setTitle($mynewpagetitle);
    ?>
    ```

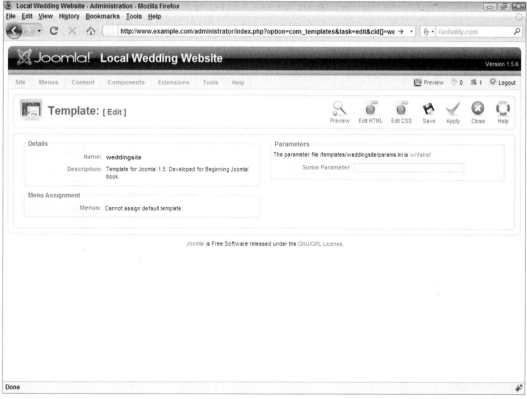

Figure 10-2

5. To shorten the number of lines of code you need to write, you can put all of the code together. Make sure that all of your page title code occurs before the header is included in your template.

```php
<?php
$this->setTitle('My Site Name - '.$this->getTitle());
?>
```

How It Works

Your Joomla! template is an instance of the JDocument object in the Joomla! framework. This object contains all the information to be presented to the end user, including the HTML title. The line in your template that includes the header loads all that information through this object, including metadata, style sheet references, script references, and the page title.

Because the template is an instance of the JDocument object, you can access all the methods and properties of that object by simply using $this. The function for retrieving the page title is $this->getTitle(), and the function for setting the page title is $this->setTitle(). Each component that is loaded on your site sets the page title either through the JDocument object or through the menu item that points to the component.

The `setTitle()` function can be used any number of times, as long as it is used before the header is included in the template. By using the `setTitle()` function in the template, you are simply setting the value of the `title` parameter in the `JDocument` object before it is included in the template's HTML output.

In this example, you edited the template through the Joomla! template editor in your administrator panel. You could also edit the template file by downloading the template's `index.php` file via FTP, modifying the file on your local system, and then uploading the modified file to replace the old file via FTP. Depending on the permissions on your server, you may have to do it this way because the file might not be writable by the template editor.

Advanced Module Position Conditions

As you learned in Chapter 1, a module position is a specific location within a template where modules can be displayed. You can assign modules to specific module positions on specific Item IDs. Module positions are loaded in a template in only two ways: with conditions and without conditions.

To load a module position without conditions, you simply add the tag to include the position:

```
<jdoc:include type="modules" name="some_module_position" style="some_style" />
```

Loading a module position with conditions means that there may be occasions that you do not wish for your template to even render the module position or the template HTML that surrounds the position, so you add some code to tell the template when to load a position and when not to load a position. This is particularly useful for "collapsible" module positions. For example, if the module position in the left column is not loaded, you might want the main column of the page to expand to the full width of the page, filling in the space left by the absent left column. To load a module position with conditions, you add a PHP `if()` statement to test your condition before loading the position:

```
<?php if ($some_condition_is_true) : ?>
<div id="some_id" class="some_class">
  <jdoc:include type="modules" name"some_module_position" style="some_style" />
</div>
<?php endif; ?>
```

The most common condition for testing whether or not to load a module position is to test if that position has any modules enabled for the current page. As you learned in Chapter 8, this condition uses the function `$this->countModules('some_position')`. The following example illustrates a typical usage of this function:

```
<?php if ($this->countModules('some_module_position')) : ?>
<div id="some_id" class="some_class">
  <jdoc:include type="modules" name"some_module_position" style="some_style" />
</div>
<?php endif; ?>
```

> ### Collapsible Module Positions
>
> Collapsible module positions are a common feature for templates. If you are looking to purchase a template, make sure that it offers collapsible module positions, because they make the template much more flexible.

For most basic websites, this condition and variations on this condition suffice. However, there may be occasions when you need to check for other conditions. The possibilities for module position conditions are virtually limitless. In this section, you learn how to apply three possible conditions:

- ❑   Loading a module position only for unregistered users
- ❑   Loading a module position only for a specific user
- ❑   Loading a module position only for a specific user group

Loading a Module Position for Unregistered Users Only

What if you wanted to display a banner encouraging visitors to sign up for a user account on your site? Once someone has signed up and signed in, there is no longer any need to display that module because you've already made the sale. After that, it's just annoying.

When you publish a module in the module manager, you can choose from three available permission settings: Public (everyone can see the module), Registered (only users who are logged in can see the module), and Special (only users with at least "author" access who are logged in can see the module). These options leave out the setting to display a module only to users who are not logged in, which is a flaw in the design of Joomla!. Fortunately, there is an easy way around this design flaw that makes it possible to show a particular module position only to users who are not logged in.

Try It Out   Loading a Module Position for Unregistered Users Only

To load a module position for unregistered users only, follow these steps:

1.   Open your template `index.php` file.

2.   At the top of the template, insert the following code:

```
<?php $myuser = Jfactory::getUser(); ?>
```

3.   At the location in your template where you want to load the position, add the following code:

```
<?php if (!$myuser) : ?>
<jdoc:include type="modules" name"some_module_position" style="some_style" />
<?php endif; ?>
```

4.   Replace "`some_module_position`" with the actual name you want to use for this position, and replace "`some_style`" with the actual style you wish to use.

5.   Save the changes you have made to your template.

How It Works

The JFactory object is an object in Joomla! that is used to call other objects. In this case, JFactory is used to call an instance of the JUser object using JFactory::getUser(). This instance of the JUser object is then assigned to a variable called $myuser. If the user is logged in, $myuser will contain an instance of the object. If the user is not logged in, $myuser will be null, meaning it will return a value of false in an if() statement.

Before the module position is loaded, $myuser is checked in an if() statement to see if it contains the JUser object or if it is null. If it is null, that means that the user is not logged in, and therefore the module position can be loaded. If it is not null, the user is logged in and the module position should not be loaded.

Some third-party extensions are available that enable you to hide certain content from users who are logged in. These extensions either extend Joomla!'s access control system, or they simply enable you to block certain content or modules from specific existing user groups. This technique can be used in conjunction with these types of extensions to gain greater control over who can and cannot access certain parts of your site.

Loading a Module Position for Only a Specific User

As you have already learned, the only permission settings for publishing a module position are Public, Registered, and Special. As the webmaster of your site, you may want to load a module that only you can see when you are logged in. Unfortunately, there is no way to do this from within the module manager, so you need to apply a module position condition so that a particular module position will only load for a specific user when that user is logged in. Applying this condition is a simple extension of the condition for loading a module position only for unregistered users.

Try It Out   **Loading a Module Position for Only a Specific User**

To load a module position only for a specific user, follow these steps:

1. Open your template index.php file.

2. Get the ID of the user account for which you want to display the module position. You can access the user ID in the user manager in the Joomla! administrator, as shown in Figure 10-3. The user ID for the first Super Administrator in the system is usually 62, which is true for this example.

3. At the top of your template, insert the following code:

```php
<?php
$myuser = Jfactory::getUser();
$myuserid = 0;
if ($myuser) :
        $myuserid = $myuser->id;
endif;
?>
```

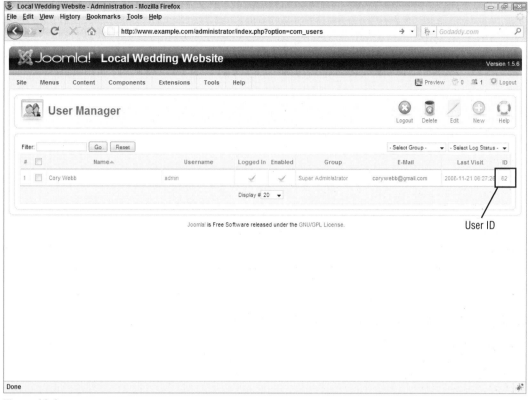

Figure 10-3

4. In the location in your template where you wish to include the module position, add the following code:

```php
<?php if ($myuserid == 62) : ?>
<jdoc:include type="modules" name"some_module_position" style="some_style" />
<?php endif; ?>
```

5. Replace "`some_module_position`" with the actual name you want to use for this position, and replace "`some_style`" with the actual style you wish to use.

6. Save the changes you have made to your template.

How It Works

This module position condition uses the same objects as the previous condition, but it goes beyond simply checking whether or not the JUser object exists. Once it is determined that the object exists (the user is logged in), the value of the user ID is taken from $myuser->id and stored in the variable $myuserid.

Before the module position is loaded, $myuserid is checked in an if() statement to determine if it is equal to the ID of the user that you want to be able to see the position. If $myuserid is equal to the designated user ID, the position is loaded. If it is not equal to the designated user ID, the position is not loaded.

You might be looking at these steps and thinking that you could cut down the number of lines of code by checking the value of $myuser->id rather than assigning it to a variable first. This would work, if you could guarantee that your users are always logged in to your site. Otherwise, you will get a PHP error because $myuser is null, and you can't have parameters on a null object. In other words, if $myuser is null, then $myuser->id can't possibly exist, so you have to first check that $myuser is not null and then assign the value of $myuser->id to a different variable, $myuserid.

Loading a Module Position for a Specific User Group

Joomla! has seven user groups (eight if you include guests): Registered, Author, Editor, Publisher, Manager, Administrator, and Super Administrator. For some reason, however, there are only three permission settings, which you already learned about. You might not want to limit the loading of a module position for a specific user, but you could possibly need a little more granularity when deciding who gets to see modules in a particular position. Applying a condition for loading a module position for a specific user group is similar to the condition for loading a position for a specific user.

Try It Out   Loading a Module Position for a Specific User Group Only

To load a module position only for a specific user group, follow these steps:

1. Open your template index.php file.

2. Decide which user group you want to be able to see the module position. For this example, only Super Administrators will be able to see the position.

3. At the top of your template, insert the following code:

```php
<?php
 $myuser = Jfactory::getUser();
 $myusergroup = '';
 if ($myuser) :
        $myusergroup = $myuser->usertype;
 endif;
?>
```

4. In the location in your template where you wish to include the module position, add the following code:

```php
<?php if ($myusergroup == 'Super Administrator') : ?>
<jdoc:include type="modules" name"some_module_position" style="some_style" />
<?php endif; ?>
```

5. Replace "some_module_position" with the actual name you want to use for this position, and replace "some_style" with the actual style you wish to use.

How It Works

This condition works almost exactly the same as the condition for loading a module position for a specific user does. The difference is that instead of testing the value of $myuser->id, you test the value of $myuser->usertype. Note that the value of $myuser->usertype is just the name of the user group to which the user belongs, if the user is logged in.

Before the module position is loaded, $myusergroup is checked in an if() statement to determine if it is equal to the name of the user group that you want to be able to see the position. If $myusergroup is equal to the designated user group name, the position is loaded. If it is not equal to the designated user group name, the position is not loaded.

Building a Split Menu

As you learned in Chapter 5, Joomla! allows you to build menus with nested menu items, also called sub or child menu items. With this feature, it is possible to build out most or all of your site's navigation hierarchy with one menu. For example, your menus might look something like this:

- ❑ Home
  - ❑ Menu Item 1
    - ❑ Sub Menu Item 1-1
    - ❑ Sub Menu Item 1-2
  - ❑ Menu Item 2
    - ❑ Sub Menu Item 2-1
    - ❑ Sub Menu Item 2-1-1
    - ❑ Sub Menu Item 2-1-2
    - ❑ Sub Menu Item 2-2

You have several ways to display a menu when it has numerous menu items in multiple levels of the menu. One such option, as shown in Figure 10-4, is to display the menu as an expanded menu tree. This option is fine if you have a relatively small menu with few submenu items. However, for larger menus with many submenu items, other options need to be considered.

Another option that is commonly used is called a Suckerfish menu, as shown in Figure 10-5. Suckerfish menus use a combination of JavaScript and CSS to display only the top level of a menu, and display each sublevel only when you hover your mouse over the parent item of a sublevel. This style of menu is a great way to display large menus with multiple sublevels that contain several submenu items each. Several variations on the Suckerfish menu idea exist, but the most common use is to have a horizontal top level with each sublevel extending vertically below the top-level menu item. If you are proficient with CSS and JavaScript, you can create a Suckerfish menu with the core menu module. Third-party menu modules are also available that create a Suckerfish menu for you. Many professional template developers build special menu styles like this into their templates, bypassing the menu module altogether.

Figure 10-4

A third option is to use a split menu. A split menu is a menu in which only the top level of the menu is displayed in one module as the main navigation of the site, and the sublevels are displayed in a separate module only when the user is on the page associated with the parent menu item in the top level or a page of one of the menu items in the sublevel. With Joomla! 1.0, some template developers included split menus as an optional feature in their templates. With Joomla! 1.5, it is possible to incorporate a split menu by using the core menu module.

Try It Out   **Building a Split Menu with Submenu Items and the Main Menu Module**

To build a split menu with submenu items and the main menu module, follow these steps:

1. Create a menu or modify an existing menu in the menu manager with a main level and one sub-level. For example:

- ❏ Home
- ❏ Menu Item 2
  - ❏ Sub Menu Item 2-1
  - ❏ Sub Menu Item 2-2
- ❏ Menu Item 3
  - ❏ Sub Menu Item 3-1
  - ❏ Sub Menu Item 3-2

2. Add a menu module in the module manager for the top level of the menu. You learned about menu modules in Chapter 5, and you learned how to add a module in Chapter 6. You can access the module manager by logging in to your administrator panel at www.yoursite.com/administrator and clicking Extensions ⇨ Module Manager.

3. Under Module Parameters in your new menu module, set the menu name to the name of the menu you wish to use. Set the start level to 0, and set the end level to 1. Set Always show sub-menu items to No. You can see these parameters in Figure 10-6.

Figure 10-5

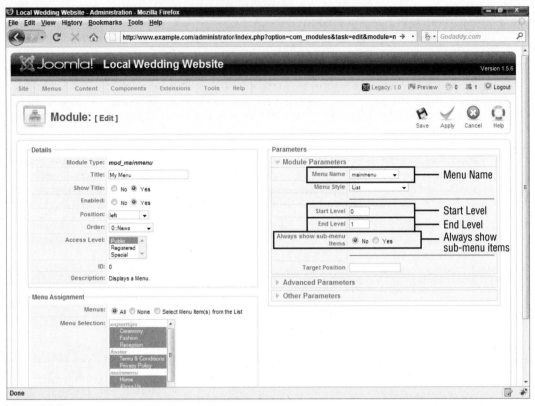

Figure 10-6

4. Under Other Parameters, set Expand Menu to No.

5. Assign this module to be published on all menu items in that menu. This menu module will only display the top-level menu items. Under Menu Assignment, shown in Figure 10-6, select Select Menu Item(s) from the List, and then select the menu items in the list for which the module should be published.

6. Add another menu module in the module manager for the sublevels of the menu.

7. Under Module Parameters, set the menu name to the name of the menu you wish to use. Set the start level to 1, and set the end level to 1. Set Always show sub-menu items to No.

8. Under Other Parameters, set Expand Menu to No.

9. Assign this module to be published on all submenu items from the menu and the parent menu items associated with the selected submenu items. This menu module will display only the submenu items that share the same parent menu item for the given page. Under Menu Assignment, choose Select Menu Item(s) from the List. For this example, you then select Menu

Item 2, Sub Menu Item 2-1, Sub Menu Item 2-2, Menu Item 3, Sub Menu Item 3-1, and Sub Menu Item 3-2.

How It Works

Joomla! 1.5 introduces a new feature in the menu module: the Start Level and End Level parameters, which enable you to choose which levels of a menu get displayed in the module. Using these parameters, you can limit the module to show only the sublevels you want it to display, blocking out all other levels.

With the example menu items given, the top-level menu module is displayed at all times, as shown in Figure 10-7. If a visitor clicks Menu Item 2 in the top-level menu module, the page associated with this menu item is displayed, and the submenu module will also be displayed, as shown in Figure 10-8. This submenu module will automatically select the submenu items under Menu Item 2 and display them and only them on the page. That way, the user can easily navigate through this section using this submenu module.

Figure 10-7

Figure 10-8

Why not just create separate menus?

Good question. I'm glad you asked. Yes, it makes a lot of sense to create separate menus for your submenu items, and you could absolutely take that approach. With that approach, you would create your main menu normally with no submenu items and publish it for all pages. Then, you would create a separate menu for each set of submenu items, and publish a separate submenu module for each submenu. There may be some cases where this approach is necessary because the split menu system simply wouldn't work with your site's information architecture. If that's the case, by all means you should take this approach.

However, several reasons exist for why the split menu approach makes sense. First, it is easier to manage one menu with multiple levels than it is to manage several menus. Imagine a situation where you have a main menu with seven or eight menu items, and each menu item has multiple submenu items, and those submenu items have multiple submenu items. If you build a separate menu for each set of submenu items, the number of menus becomes too large to manage easily.

Second, having submenu items within one menu shows the navigation hierarchy of the site more naturally. Giving users the ability to see the tree structure created by menu and submenu items in one menu helps them visualize how your site's navigation is structured.

Finally, SEF URLs are affected by the way your menus are organized. If you use Joomla!'s default SEF URL functionality, it generates the name of the URL based on the aliases of menu items. For example, if you set the alias for Menu Item 2 to menu-item-2, the URL that links to this menu item would be `http://www.yoursite.com/menu-item-2.html`. If you set the alias for Sub Menu Item 2-1 to sub-menu-item-2-1, the URL that links to this menu item would be `http://www.yoursite.com/menu-item-2/sub-menu-item-2-1.html`. Note that Joomla! automatically adds menu-item-2 to the URL path because it is the parent item to Sub Menu Item 2-1. If Sub Menu Item 2-1 had just been a top-level menu item in a separate menu, its SEF URL would have been `http://www.yoursite.com/sub-menu-item-2-1.html`, which does not reflect the true navigation hierarchy.

Organizing Content in Multiple Levels

One of the biggest limitations in Joomla! is the way it organizes content into a two-level hierarchy of sections and categories. For larger, more complex sites, this type of organization is not sufficient. Take an "About Us" section, for example. You could organize a section like this into several levels:

- ❑ About Us (Section)
  - ❑ Our History (Category)
    - ❑ Our Founding (Article)
    - ❑ Our Philosophy (Article)
    - ❑ Our Mission (Article)
  - ❑ Our People (Category)
    - ❑ Management (Sub-Category)
    - ❑ Manager 1 (Article)
    - ❑ Manager 2 (Article)
    - ❑ Engineering (Sub-Category)
    - ❑ Engineer 1 (Article)
    - ❑ Engineer 2 (Article)
    - ❑ Marketing (Sub-Category)
    - ❑ Marketing Personnel 1
    - ❑ Marketing Personnel 2

Even with this basic example, you can easily get beyond the constraints of Joomla!'s content hierarchy. Because Joomla! does not have subcategories, you would not be able to subdivide the "Our People" category into "Management," "Engineering," and "Marketing." If you stuck strictly to Joomla!'s sections and categories for this section, you would be forced to put all personnel under the "Our People" category, and you would lose the benefits of organizing this content into subcategories.

Fortunately, there are ways around this limitation. One way around this limitation is to use a third-party component for managing content items. Some components allow for organizing content differently than the core content component, and the availability of such components gives you options for how you organize your content. You can find such components in the JED under the Content Management category.

Another way to handle this is to use your menu structure to give the appearance of categories and subcategories. This method is useful for sections with relatively static content because it is not regularly updated in the same way that a news or blog content would be updated. With this method, you create a menu with multiple levels of menu items and submenu items that point to either a section layout, a category layout, or an article layout.

Try It Out   Organizing Content to Look Like Nested Categories

To organize content using your menu structure, follow these steps:

1. Organize your content into categories and subcategories. For this example, use the "About Us" content structure presented earlier.

2. Determine which content is static and which content is dynamic in nature. For this example, all of the content is static, because it will not be updated regularly like a blog or news. Because the content is static, each menu item simply points to an article.

3. Create all of your articles, categories, and sections. Because the example requires only articles, sections and categories are not necessary. The articles for this example will just be uncategorized. (Note: You may find that you need to build the structure of your site before the copy is written. If that is the case, you can just use filler text like the "Lorem Ipsum" text you learned about in Chapter 8.)

4. Create the menu items to point to the articles, categories, and sections, which you learned to do in Chapter 5. Even though a menu item is acting as a category or subcategory level, that does not mean that it needs to point to a category layout. Remember, this is just creating the appearance of nested categories. For example, the sample content would only have menu items that point to articles, even though it appears to be nested categories.

How It Works

The end user does not necessarily see your content organization the same way that Joomla! stores the data. To the end user, your content is organized the way that it is presented on the screen, so if the user sees nested categories in the form of nested menu items, then in effect you have created nested categories.

Strict adherence to Joomla!'s content organization does not make sense in all cases, so sometimes it is necessary to circumvent standard protocol and think outside the box. The point of this organization trick is not to convince you that using nested menu items is the only way to create the appearance of nested categories. The point is to demonstrate that other methods exist for organizing your content outside of the standard section/category/article hierarchy. With a little creativity and an understanding of how the different parts of Joomla! work together, many possible ways exist to overcome the restrictions imposed by Joomla!'s content structure.

There are limits to this particular method of creating the appearance of nested categories. For instance, this method is particularly useful for static content, but it doesn't always make sense to use this method for regularly updated content such as news or a blog. The fact that you have to create a menu item for each article would limit the efficiency of the management of your content because it would add a step to the process of adding articles to a blog or news section. However, using content sections and categories as part of your menu item structure would remove this limitation because you would not need to add a separate menu item for each categorized article, because each article would be presented within its respective category layout.

Loading Components in Different Areas of the Template

Joomla! templates are infinitely flexible in the number of things you can do with them. One way to customize a template is to use different conditions to load components in different areas of the template. For example, you might want to load all components in a main area of the template except for the contact component, which you might want to load below the footer. This situation is not a very practical, but it illustrates the fact that you can load each component differently in your template based on which particular template is being loaded.

Try It Out   **Loading Only the Contact Component below the Footer**

To load only the contact component below the footer:

1. Open your template `index.php` file.

2. At the top of the `index.php` file, add the following code to get the name of the current component:

```php
<?php
  $myoption = JRequest::getVar('option', '');
?>
```

3. In the location where all components are loaded except for the contact component, add the following code:

```php
<?php if ($myoption != 'com_contact') : ?>
  <jdoc:include type="component" />
<?php endif; ?>
```

4. In the location where the contact component is loaded, add the following code:

```php
<?php if ($myoption == 'com_contact') : ?>
  <jdoc:include type="component" />
<?php endif; ?>
```

5. Save the changes you have made to the file.

How It Works

The first thing you add to the template is code to get the name of the component being loaded. Only one component is loaded at a time, so there will be only one component name. The name of the component is in the page URL in the `option` parameter. For example, if the contact component is loaded, then `option=com_contact`.

The `JRequest` object is a Joomla! PHP object that has several functions used to get the value of HTTP request variables. It is preferred over the PHP methods `$_GET`, `$_POST`, and `$_REQUEST` because the `JRequest` object sanitizes incoming request variables to help make your site more secure.

The method `JRequest::getVar('option', '')` gets the value of the request variable `option`, and if no value exists it sets the default as an empty string. This value is then stored in the variable `$myoption` for use later in the template.

Before the component is loaded, the template checks the value of `$myoption` to see if it is equal to `com_contact`. If it is equal, the contact component is loaded. The component is loaded in one area of the template if the contact component is the current component and in another area of the template if the contact component is not loaded. You can easily use this technique to perform other component-specific functions in your template, such as loading component-specific CSS or loading component-specific module positions.

Using Different WYSIWYG Editors for Different Users

Approximately a dozen WYSIWYG editors are available for Joomla!, and different people prefer different editors. Some people may find one editor easier to use than another one, and others might just like the features of one better than the features of another. Whatever the reason, if multiple users on your site will be adding and managing articles, it makes sense to give them a choice of which WYSIWYG editor they use.

Try It Out   Assigning Different WYSIWYG Editors to Different Users

To assign different WYSIWYG editors to different users, follow these steps:

1. Install multiple WYSIWYG editors. Joomla! comes with three editor options pre-installed: No Editor, TinyMCE 2.0, and XStandard Lite 2.0. (Note: XStandard Lite 2.0 is disabled by default, and to use it you must enable the XStandard Lite 2.0 Editor plugin.) You can find several more options to download in the JED at `http://extensions.joomla.org/component/option,com_mtree/task,listcats/cat_id,1773/Itemid,35/`. WYSIWYG editors come packaged as plugins, so you just install them like you would any other plugin.

2. In the user manager, as shown in Figure 10-9, set a different editor for each user.

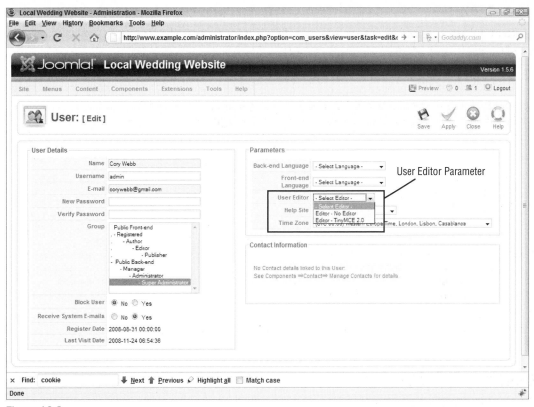

Figure 10-9

3. In the global configuration under the System parameters tab in the User Settings, as shown in Figure 10-10, set Front-end User Parameters to Show to enable your users to select which WYSI-WYG editor they each prefer to use.

4. Save the changes you have made to the global configuration.

How It Works

In the global configuration, you can set a default WYSIWYG editor that will be used by all users by default unless you set a different WYSIWYG editor for each user or allow each user to select their own editor. Each user account has its own unique set of parameters including which editor the user prefers.

When Joomla! is loading a form that contains a WYSIWYG editor, it checks the user's parameters to determine if the user accessing the form has selected a different editor than the default. If the user has selected a different editor, Joomla! loads that editor. Otherwise, Joomla! loads the default editor. Some WYSIWYG editors take this one step further by turning certain features on or off for particular users or user groups.

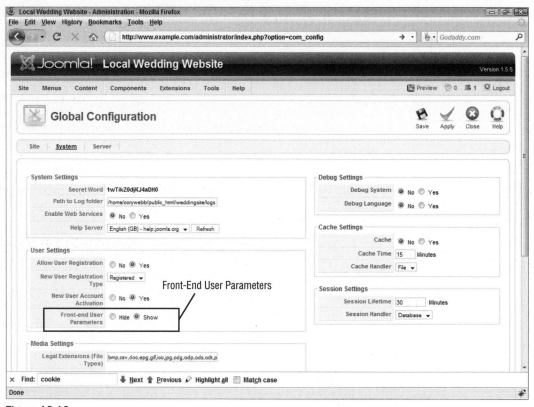

Figure 10-10

Using Multiple Templates

The template is the main piece of the presentation layer of any Joomla! website. It dictates how things look on a site, and it includes menu styles, fonts, colors, module positions, and much more. As you have learned, templates offer you infinite flexibility in customizing presentation details. Another level of flexibility is the ability to load different templates for different sections of your site.

There are several reasons for doing this. For example, you might have a news site with different categories, and you might want to have a different color scheme for each category. To achieve this, you could load a separate template for each category on your site. You might also include a component on your site that needs to have a completely different look and feel from the rest of the site. To do this, you would simply load a separate template for that component.

However, if you intend to use the multiple template feature to create the appearance of multiple sites within one installation of Joomla!, you should probably reconsider this approach. Joomla! was not made to handle multiple sites with one instance, and attempting to do this could lead to unnecessary complexity in managing your site and your content.

Try It Out   **Using Multiple Templates**

To use multiple templates, follow these steps:

1. Install all of the templates you want to use.

2. Go to your template manager, as shown in Figure 10-11, by logging in to your administrator panel at www.yoursite.com/administrator and clicking Extensions ⇨ Template Manager. Set your default template by selecting the template and clicking the Default button in the toolbar. The default template will have a star by its name in the "Default" column of the template manager.

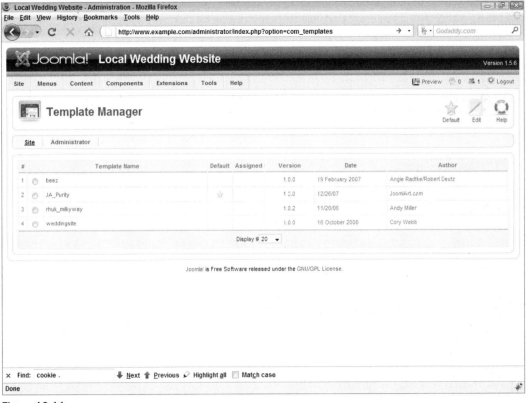

Figure 10-11

3. For each template that you want to use (besides the default template, which will be used for every page unless you assign a different template to a particular page), click the template name in the list to open the template editor, which is shown in Figure 10-12.

4. Under Menu Assignment in the template editor, choose Select from List and then select all of the menu items to which you wish to assign the template. You can only assign one template per menu item, and you can't assign the default template because it is assigned to all unassigned menu items by default.

Figure 10-12

How It Works

Whenever a page is loaded, Joomla! checks to see if a template is assigned to that page via its menu item. If a template is not assigned, the default template is loaded. Assigning different templates to different sections of your site is a great way to have a unique look and feel for each section of your website.

There are some disadvantages to assigning multiple templates on your site. First of all, if there is no consistency among the different templates you assign, you run the risk of losing the brand image that you are trying to project and confusing your site's visitors by giving them an inconsistent experience for each section of your site. Another disadvantage is, if there is consistency among the various templates, it becomes more difficult to make changes to the look of your site because you may have to make a change to each template that you use. If you end up using several templates, the task could quickly become overwhelming. A better approach might be to build a smart template that changes its color scheme based on which area of the site is accessed. This approach keeps all of your template code in one place, so you only have to make a change once when necessary. The next section describes a technique that makes this type of smart template possible.

Using Page-Specific CSS in a Template

If assigning multiple templates does not work with the needs of your site, but you need to have a slightly different look and feel for different pages on your site, you might want to consider using page-specific CSS within your default template. With page-specific CSS, you can change the look and feel of different pages by creating unique styles for each page of the site.

You have several ways to create unique styles for each page of a site, but the two easiest ways to do this are to use page-specific CSS classes, or to load page-specific CSS files. Either of these options will work, but for the purposes of this example, try using page-specific CSS classes.

The quickest way to use page-specific CSS classes is to give the <body> tag a unique CSS class for each page on the site. You could put unique classes throughout the page, but only adding one to the body tag keeps the code simpler in the index.php file.

Try It Out **Using Page-Specific CSS Classes in Your Template**

To use page-specific CSS classes in your template:

1. Open your template index.php file.

2. At the top of the file, add the following code:

```php
<?php
 $myitemid = JRequest::getVar('Itemid', '');
 $myoption = JRequest::getVar('option', '');
 $myview = JRequest::getVar('view', '');
 $mypageclass = 'itemid'.$myitemid.' option'.$myoption.' view'.$myview;
?>
```

3. In the <body> tag, add the following attribute:

```
class="<?php echo $mypageclass; ?>"
```

4. Save the changes you have made to the file.

5. Open your template CSS file.

6. For each item that you wish to customize for a specific page, add a new CSS element with the body tag and class selector(s) for that page before the item's selectors. For example:

```css
body.itemid1 div.somediv {
 /* SOME CSS CODE */
}
body.itemid1.viewarticle div.somediv {
 /* SOME CSS CODE */
}
body.optioncom_content div.somediv {
 /* SOME CSS CODE */
}
```

7. Save the changes you have made to the CSS file.

How It Works

The request variables `Itemid`, `option`, and `view` are retrieved using the `getVar` function in the `JRequest` object. The values of these variables are stored in `$myitemid`, `$myoption`, and `$myview`, respectively. These variables are then used to create a set of custom classes for the `<body>` tag, and are stored in the variable `$mypageclass`. This variable is then added to the `class` attribute of the `<body>` tag.

For example, if the current page's URL is `http://www.yoursite.com/index.php?option=com_content&view=article&layout=article&id=1&Itemid=1`, the body tag would look like this:

```
<body class="itemid1 optioncom_content viewarticle">
```

Using class selectors for the body element in your CSS file, you can then customize any element on the page with basic CSS rules.

Summary

Joomla! provides a flexible framework that makes advanced customization achievable with virtually infinite possibilities. An advanced developer can extend and customize Joomla! far beyond what Joomla!'s core can do on its own, and by learning a few advanced tips and tricks, you can start to get an appreciation for all that is possible with Joomla!.

In this chapter, you have learned the following advanced tips and tricks:

- ❑ Changing the HTML title from the template
- ❑ Advanced module position conditions
- ❑ Building a "split menu" with one menu and the main menu module
- ❑ Organizing content in more levels than just sections and categories
- ❑ Loading different components in different areas of the template
- ❑ Using different WYSIWYG editors for different users
- ❑ Using multiple templates
- ❑ Using page-specific CSS in a template

Now that you have learned how to build a Joomla!-powered website and learned some advanced tips and tricks for customizing your site, you know all there is to know about Joomla!. And if you believe that, you haven't been paying attention. You can build websites with Joomla! for years and still learn something new every day. The best way to learn Joomla! is to keep digging and trying new things, so now it is time to take what you have learned in this book and start applying it to the sites that you build. First, please take a few moments and complete the following exercises to test your understanding of the concepts in this chapter. You can find the solutions to these exercises in Appendix A.

Exercises

1. List three conditions you could use for loading a module position. Try to think of some possible conditions not listed in this chapter.

2. What is a split menu, and why might you want to use it?

3. What is the `JRequest` object, and what should it be used in lieu of?

Exercise Solutions

Chapter 1

Exercise 1 Solution

The highest level in the content hierarchy is a section. The next highest level is a category.

Exercise 2 Solution

Modules are extensions that perform simple, specific tasks that cannot be handled efficiently by a component. Module positions are locations in a template where modules are loaded.

Exercise 3 Solution

The four applications that come with Joomla! are the site application, the administrator application, the Joomla! installer, and the XML-RPC application.

Exercise 4 Solution

The benefit of having a table prefix is that you can have multiple installations of Joomla! on the same database without resulting in data interference.

Exercise 5 Solution

An Item ID is automatically assigned to a menu item when it is created.

Chapter 2

Exercise 1

Three layouts for the core content component are Section Blog, Category Blog, and Article layouts.

Exercise 2

Plugins are necessary for this task because each component's data is structured differently, and therefore they must be searched differently. Building all of the possibilities into one component would be impossible, but making the component extensible with the use of plugins makes it possible to search a virtually unlimited number of components.

Exercise 3

The e-mail cloaking plugin hides e-mail addresses in content items from spammers using JavaScript.

Exercise 4

The JA_Purity template is in the Joomla! distribution as a result of winning a contest.

Chapter 3

Exercise 1

The three main sections in the global configuration are site, system, and server.

Exercise 2

Caching is used to improve your site's performance. It makes it possible to greatly decrease the load on your MySQL server, thereby increasing your site's response speeds.

Exercise 3

The "Read more" link lets the reader know that there is more text in the article, and it links to the full text of the article.

Exercise 4

Gathering search statistics can be useful in determining what people are looking for when they visit your site, but it can also use up a lot of resources as more and more searches are recorded.

Chapter 4

Exercise 1 Solution

An article can only belong to one category at one time.

Exercise 2 Solution

One way is by editing the category and changing the category's section within the edit form. The other method is selecting the category in the list of categories and clicking the Move button in the category manager toolbar.

Exercise 3 Solution

Categorize the article in the uncategorized category. Categorize the article in the uncategorized category. Categorize the article in the uncategorized category. Categorize the article in the uncategorized category. Categorize the article in the uncategorized category.

For the rest of Exercise 3, you can create an uncategorized article on your own hosted server or XAMPP server.

Exercise 4 Solution

Three options available if your planned content structure does not fit into Joomla!'s content architecture are:

1. Make some compromises with your plan so that it fits into Joomla!'s architecture.
2. Use a third-party component that will help you organize your content the way you need to.
3. Use a different CMS that handles your specific content structure.

Chapter 5

Exercise 1

Technically, it is possible, but only for very advanced users who have a very good reason for attempting something so foolish. For everyone else, no, it is not possible to build a Joomla! site without a menu.

Exercise 2

The Unique Name field is only used to identify each menu from within Joomla!'s code, so you can name this whatever you want to name it as long as it is different than all of the other menus' unique names.

Exercise 3

The default menu item is the menu item of the component view that is the first thing a visitor sees when he or she visits your site at www.yoursite.com.

Exercise 4

The Item ID tells Joomla! which menu item is currently active on the site, which tells it which menu items to highlight and which menu item parameters to load in the active view. It also tells Joomla! which modules to display on the site because each module can be set to display for all menu items or for a select few specific menu items.

Chapter 6

Exercise 1

The five types of extensions are components, modules, plugins, templates, and languages.

Exercise 2

The three methods for installing extensions are uploading an installation package via the extension installer, installing from a directory on the server, and installing from a URL.

Exercise 3

The first method is by clicking the up or down green arrows in the "Order" column of the module manager. The second method is to change the order numbers in the boxes in the "Order" column. The third method is to click on the module title or check the box and click the Edit button in the toolbar to open the module editor and change the "Order" parameter.

Exercise 4

As of this writing, 3,821 extensions are listed in the directory. You can see this number in the top-right corner of the JED, just under the main menu.

Exercise 5

As of this writing, Joomla! has been downloaded from JoomlaCode.org 6,776,436 times. You can find the current number on the home page of JoomlaCode.org in the right column under "Top Downloads."

Chapter 7

Exercise 1

In Joomla! 1.5, the following items can be syndicated: Content Front Page Blog Layout data, Content Section data, Content Category data, Contact Category data, and Web Links Category data.

Exercise 2

With the "For each feed item show" parameter, you can choose to display just the introductory text for each article or the full text of each article.

Exercise 3

In most of the newer web browsers, the browser can detect if a feed is available on a particular page based on a line of HTML markup entered into the header of the HTML document. The "Show a Feed Link" parameter includes the feed link in the HTML header, which helps the browser detect the presence of the feed.

Chapter 8

Exercise 1

Filler text is text used as a placeholder in comp design or mock-up for the purposes of seeing how the design will look. Designers commonly use "Lorem Ipsum" text as filler text, which you can generate at http://www.lipsum.org.

Exercise 2

The only two files required for building a functioning template are templateDetails.xml and index.php.

Exercise 3

The file named offline.php is a template for what displays when the site is taken off-line.

Exercise 4

A module chrome function follows this pattern:

```
function modChrome_stylename($module, &$params, &$attribs)
{
   // Module Chrome PHP Code}
```

Chapter 9

Exercise 1

Some common problems encountered with Joomla! websites are:

❑   Lack of control over module positions on search results pages when the search module is used but no menu item exists for the search component.

❑   SEF URLs not working properly.

❑ Inability to add JavaScript to articles.

❑ Unable to get "Welcome to Frontpage" off of the front page.

Exercise 2

Three websites you can go to for help are:

❑ Joomla! Documentation — `http://docs.joomla.org/`

❑ Joomla! 1.5 API Reference — `http://api.joomla.org/`

❑ Joomla! Community Forums — `http://forum.joomla.org/`

Exercise 3

a) It is important to try and solve a problem yourself through trial and error because that is one of the best ways to learn your way around the system.

b) It is important to do some research before asking for help in the forum because chances are your question has already been answered somewhere in the forum, and it saves everyone time from having to answer the same question multiple times.

Chapter 10

Exercise 1

The three advanced module position conditions listed in this chapter are:

❑ Loading a module position only for unregistered users

❑ Loading a module position only for a specific user

❑ Loading a module position only for a specific user group

The number of possible conditions you could use for determining whether or not to load a module position are virtually limitless. Some other possible conditions are loading a module position for a specific component, loading a module position on a specific day, or loading a module position for a specific item within a specific component.

Exercise 2

A split menu is a menu in which only the top level of the menu is displayed in one module as the main navigation of the site, and the sublevels are displayed in a separate module only when the user is on the page associated with the parent menu item in the top level or a page of one of the menu items in the sublevel.

The split menu approach makes sense for several reasons. First, it is easier to manage one menu with multiple levels than it is to manage several menus. Imagine a situation where you have a main menu with seven or eight menu items, and each menu item has multiple submenu items, and those submenu items have multiple submenu items. If you build a separate menu for each set of submenu items, the number of menus becomes too large to manage easily.

Second, having submenu items within one menu shows the navigation hierarchy of the site more naturally. Having the ability to see the tree structure created by having menu items and submenu items in one menu helps users visualize how your site's navigation is structured.

Finally, SEF URLs are affected by the way your menus are organized. If you use Joomla!'s default SEF URL functionality, it generates the name of the URL based on the aliases of menu items. For example, if you set the alias for "Menu Item 2" to "menu-item-2," the URL that links to this menu item would be http://www.yoursite.com/menu-item-2.html. If you set the alias for "Sub Menu Item 2-1" to "sub-menu-item-2-1," the URL that links to this menu item would be http://www.yoursite.com/menu-item-2/sub-menu-item-2-1.html. Note that Joomla! automatically adds "menu-item-2" to the URL path because it is the parent item to "Sub Menu Item 2-1." If "Sub Menu Item 2-1" had just been a top-level menu item in a separate menu, its SEF URL would have been http://www.yoursite.com/sub-menu-item-2-1.html, which does not reflect the true navigation hierarchy.

Exercise 3

The JRequest object is a Joomla! PHP object that has several functions used to get the value of HTTP request variables. It is preferred over the PHP methods $_GET, $_POST, and $_REQUEST because the JRequest object sanitizes incoming request variables to help make your site more secure.

Appendix B

Exercise 1

The correct answer is blue.

Exercise 2

Two packages you could use to install a web server on your home or office computer are XAMPP and WAMP.

Exercise 3

You need to know your host name (usually "localhost"), database name, database username, and password before you can run the Joomla! installer.

Exercise 4

Two reasons you might want to move your entire Joomla! Installation from one server to another rather than start with a fresh installation on your new server are:

1. Your site has accumulated a large amount of data in the database over time (sections, categories, content items, contacts, news feeds, etc.).

2. Your site uses multiple third-party extensions already configured and/or customized for your site.

Installing Joomla!

Installing Joomla! is essentially a three-step process: 1) unpack the Joomla! installation package and upload the files to your server; 2) set up your database server, and 3) run the Joomla! installer. You can install Joomla! on any Windows or Linux computer running Apache or Microsoft Internet Information Server (IIS), PHP, and MySQL. In this appendix, you learn how to install Joomla! locally and how to install it remotely in a shared hosting environment. You also learn how to move an entire Joomla! installation from one server to another without rebuilding your site from scratch.

The first section in this chapter covers the basic requirements of a web server for installing Joomla! and where to find installation packages to set up a local web server on your home or office computer. It then covers installing a web server on your system and installing Joomla! on that web server.

The next section covers what to look for in a web host. It then covers how to install Joomla! on a web server in a shared hosting environment with cPanel.

Finally, this chapter covers the process by which you can copy an entire Joomla! installation from one server to another or from your local system to your remote hosting environment.

Download Joomla! at `http://joomlacode.org/gf/project/joomla/frs/`. As of this writing, the latest version is Joomla! 1.5.8, but that is subject to change as regular releases are made by the core team.

Setting Up a Local Web Server on Your Home or Office Computer

Joomla! 1.5 can be installed on web servers that meet the following minimum requirements:

- ❑ Apache 1.3 or above or Microsoft IIS (Apache 2.2 or above is optimal)
- ❑ PHP 4.3.10 or above (PHP 5.x or above is optimal)
- ❑ MySQL 3.23.x or above (MySQL 5.x is optimal)

Fortunately, these minimum requirements are easy to find and easy to set up. Several installation packages are freely available with which you can install and set up a web server on your home or office computer. In this section, you learn where to find these installation packages and how to install a web server on your computer for the purpose of installing Joomla! on your home or office computer as a test environment.

Local Web Servers

Four main options are available for installing a local web server on your home or office computer:

❑ XAMPP is a distribution of the Apache web server that contains MySQL, PHP, and Perl. XAMPP can be installed on Linux, Windows, Mac OSX, or Solaris, and it is free. You can download the installation package at http://www.apachefriends.org/en/xampp.html and easily install on your Windows PC. XAMPP is not intended for use on a "live" site and should be used only for testing purposes. For this section, you will be installing XAMPP on Windows Vista.

❑ WAMP is another distribution of the Apache web server that contains MySQL and PHP. WAMP is available only for Windows PCs, so it is not as versatile as XAMPP. This is a popular choice for setting up an Apache server as a test environment, but should also not be used for a "live" site. You can download WAMP for free at http://www.wampserver.com/en/.

❑ MAMP is the Mac OSX-compatible distribution of Apache with MySQL and PHP. You can download MAMP at http://www.mamp.info.

❑ JSAS is an acronym that stands for "Joomla! Stand Alone Server," and it is a complete Apache web server distribution with MySQL and PHP. It also comes with Joomla! pre-installed. However, it is not freely available, and according to its own changelog found at http://www.jsasonline.com/jsas-changelog.html it is not regularly updated. You can find JSAS at http://www.jsasonline.com/.

Downloading XAMPP

To download XAMPP for Windows, go to http://www.apachefriends.org/en/xampp-windows.html and download the installer to your desktop. Several download options are available on this page, but you only want to download the installer for the basic package.

Installing XAMPP

1. Once you have successfully downloaded the XAMPP installer, it is time to install it on your system. First, double-click the setup file to activate the installer.

2. After you click Allow on Vista's User Access Control, you will be prompted to select your language like in Figure B-1.

Figure B-1

3. Next, you will see the warning shown in Figure B-2 that states that due to permissions issues in Windows Vista, XAMPP must be installed in a directory other than the Program Files directory. Simply click OK to proceed to the next step.

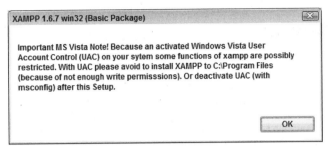

Figure B-2

4. Next, you should be in the XAMPP Setup Wizard shown in Figure B-3. Click Next to continue.

Figure B-3

5. On the next screen, shown in Figure B-4, you will be prompted to choose an installation location. I have chosen to install XAMPP at `c:\xampp`, because that is the default location set by the installer. You can install XAMPP anywhere on your system, but the default location will suffice for testing purposes. Choose your location and click Next.

6. On the XAMPP Options screen shown in Figure B-5, simply click Install to proceed with the installation.

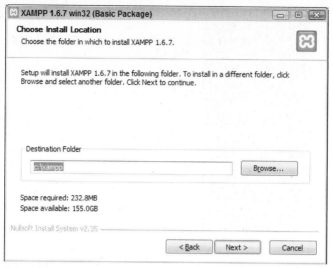

Figure B-4

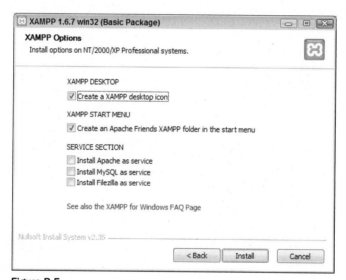

Figure B-5

7. On the next screen shown in Figure B-6, click Finish to complete the installation of XAMPP on your system.

Running and Configuring XAMPP

Once you have successfully installed XAMPP, you will be given an option to launch the server.

1. Click Yes to launch the server, or click No and then launch XAMPP by clicking the shortcut on your desktop. You will then see the XAMPP control panel like in Figure B-7.

Figure B-6

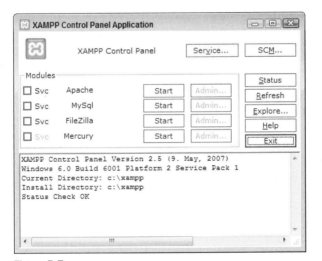

Figure B-7

2. Within the control panel, you can start the necessary parts of the server for installing Joomla!. Click the Start buttons next to Apache and MySQL to launch the web server and the database server.

3. Once the Web server and the database server are running, you can access your server through your web browser by visiting http://localhost/. You will then be automatically redirected to http://localhost/xampp/, which gives you access to server tools like phpMyAdmin.

The root of your web server is located at c:\xampp\htdocs\. You install Joomla! 1.5 in a subdirectory at c:\xampp\htdocs\j15\, which you will then be able to access at http://localhost/j15/.

Installing Joomla! on Your Local Server

Once you have downloaded the Joomla! installation package from `JoomlaCode.org`, installing Joomla! can be broken down into three steps: 1) unpack the Joomla! installation package and upload the files to your server; 2) set up your database server; and 3) run the Joomla! installer.

Unpack and Upload

The first step in the process is to unpack and upload the Joomla! files to your server. In this case, because the server is your home or office computer, you can simply unpack the files and move them to the proper directory. With a site hosted remotely on a server, you would normally upload these files using an FTP client, which you learn about later in this appendix.

1. Create the directory where the test site will be stored. For this example, create a directory at `c:\xampp\htdocs\j15\`.

2. Unpack the Joomla! installation package to the directory you just created. I am installing version 1.5.6, so my installation package is `Joomla_1.5.6-Stable-Full_Package.zip`. Several tools are available for unpacking zip files, and you can use whichever one you prefer. I am using ALZip from `http://www.altools.com/`.

3. Within the directory `c:\xampp\htdocs\j15\`, you should now have the following file structure:

- ❑ `administrator/`
- ❑ `cache/`
- ❑ `components/`
- ❑ `images/`
- ❑ `includes/`
- ❑ `installation/`
- ❑ `language/`
- ❑ `libraries/`
- ❑ `logs/`
- ❑ `media/`
- ❑ `modules/`
- ❑ `plugins/`
- ❑ `templates/`
- ❑ `tmp/`
- ❑ `xmlrpc/`
- ❑ `CHANGELOG.php`
- ❑ `configuration.php-dist`
- ❑ `COPYRIGHT.php`
- ❑ `CREDITS.php`
- ❑ `htaccess.txt`
- ❑ `index.php`
- ❑ `index2.php`

❑   `INSTALL.php`

❑   `LICENSE.php`

❑   `LICENSES.php`

❑   `robots.txt`

Now that the files are unpacked and uploaded to the server, you are ready to set up the database.

Setting Up the Database

XAMPP comes with a version of phpMyAdmin pre-installed. phpMyAdmin is the leading web-based system for managing MySQL databases; it is a very useful tool for setting up a database on your local server.

1.   Open your web browser, and browse to `http://localhost/xampp/`. You will then be prompted to select a language. Select your language, and then you will be redirected to the XAMPP control panel.

2.   In the left column Tools menu, click phpMyAdmin to launch the database manager. Figure B-8 shows the phpMyAdmin home screen. In the middle of the page, there is an option to create a database. In the first box, set the name of the database to `j15`. In the Collation drop-down, select `utf8_bin`, because this is the standard that Joomla! uses. Then, click Create to create the database.

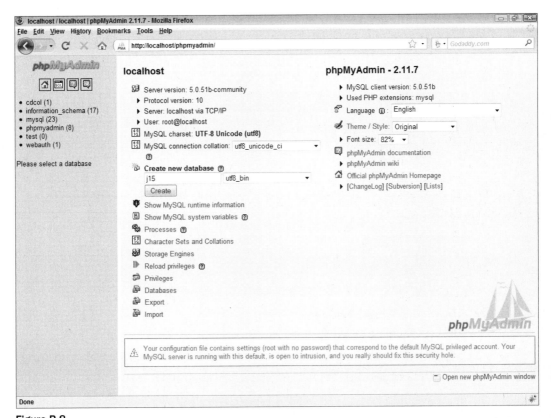

Figure B-8

3. Next click the home icon in the top-left corner of the page under the phpMyAdmin logo. This returns you to the phpMyAdmin home page so that you can set up a database user. Seven links below the `Create new database` form you just used is a `Privileges` link. Click that link to manage the privileges for the database on the screen in Figure B-9.

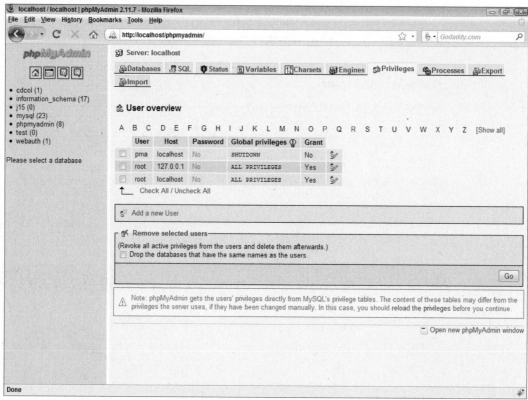

Figure B-9

4. In the middle of the page, click the Add a New User link to add a new user to your database. On the next screen enter the following settings:

❑ **Username:** Select Use Text Field from the drop-down box, and enter **j15** in the text box.

❑ **Host:** Select Local from the drop-down box, and localhost should automatically be entered into the text box.

❑ **Password:** Select Use Text Field from the drop-down box, and enter **j15** in the text box.

❑ **Re-type:** Enter **j15** in the text box.

❑ **Generate Password:** Ignore this.

❑ **Database for User:** Select Grant All Privileges on Wildcard Name (username_%).

❑ **Global Privileges:** Click Check All to grant all privileges to this user.

5. Once you have entered your user information, scroll down to the bottom of the page and click Go.

You now have a database and a user with all privileges on that database. The key pieces insert of information you need to take from this process to the next are host (localhost), database name (j15), username (j15), and password (j15). Note that I used j15 for the database name, username, and password for the sake of keeping it simple. In a live site environment, you will want to choose a more descriptive database name and a more secure username and password. The next step is to run the Joomla! installer.

Running the Joomla! Installer

The installer walks you step-by-step through the process of installing Joomla!. To begin the installation process, open your web browser and navigate to your local web server and the directory to which you loaded your Joomla! files. For this example, the Joomla! files are located at `http://localhost/j15/`.

1. The first step in Figure B-10 prompts you to select a language. US English is selected by default. Once you have selected your language, click Next to move on to the next step.

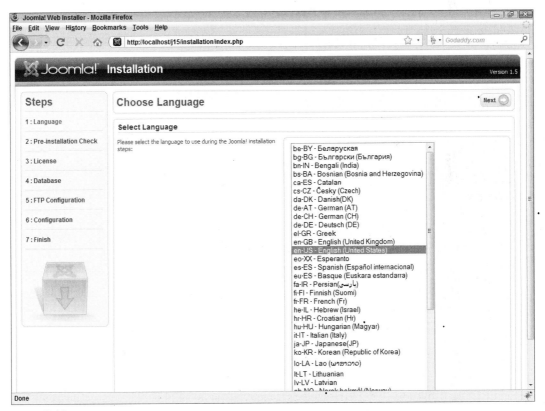

Figure B-10

2. The next step in Figure B-11 is the Pre-installation Check. In this step, Joomla! automatically checks your server's settings to determine if it meets the minimum requirements and if it has the recommended settings for optimal performance. If any of the requirements listed on the top half of the page say "No," your server does not have the minimum requirements to install Joomla!.

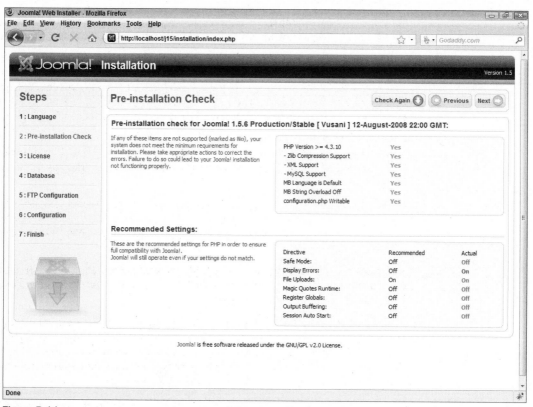

Figure B-11

The minimum requirements listed in the Pre-installation Check are:

❑ **PHP Version >= 4.3.10:** Most web hosts meet this requirement. If your web host does not meet this requirement, you need to consider switching hosts.

❑ **Zlib Compression Support:** Joomla! uses Zlib compression for installing extensions. If your server does not have Zlib Compression support, you cannot use the extension installer.

❑ **XML Support:** Joomla! uses XML for extension installation, and for managing extension parameters.

❑ **MySQL Support:** Joomla! uses the MySQL database engine to store and retrieve data.

❑ **MB Language is Default:** MB stands for multibyte. Multibyte language support allows for supporting languages that use so many characters that they cannot be contained in a single byte like English can.

❑ **MB String Overload Off:** MB String Overload is a PHP setting that enables programmers to use standard string functions for handling multibyte strings. Joomla! requires this setting to be off.

❑ **configuration.php Writable:** You can actually go through the installation process if `configuration.php` is not writable, but it makes installation easier if it is writable.

The bottom half of the screen contains a list of recommended settings. Joomla! will still operate if these settings do not meet its recommendations, but adhering to the recommended settings will ensure that the server is configured optimally for running Joomla!. You should work with your hosting provider to make sure these settings match. In a local testing environment, it is not as important that these settings match. The recommended settings are:

❑ **Safe Mode Off:** *Safe mode* is a setting that limits PHP so that it can only perform actions on files and folders with the same owner as the one PHP uses. This should be turned off so that Joomla! can perform actions on any file or folder with the proper permission settings.

❑ **Display Errors Off:** For a live site, you want the PHP display errors setting turned off because if there is a PHP error, you want to be able to control the display of that error. For testing, it actually makes sense to have Display Errors On so that you can debug potential issues in your site.

❑ **File Uploads On:** If your server prevents file uploads via HTTP, you cannot use the powerful extension installer built into Joomla!. Other ways exist to install extensions, but the installer makes it so much easier.

❑ **Magic Quotes Runtime Off:** Magic Quotes is a setting in PHP that automatically adds slashes to strings to escape quote characters for the purpose of saving the string to a database. The problem with this setting is that it can potentially add slashes to strings where you do not want slashes. Joomla! has built-in libraries for handling strings for saving them to the database, so Magic Quotes is not necessary.

❑ **Register Globals Off:** Having Register Globals on leaves your site open to security vulnerabilities. You can read more about Register Globals at `http://us.php.net/ register_globals/`. Joomla! has libraries that emulate the Register Globals setting, so it is not necessary.

❑ **Output Buffering Off:** Output buffering can enhance performance, but the directive should be set to off and output buffering should be explicitly enabled in the program code.

❑ **Session Auto Start Off:** The session auto start directive enables PHP scripts to work with sessions without requiring the script to explicitly start the session. The problem with session auto start is that if it is enabled in PHP, objects in the session classes must be loaded before the session starts. This can cause issues if the objects are not loaded, so Joomla! starts sessions explicitly to maintain control over the session starting process.

3. The third screen in the installation process, shown in Figure B-12, is the GNU/GPL, the license under which Joomla! is released. You may recall the definition of the GNU/GPL in Chapter 1. Simply click Next to indicate that you agree to the terms of the license and to navigate to the next step in the process.

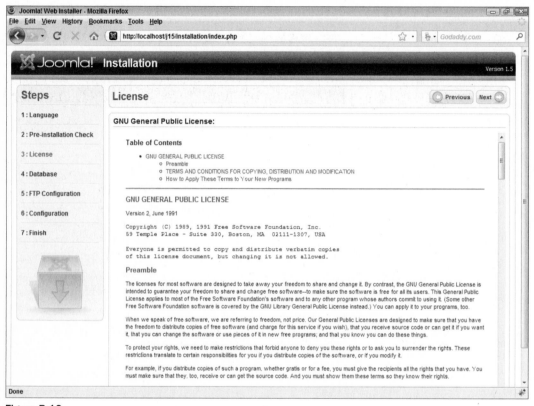

Figure B-12

4. The fourth step is database configuration, as shown in Figure B-13. For the basic settings, enter the database information you established when setting up the database:

- ❑ Database Type: **MySQL**
- ❑ Host Name: **localhost**
- ❑ Username: **j15**
- ❑ Password: **j15**
- ❑ Database Name: **j15**

For the advanced settings, you can optionally erase or back up existing tables from a previous Joomla! installation in the database. This is also where you set the database table prefix. Click Next on this screen to remove or back up any existing tables in the database and insert the Joomla! data tables into the database. If your database settings are incorrect, the installer will display an error message.

Figure B-13

5. The fifth step in the installation process is FTP configuration, as shown in Figure B-14. The FTP layer in Joomla! enables file manipulation on the server through the browser when permissions restrictions might otherwise prevent file manipulation. The FTP layer is optional, and you do not need FTP for your local environment, so leave this blank for now. In the section that covers installation in a shared hosting environment, you learn how to obtain your FTP information for setting up this layer.

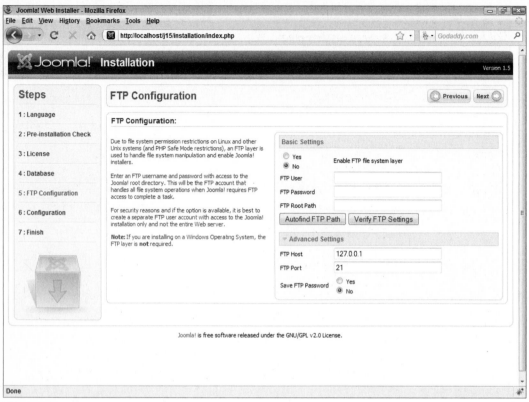

Figure B-14

6. The sixth step is configuration. In this step, you can set the name of your site and the administrator e-mail and password (the administrator username is "admin" by default) as shown in Figure B-15. You can also install default sample data or data migrated from the Joomla! 1.0 installation. To install the default sample data, simply click Install Sample Data.

7. To load the migration data, you must first create a migration script on your Joomla! 1.0 site using the com_migrator component that you can find at `http://extensions.joomla.org/component/option,com_mtree/task,viewlink/link_id,4223/Itemid,35/`. Then, select the circle next to Load Migration Script and enter the old table prefix and old site encoding from your previous site. Next, you browse your system for the migration script, check the box labeled "This script is a Joomla! 1.0 migration script" in Figure B-16, and click Upload and Execute.

8. The final screen in the installer, as shown in Figure B-17, contains a reminder that you must remove the installation directory before you can run Joomla!. To do this on your local system, navigate to `c:\xampp\htdocs\j15\` using Windows Explorer, and delete the directory named `installation`. Once you have removed the installation directory, you have successfully installed Joomla! on your home or office computer. You are now ready to install Joomla! in a shared hosting environment.

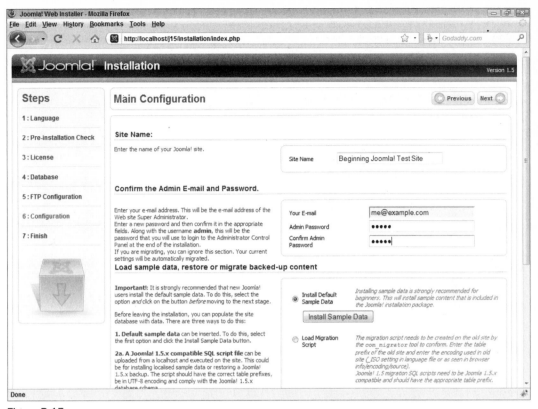

Figure B-15

9. Now that you have installed Joomla!, click the Site button in Figure B-17 to visit your new installation and enjoy the satisfaction of knowing that you have just successfully installed Joomla!.

Installing Joomla! in a Shared Hosting Environment

Unless you host your site with your own server, you will likely use one of three types of hosting configurations: shared hosting, virtual private server (VPS) hosting, and dedicated server hosting. Shared hosting is the most affordable configuration and is one in which many websites are hosted on the same server. You usually do not have root access to the server, but your hosting company gives you FTP access and a web-based control panel with which you can manage files, databases, e-mail addresses, and other items associated with hosting a website.

The next level up from shared hosting, both in terms of price and options, is VPS hosting. In this configuration, the server resources are still technically shared by multiple sites, but you typically have fewer sites per server. Another feature of VPS hosting is that you have root access to your piece of the server, so you have more control over the configuration and the resources allocated to your account.

Figure B-16

Dedicated server hosting is the most expensive option, but you get an entire server dedicated to your site's needs. You do not have to share server resources with other sites on the server, and usually you have root access to the server. With root access, you have complete control over of the configuration of your server.

Because shared hosting is the most affordable option, shared hosting environments are the most common setups for running Joomla!-powered websites. Web hosting companies that offer shared hosting are ubiquitous on the Internet, so it is important to know what to look for in a web host. This section covers how to install Joomla! in a shared hosting environment with cPanel.

What to Look for in a Web Host

One of the first things people often look for when seeking a web hosting provider is price. Price is important because it affects the bottom line, but I've always believed in the old adage that "you get what you pay for." Some really good hosting providers out there offer high-quality shared hosting for a low price, but you need to know what to look for and the right questions to ask when you are looking for a web

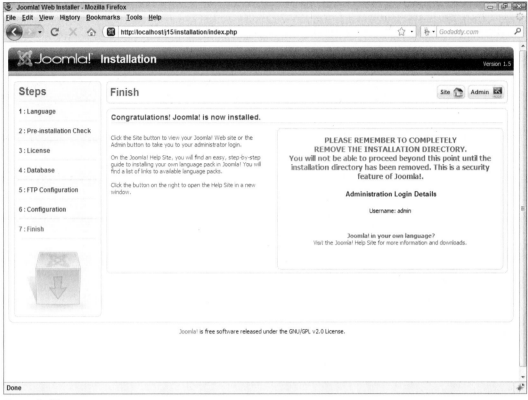

Figure B-17

host. Besides meeting the basic minimum requirements for Joomla! as discussed earlier in this chapter, research the following four qualities in addition to price:

❑ **Bandwidth:** Bandwidth is a measure of the amount of data that can be passed to and from your hosting account per month. If you anticipate a lot of traffic to your site, or if you plan on streaming media such as videos or audio directly from your server, you need to make this number as high as possible. If you are building a site to share information with the Little League baseball team you are coaching, bandwidth is probably not a huge concern. You can find affordable hosting that offers at least 1 terabyte (1,000 gigabytes) of bandwidth.

❑ **Storage:** A single installation of Joomla! requires less than 10 megabytes, and most hosts offer more than 100 megabytes of storage. The question of how much storage you need really comes down to the type of site you are building. If you plan on hosting a large number of pictures, videos, or audio files, you will need a lot of storage. If you're that Little League coach, you probably won't need a lot of storage space. Get as much storage as you think you need, and make sure your hosting provider can easily upgrade your storage without significantly disrupting your site.

❑ **Reliability:** Uptime is the most commonly used measure of reliability. Uptime is the measure of the percentage of time that your site can be accessed. Look for a host with a service level agreement (SLA) that offers refunds for downtime, so that you can feel assured that your site will be up at least 99% of the time.

❑ **Support:** Most web hosts promise great reliability, but the reality is that things happen. Servers go down. Networks go down. A couple of years ago, a car accident caused a power line to go down in Dallas bringing down the data center of a top-tier web host for several hours. This outage affected several high-profile sites, which undoubtedly spend thousands of dollars a month for hosting. You never know what could happen, so you want to know that your host will be there to solve unforeseen issues. Try and find out if your hosting provider offers 24/7 telephone or e-mail support, and look for existing customers to see if they have been satisfied with the support they have received.

Another important consideration is how easy it is to manage your account. Most hosting companies offer management tools like cPanel or Plesk, which make managing your hosting account easy with a web-based interface for managing files, databases, e-mail accounts, and so forth on your account. In the next section, you learn how to set up your database using cPanel.

Setting Up Your Database with cPanel

cPanel is one of the most popular tools used by hosting companies to give customers control of their hosting accounts. With most hosting companies, cPanel is available for shared, VPS, and dedicated hosting accounts. In this section, you learn how to use cPanel to set up a database for use on your site.

Try It Out   **Setting Up Your Database with cPanel**

cPanel enables you to control almost every aspect of your account. To use it to set up a database on your site, follow these steps:

1. Log in to your cPanel account and scroll down and click the "MySQL Databases" link as shown in Figure B-18. Different hosts use different themes or skins for their cPanel implementation, so the appearance might be different from what is shown in Figure B-18, and the link might be in a different location.

2. The next page is the MySQL Account Maintenance page, as shown in Figure B-19. Notice that this server already has a database installed named example_blog. This hosting service allows unlimited MySQL databases, so the Joomla! database will be a separate database. You could just use a pre-existing database to install Joomla!, and it will not interfere with the data that is already there. The best practice is to put each installation of Joomla! on its own database unless you have a reason not to.

3. To create the database, you simply need to give it a name. Enter the name of your database into the New Database box, and click Create Database. Because the sample site for this book is a wedding site, the name used here is "weddingsite." Because the server is in a shared hosting environment, other sites are using the same MySQL database server, so cPanel automatically prefixes the database name with a name unique to your hosting account. In this case, the resulting name will be example_weddingsite. Remember this name because you will need it for the Joomla! installer.

4. The next step is to create a user for the database. Go back to the MySQL Account Maintenance page and scroll down to Current Users. Enter a username and a password for the database user, and click Create User. For the sample site, the database user will be wedding, and the password will be 12345, but you should try to come up with a better password than this. As with the database name, the username will be given a prefix to keep it from using the same username as someone else on the server. In this case, the username becomes example_wedding, and the password remains 12345. Remember this information because you will need it for the Joomla! installer.

Figure B-18

5. Now that your database and user are created, you need to give the user account all access to the database. Go back to the MySQL Account Maintenance page and scroll down to Add Users To Your Databases. Select example_wedding from the User drop-down list, and select example_weddingsite from the Database drop-down list. Make sure All is checked under Privileges and click Add User to Database. You now have a database named example_weddingsite and a user account named example_wedding with the password 12345 and are ready to unpack and upload your Joomla! files to the server.

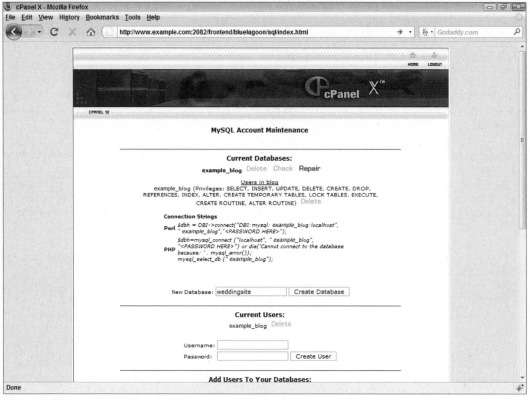

Figure B-19

Unpack and Upload

If you have not already done so, you should unpack your Joomla! installation package as you learned in the first section of this chapter. Unlike uploading your files to your local computer, uploading to a remote server requires the use of FTP, or File Transfer Protocol. Your host should come equipped with FTP server capabilities, and you should have an FTP user account from your host. The only thing missing is an FTP client, which is software you load on your computer to access an FTP server.

Several options exist for FTP clients, but my favorite is an open source application called FileZilla, which you can download at `http://filezilla-project.org/`. Once you have downloaded and installed FileZilla, you need to enter your FTP information including the host server (usually your domain name without the "www"; for example, `example.com`), your FTP username, and your FTP password.

Using FileZilla, upload all of the files from your unpacked Joomla! installation package to the directory where you wish to install Joomla! (for example, `example.com/joomla/`). For the test site, Joomla! will be installed in the root web directory, usually `public_html` or www on your server. Depending on the speed of your Internet connection, allow several minutes for the upload because there are more than 3,000 files in the Joomla! installation package. Once all of the Joomla! files are uploaded to your server, you are ready to run the Joomla! installer.

Running the Joomla! Installer

To run the Joomla! installer, open your web browser and navigate to the directory where you uploaded the Joomla! files. If the site is in the root directory like the example site, simply navigate to the root of your site by entering your domain name into the address bar. You will automatically be redirected to the installer.

Running the installer in a shared hosting environment is exactly the same as running it on your local system, but a couple of minor differences for the example site should be pointed out here.

First, the database configuration details are different. For the local test server, the database name, username, and password were j15. For the example site on the hosted server, the database name is example_weddingsite, the username is example_wedding, and the password is 12345.

Second, now that there is an FTP server, you can enable the FTP layer in Joomla!, as shown earlier in Figure B-15. Enabling this layer is optional, but to do so, you simply check Yes next to Enable FTP System Layer; enter your FTP username and password; click Autofind FTP Path and Verify FTP Settings; and click Next. You need to modify the advanced settings on this screen only if your FTP server host or port number is anything other than what the normal default would be. Note that your host defaults to 127.0.0.1, which is the localhost. This is different from what you entered into FileZilla because PHP is accessing the FTP server from within the host server, whereas FileZilla is accessing the FTP server from outside the host server.

Finally, on the Main Configuration screen shown earlier in Figure B-16, the site name is different and the sample data will not be installed. The site name will be Local Wedding Website, to go along with the subject of the example site. The sample data is not installed this time because it can become a hindrance when trying to set up your site. You will spend more time removing sample data to make room for your own data, and it really slows your progress.

Now that you know how to install Joomla! on a local server on your home or office computer and on a shared web hosting account, you can learn how to move an entire Joomla! site from one server to another, or from your local server to a hosted server.

Moving Your Joomla! Installation from One Server to Another

Things happen. Plans change. Websites outgrow current servers and need new servers. Hosting companies provide poor service, prompting a web master to decide to change servers. Or you might develop your site on a local development or test server before launching it, and you need to move it to your live server. Whatever the reason, you might need to move your Joomla! installation from one server to another.

If you've been running a website for a while, you have probably already accumulated quite a bit of content and several third-party components and/or modules, and you do not want to start fresh with a new Joomla! installation. This section explains the process of moving your entire site — files, database, and all — from one server to another. An important thing to understand about Joomla! 1.5 is that an installation can reside on any domain with only a few minor changes to the global configuration. This section covers the necessary changes that you must make to the configuration for Joomla! to run on a different server and different domain.

Why not create a fresh installation?

In many cases, creating a fresh installation of Joomla! makes sense. For instance, if your site has relatively few articles and only a handful of third-party extensions, you might consider installing Joomla! and simply rebuilding the site. However, if you fit into one of the following categories, you will want to consider moving your entire site:

- ❏ Your site has accumulated a large amount of data in the database over time (sections, categories, content items, contacts, news feeds, and so on).

- ❏ Your site uses multiple third-party extensions already configured and/or customized for your site.

- ❏ You have a development server and a live server, and you want to have an exact copy of the site on both servers.

- ❏ You just feel like trying it out to see if you can do it.

Try It Out   **Moving Your Joomla! Installation from One Server to Another**

Moving your Joomla! installation comes down to six steps:

1. **Check server settings:** Compare the server settings of your current host to the settings on the new host to make sure that your new server is compatible with Joomla! and the extensions you have already installed.

2. **Back up everything:** This includes all Joomla! files, third-party component files, and any other files that you have added to your site such as images, videos, and so on. Create a folder on your local system, and download all files to that folder using your FTP client application.

3. **Export your database:** The third thing you need to do is export your Joomla! database. The best thing to do is to export it into an SQL file, which makes importing it easier in a later step. The SQL file will contain all of the necessary SQL commands for creating your database tables and filling them with your data. Be sure you export the entire database.

   Using phpMyAdmin on both servers makes this step easier, because it offers the ability export your entire database to an SQL file. It also makes importing your files easier in step 5.

4. **Modify** `configuration.php`: Every Joomla! installation has a configuration file in its root directory called `configuration.php`. This file stores basic configuration information that Joomla! uses throughout the system. Most of the parameters in the file will stay the same, but some will change due to the different settings on the two servers:

   - ❏ `$host`: This value is the database host. In most cases, this will be "localhost," but if you are using a different server for your database, you will need to change this.

- ❏ $user: This is the database user. Change this if it is different from the user on your other server.

- ❏ $password: This is the database user's password.

- ❏ $db: This is the database name.

- ❏ $ftp_host: In most cases, the FTP host will be "127.0.0.1," but if you are using a different setting you will change it here.

- ❏ $ftp_port: In most cases, the FTP port will be "21," but if your server uses a different port you will change it here.

- ❏ $ftp_user: This is your FTP username.

- ❏ $ftp_pass: This is your FTP password.

- ❏ $ftp_root: This is the root path to which your FTP user has access.

- ❏ $tmp_path: This is the absolute path to the tmp directory on your server. It will probably look something like "/path/to/joomla/installation/tmp."

- ❏ $log_path: This is the absolute path to the logs directory on your server. It will probably look something like "/path/to/joomla/installation/logs."

- ❏ $offset: This is the time zone offset for your server. For example, if your company is in one time zone, but your server is in a time zone two hours ahead, you will need to see this to "-2."

- ❏ $live_site: This parameter is optional. You can probably leave it blank, but if you use it, this is the URL of your site. It will probably look something like "http://www.example.com" or "http://www.example.com/joomla."

- ❏ $sendmail: This is the path to the sendmail program on your server. If you are not using sendmail, you can ignore this.

- ❏ $smtpuser: This is the username for your SMTP server. If you are not using your SMTP server for sending e-mails from your site, you can ignore this.

- ❏ $smtppass: This is the password for your SMTP server. If you are not using your SMTP server for sending e-mails from your site, you can ignore this.

- ❏ $smtphost: This is the host name or IP address for your SMTP server. If you are not using your SMTP server for sending e-mails from your site, you can ignore this.

5. **Upload all of your files to the other server:** Using an FTP client application (like FileZilla), upload all of your files to the location on your new server where you want to install Joomla!.

6. **Import your database to the new MySQL database:** Using phpMyAdmin (or console commands if you are an advanced database administrator) and the SQL file you generated in step 2, import your old database into your new database.

7. **Test your new installation:** Your move should now be complete, but please don't take my word for it. Test your site to make sure that everything is in its proper place and working the way you expect it to. For example, if you did not use relative URLs for your links on your old server, they may not work properly on your new server.

Summary

In this chapter you learned how to set up a web server on your home or office computer and install Joomla! on that server. You also learned what to look for in a web host, and how to install Joomla! in a shared hosting environment. Installing Joomla! boils down to three basic steps:

1. Unpack and upload.
2. Set up the database.
3. Run the Joomla! installer.

Finally, you learned the six steps to moving your Joomla! installation from one server to another.

Work through the following exercises to test your understanding of the Joomla! installation process. You can find the solutions to these exercises in Appendix A.

Exercises

1. What is your favorite color?
2. List two packages you could use to install a web server on your home or office computer.
3. What four pieces of information do you need about your database before you can install Joomla!?
4. List two reasons listed in this chapter why you might want to consider moving your entire installation from one server to another rather than start with a fresh installation of Joomla!. Can you think of any other possible reasons?

Must-have Extensions

One of Joomla!'s greatest strengths is the abundance of extensions available to help your site perform almost any function you can think of. Need a social network? There's a component (or two or three) for that. Need a blog? It's covered. Need a document management system? No problem. A project management system? You've come to the right place. A photo gallery? Check.

You get the idea. The Joomla! framework is infinitely extensible to do anything you need, and many industrious individuals, groups, and companies have already taken the time to build some excellent extensions that anyone can download and use for free or a small fee. As you have already learned throughout this book, the Joomla! Extensions Directory (JED) is the best place to look when hunting for extensions. It lists thousands of extensions in more than 200 categories. You can find the JED at `http://extensions.joomla.org`.

Commercial vs. Free Extensions

There are many advantages and disadvantages to using both commercial and free extensions. In many cases, there is a commercial extension and a free extension that perform basically the same function. You should decide on a case-by-case basis which extension is right for your website.

Commercial extensions are extensions for which you must pay a small fee to use on your site. Commercial extensions might be offered under a proprietary license, or they might be offered under the same open source license under which Joomla! is released, the GNU/GPL. The main benefit of using a commercial extension is support. When you pay for an extension, you have a reasonable expectation of receiving a certain level of support. You should also expect to get a higher quality product if you are paying for it, but there is no guarantee that the quality will be any better than what you could get with a free alternative. Some commercial extensions are encrypted, meaning you cannot access or modify certain parts of the code. Encryption is one of the drawbacks of these extensions, because you are not as free to customize the extensions to suit your needs.

The JED is full of free extensions. Most of them are open source extensions released under the GNU/GPL. The main benefit of free extensions is that they are free. You get to add functionality to your site without having to pay for it. Another advantage is that

---

Continued

their code is open source, so you can modify and customize the code however you need to. The biggest disadvantages in most cases are a lack of support and documentation. Some of the free extensions available do not have the same community involvement as the entire Joomla! project, so there is not the same level of support or documentation that you might expect.

This appendix contains a list of some of the best and most popular extensions available for Joomla! and where you can find them. The extensions in this appendix are organized by their primary function, and the functions listed are:

- ❑ Social Networking
- ❑ Blogging
- ❑ Forums
- ❑ File Management
- ❑ Document Management
- ❑ Business Directory
- ❑ Photo Galleries/Slideshows
- ❑ Form Creation and Management
- ❑ WYSIWYG Editors
- ❑ E-Commerce
- ❑ Real Estate
- ❑ Events/Calendars
- ❑ SEF URLs
- ❑ User Management
- ❑ Other Utilities

Currencies

Some of the commercial extensions listed in this appendix have varying currencies. Joomla! is a global project, and as such, many companies that sell Joomla!-related products and services are in different countries. The prices listed in this appendix are in the currency listed by the vendor, because any attempt to convert the price to a common currency would most certainly be inaccurate due to the natural fluctuation in the relative values of currencies.

Social Networking

Social networking is not available in Joomla!'s core, and the core user management leaves a lot to be desired. Fortunately, you have some choices available if you want to add social networking functionality to your site.

Extension	License/Price	Description
Community Builder	GPL/Free €25.00 for a documenta-tion subscription	Community Builder is the original social networking component for Joomla!. There were components that came before Community Builder that extended the user profile to enable gathering more information about users, but Community Builder was the first to incorporate social interaction along with an extended user profile. After it was first released Community Builder quickly gained a huge following, with almost as many people registered at its website, Joomlapolis.com, as there are registered in the official Joomla! forums. Few extensions have achieved the same level of success as this component.
		Community Builder offers the ability to create custom user fields to extend your users' profiles any way you want. It enables your users to connect with other users on the site, similar to the Friends features on popular social networking sites like Facebook and MySpace. It recently joined forces with another popular component, GroupJive, to give users the ability to create and maintain custom user groups, also like other popular social networks.
		It also has its own plugin system so that developers can extend its functionality and integrate it with other components. There is an active development community that has built many plugins that provide a wide range of functionality for your site.
		You can find more information about Community Builder and download it at its website, `http://www.joomlapolis.com`.
JomSocial	Commercial/ $99 Standard or $149 Pro	JomSocial is a newcomer to social networking with Joomla!. It is developed by a company from Malaysia called Slashed & Dots, whose website is Azrul.com. This company is perhaps best known for its very popular extensions, JomComment, which you learn about later in this appendix.
		The price may seem a little steep, especially since Community Builder is available for free, but JomSocial's feature set along with Slashes & Dots' reputation for building high quality Joomla! extensions make it well worth the price.
		JomSocial offers a custom extended profile like Community Builder. It also offers a built-in private messaging system, which Community Builder does not have. It has a built-in friend system, and an activity stream like you would see on Facebook. Users can also write on each other's "walls," much like Facebook's "walls." It also has built-in groups functionality, photo and video hosting, and an API for developing applications (plugins) that work directly with it.
		This component was built specifically for Joomla! 1.5, so it has better, cleaner integration than Community Builder. It is also backed by a company with a great reputation for quality products and support.
		You can find out more about JomSocial at its website, `http://www.jomsocial.com`.

Other Social Networking Tools: Joomunity (`http://www.joomunity.com`) and JoomSuite People Touch (`http://www.joomsuite.com`)

Blogging

For as long as Joomla! has been around, blogging has been its Achilles heel. Systems like Wordpress, which was developed specifically for blogging or personal publishing, have a huge advantage over Joomla! because it does not do blogging very well out of the box.

Some of the features lacking in Joomla!'s core are the ability to comment on posts, user blogs, and track-backs, just to name a few. Other platforms have these features standard, which leaves Joomla! behind as a second-tier blogging platform at best. The following extensions have helped close the functionality gap between Joomla! and other personal publishing platforms.

Extension	License/Price	Description
MyBlog	Commercial /$45	MyBlog is a blogging component developed by the same people who develop JomSocial. It offers a major step toward providing many of the blogging features that Joomla! is missing.
		With MyBlog, you get user blogs, RSS feeds, tags, pings, and a user-friendly interface for managing personal blogs. It makes writing blogs easier with Joomla! because it brings together so many of the features that are necessary for blogging.
		You can find out more about MyBlog and purchase it at `http://www.azrul.com`.
JomComment	Commercial /$35	One thing that MyBlog does not have is a commenting function. You can't really have a blog without giving your readers the ability to comment on your posts. The team at Azrul.com know this, which is why they developed JomComment.
		JomComment is a component and a plugin that integrates seamlessly with Joomla!'s core content component for enabling users to comment on articles. It also integrates seamlessly with MyBlog, so the two products combined offer the best blogging solution available for Joomla!. Many third-party developers enable their components to integrate with JomComment, which enables commenting on things other than just articles.
		JomComment offers many features you need for comment functionality. You can enable commenting on all articles, and you can limit it to certain categories. It has RSS feeds for comments on each article, and it enables users to subscribe to an article's comments, so they will be notified when someone posts a new comment to the thread.
		It also displays an optional hit counter and social bookmarking feature along with a link to enable users to set an article as one of their favorites. It provides SPAM protection with its own built-in algorithms, IP blocking, and user blocking, and it also integrates with the popular anti-spam service, Akismet. Another great feature is the ability for users to vote a comment up or down, so unpopular comments get hidden.
		You can find out more about JomComment and purchase it at `http://www.azrul.com`.

Other Blogging Tools: I Do Blog (`http://www.idojoomla.com`), Disqus comment system (`http://www.joomlaworks.gr/`), and JXtended Comments (`http://www.jxtended.com`)

Forums

Forums are one of the oldest ways people interact online. Some would call them the "Web 1.0" predecessor to social networks. A forum is arguably a social network in and of itself because it usually offers many of the same features, such as user profiles, friends, groups, and user interaction.

Joomla! has never had anything close to a forum as part of its core, but there have always been options. The two main options for forums in Joomla! are integrated forums (forums built specifically for Joomla!) and forum bridges (extensions that bridge Joomla!'s user database with that of a third-party forum such as phpBB). Integrated forums are often easier to set up and get working on your site, but they are limited in functionality. Bridging between Joomla! and a third-party forum is more difficult to set up, but you generally get a more feature-rich forum application than what you can get with integrated forums. This list contains the forums that are currently the most popular forum options available for Joomla!.

Extension	License/Price	Description
FireBoard	GPL/Free	FireBoard comes from one of the oldest forum components available for Joomla!. When the developers of JoomlaBoard stopped developing and supporting the component, the team from BestOfJoomla.com took up the reins and continued its development under a new name, FireBoard.
		FireBoard is a feature-rich forum component that is fully integrated with Joomla!. Unlike stand-alone forum applications like Simple Machines Forum and phpBB, FireBoard is developed specifically to work with Joomla!, so it shares a user database with Joomla! without the need for any kind of bridges.
		This component offers unlimited levels of nested forums, forum moderation, user profiles, avatars, custom themes, user ranks, and many other features common to forum applications. FireBoard is the best solution for a quick and easy but feature-packed forum that is integrated with Joomla!.
		You can find out more about FireBoard at http://www.bestofjoomla.com.
RokBridge + phpBB3	GPL/Free	RokBridge is a Joomla! application combined with authentication and user plugins that synchronizes the user databases between Joomla! and a stand-alone installation of phpBB3.
		PhpBB has been around for many years, and it is one of the best open source forum applications available. The benefit of using RokBridge and phpBB3 is that you get a mature forum product backed by years of development and an active development community, and you get all of the benefits of building your site with Joomla!. It's the best of both worlds. PhpBB3 has all of the features you need to run a forum, and you know that you are using a high-quality product.

(continued)

(continued)

Extension	License/Price	Description
		The biggest drawback of this solution is that it is not a true integration with Joomla! in the same sense that a forum component like FireBoard is. The main issue is that you have to build a phpBB3 theme to match your Joomla! template in order for your site and your forum to have the same look and feel. You can find out more about RokBridge at `http://www.rocketwerx.com`, and you can find out more about phpBB3 at `http://www.phpbb.com/`.
Agora	GPL/Free	Agora is a feature-rich integrated forum built upon a stand-alone forum called punBB. Like FireBoard, it is integrated with Joomla!, so there is no need for bridges to synchronize user databases. Like RokBridge, it makes use of a pre-existing forum application, so it has many of the features common to forums. Agora is a relative newcomer to Joomla!, so it is not as widely used as FireBoard. However, it is under active development and has a lot of great features. This forum is definitely worth taking a look at when you search for a forum solution for your website. You can find out more about Agora at `http://www.joomlame.com/`.

Other Forum Extensions: JooBB (`http://www.joobb.org`), SimplestForum (`http://simplestforum.org`), Rapid Forum (`http://www.joomlasimple.com`), and Nice Talk (`http://www.azrul.com`)

File Management

Traditionally, you manage the files on your server with FTP, SSH, or some web-based control panel offered by your web host. These are still great options, but as a Joomla! administrator, it's nice to have a solution for managing your files in Joomla!'s administrator application. This list contains components that provide a web-based interface for managing files on your server.

These components are only accessible in the administrator panel to users who have Super Administrator access to your site. There is a security risk in providing direct edit capabilities to every file on your site through these types of extensions, but because they are accessible only to users with Super Administrator access, the security risk is minimized.

Extension	License/Price	Description
NinjaXplorer	GPL/Free	NinjaXplorer is the successor to a popular file management component called JoomlaXplorer. Development for JoomlaXplorer stopped, so it did not support Joomla! 1.5 natively. The team at NinjaForge decided that the component was useful enough that they continued the development of this component for the benefit of the community.
		NinjaXplorer is based on an open source application called QuiXplorer, which is a web-based multi-user file management and file sharing system. It lists files and directories starting at the root web directory of your web server. It allows you to upload, copy, move, delete, and edit files on your server through an intuitive user interface in your Joomla! administrator panel. As a security precaution, it allows only users with Super Administrator access to gain access to it, so only the highest-level users have access to manage files.
		It offers an editor screen so that you can edit text-based files such as HTML, PHP, and XML files. The editor has an option syntax highlight mode that automatically color codes syntax within the code of your files based on the type of file you are editing and the code/markup within that file.
		You can find out more about NinjaXplorer at http://www.ninjaforge.com.
eXtplorer	GPL/Free	eXtplorer is a stand-alone web-based file management system that also has a Joomla! component that integrates it into the Joomla! administrator. This component offers the same file management features as NinjaXplorer, but it has a JavaScript-powered interface that gives it the look and feel of a Windows GUI application. It also has an FTP layer, so you can access your files with an FTP account just like a regular FTP client application. See Figure C-1.
		You can find out more about eXtplorer at http://extplorer.sourceforge.net/ and http://joomlacode.org/gf/project/joomlaxplorer/frs/.

Other File Management Extensions: JoomlaXplorer (http://joomlacode.org/gf/project /joomlaxplorer/)

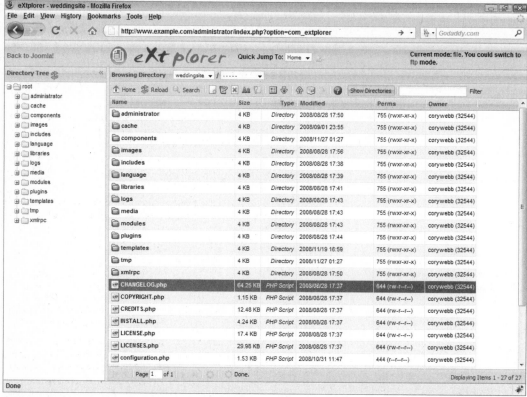

Figure C-1

Document Management

Many websites need an easy and efficient way to share downloads with their users. Software companies offer their products for download. Publishers might offer e-books for download. Designers might have graphic packs that their visitors can download. Whatever the purpose, downloads can be an important aspect of many sites. The components in this list provide solutions for managing documents and making them available for users to download.

Extension	License/Price	Description
DocMan	GPL/Free	DocMan (short for "Document Manager" or "Document Management") has been around for more than 5 years. It is an open source document management system that was originally developed for Mambo, but is now being developed for the Joomla! platform.
		DocMan has a number of features that help it to stand out as a must-have component. With DocMan, you can organize your downloads into unlimited categories and subcategories. Unlike the core content component, you can have as many levels of nested subcategories as you need, so you have greater flexibility in how you organize your documents available for download. DocMan also has its own permissions system, so you can control who is able to access, download, add, edit, and delete documents in the system.

Extension	License/Price	Description
		DocMan allows you to manage documents and files both on your server and also on remote servers, and it also keeps statistics of how many times a document has been viewed and downloaded. You can log this information by user, IP address, web browser, and by date and time. The system can be searched, so your visitors can easily find the files they are looking for.
		DocMan also has an "anti leeching" system, so that you do not have to provide direct links to your documents. This enables you to share documents with your visitors without giving them the exact location of your documents on your server. Another great feature of DocMan is that it has its own template system, so you can easily customize the look and feel of the user interface on the front end.
		DocMan is developed by a team of programmers led by Johan Janssens. Johann is one of the lead architects of the Joomla! 1.5 framework, and according to him, much of the work that went into developing the DocMan framework went into Joomla! 1.5.
		You can learn more about DocMan at `http://www.joomlatools.org/products/docman.html`.
RokDownloads	GPL/Free	RokDownloads is another component developed by the team at RocketWerx.com. It is a download/file management component that makes sharing files as easy as uploading files to your server.
		Files are organized in RokDownloads based on the directory/file structure in your designated RokDownloads directory. The system automatically detects files and directories within the root RokDownloads directory and displays them in the RokDownloads administrator interface. As the webmaster, you then have control over which files are published to the front end of the site for users to download.
		You can give each directory and file a custom name and description that will be displayed to the users on the front end of the site. You can use icons, thumbnails, and other images for each file and file type, and you can easily customize the look and feel of the user interface. You can also track the number of times a file is downloaded. Overall, RokDownloads offers an intuitive, easy-to-use interface for managing document downloads. It does not have as many features as DocMan, but it is arguably much easier to use for a beginner.
		You can find out more about RokDownloads at `http://www.rocketwerx.com/products/rokdownloads /overview`.

Other Document Management Extensions: RS Files (`http://www.rsjoomla.com`) and Remository (`http://www.remository.com`)

251

Business Directory

Business directories are a means to categorize and list businesses, almost like a phone book for the web. They can also be used to categorize, list, rate, and comment on almost anything you can think of. You could conceivably use Joomla!'s core content component and menu navigation structure (see Chapter 10) to build a business directory, but that would amount to using that component in a way that it was not meant to be used.

The business directories in this list are components that were built specifically for creating an online directory of business, products, services, and so on. They provide functionality far beyond what the core content component could manage, such as allowing users to rate and comment on items listed in the directory and allowing businesses to own and maintain their own listings.

Extension	License/Price	Description
SOBI 2	LGPL/Free	SOBI 2 (Sigsiu Online Business Index 2) is a business directory component that can be used to display a directory of businesses, products, people, and whatever else you might want to present to your visitors in a directory format. It offers many features common to online directory systems that make it an excellent choice for building an online directory with Joomla!.
		With SOBI 2, you can have unlimited nested categories, user-submitted/ user-managed listings, RSS feeds, custom data fields, search engine optimization (SEO) features, and many more features. The system also has its own plugin architecture for extending its functionality, and several add-ons are available such as a download plugin for managing documents and downloads, a listing expiration plugin, a reviews and ratings plugin, and several more. Although SOBI 2 is free, many of the add-ons for SOBI 2 are commercial add-ons that are available for a fee.
		You can find out more about SOBI 2 at http://www.sigsiu .net/sobi2.html.
Mosets Tree	Commercial /$119	Mosets Tree is a commercial directory component with many of the same features as SOBI 2, plus some features that are only available for SOBI 2 as commercial add-ons. With Mosets Tree, you can build a full-featured directory for your site. You can have unlimited nested categories, user-submitted/user-managed listings, ratings and reviews, custom layouts, cross-categorized listings, and much more.
		Unfortunately, this component does not work natively in Joomla! 1.5, and it only works with the legacy plugin enabled on Joomla! 1.5 because it was written for an older version of Joomla!. The team at Mosets is working on a version of Mosets Tree that works natively in Joomla! 1.5, and when they release it they will change the license to release it under the GNU/GPL license.
		The Joomla! Extension Directory (JED) runs on Mosets Tree, and you can view it at http://extensions.joomla.org. This is a great example of what can be done with a directory component and Joomla!.
		You can find out more about Mosets Tree at http://www.mosets .com/tree.

Other Business Directory Extensions: JXtended Catalog (http://www.jxtended.com) and JoomSuite Resources (http://www.joomsuite.com)

Photo Galleries/Slideshows

Photo gallery and slideshow extensions offer a way to manage and display photographs to your visitors in an interesting format. Several photo gallery and slideshow extensions are available for Joomla!, and this list contains some of the most useful ones.

Extension	License/Price	Description
RSGallery2	GPL/Free	RSGallery2 is a full-featured photo gallery component for Joomla!. It enables photo uploads, batch uploads (uploading more than one photo at once), automatic thumbnail creation, user albums, front-end display templates, and more.
		With the front-end display templates, you have unlimited options for how your photos are displayed. You can have a basic gallery/album layout, a MooTools-powered slideshow, a Flash slideshow, or any other display option you can come up with. You are limited only by skill and creativity. The component is actively developed and supported by a team of volunteers who are passionate about developing open source software.
		You can find out more about RSGallery2 at http://www.rsgallery2.net.
JoomlaShack Flash Rotator	Commercial /$19.95	The JoomlaShack Flash Rotator is a module that displays between 3 and 15 images in a module through a Flash-based interface that rotates through the images on a regular interval. It offers several configuration options including eight transition effects. It is based on the popular Flash image rotator from http://www.jeroenwijering.com/.
		You can find out more about the JoomlaShack Flash Rotator at http://www.joomlashack.com.
RokSlideshow	GPL/Free	RokSlideshow is a slideshow module built by the team at RocketWerx.com. Like the JoomlaShack Flash Rotator, this module displays images in a slideshow format with a number of transitions to choose from. However, RokSlideshow uses the popular MooTools JavaScript framework as its engine rather than Flash.
		The slideshow is based on the MooTools Slideshow written by Aeron Glemann (http://www.electricprism.com/aeron/slideshow). It offers six optional image transitions, and you can use a virtually unlimited number of images in the slideshow.
		You can learn more about RokSlideshow at http://www.rocketwerx.com/products/rokslideshow/overview.

Other Photo Gallery/Slideshow Extensions: Simple Image Gallery (http://www.joomlaworks.gr), YooGallery (http://www.yootools.com), and AJAX Photo Album (http://www.sakic.net)

Form Creation and Management

Creating a truly interactive website means giving your users the ability to communicate directly with you through online forms. One way to create a form is to build a custom component to handle a specific type of interaction. Another way is to use one of the following extensions for building custom, interactive forms that can send submitted data via e-mail or store it in your site's database. Besides offering the ability to build custom forms, these extensions also offer anti-spam measures to help prevent your form from becoming a tool of spambots to send you unwanted messages.

Extension	License/Price	Description
Joomla! Forms	Commercial/£29.99	Joomla! Forms is a popular form creation and management component by the team at Blue Flame IT (Jersey) Ltd. It is the successor to the popular Phil-a-Form component, which has been discontinued in favor of Joomla! Forms.
		With Joomla! Forms, you can create a custom form to suit any specific needs. You can create anything from a simple contact form to an event registration or custom user registration form.
		You can set up your forms to send data to any e-mail address and to store data in a custom database table. You can create unlimited custom fields for your forms, so the data you collect can be tailored to your specific needs. Capturing data is made easy with predefined and custom form actions, so you do not have to be a PHP or HTML expert to create your own data forms.
		You can learn more about Joomla! Forms at http://www.joomla-forms.com.
RS Form	Commercial/ €9.00–€19.00	RS Form is a form creation and management component by the team at RSJoomla!. It offers many of the same features as Joomla! Forms, but it does not have the same built-in form actions that Joomla! Forms has. It does offer the ability to write custom PHP scripts to handle form submissions, so you have a lot more flexibility in how you can customize your forms.
		You can learn more about RS Form at http://www.rsjoomla.com.
Breezing Forms	GPL/Free	Breezing Forms is the successor to the very popular Facile Forms. Breezing Forms can be used to build anything from simple forms to full-blown applications. It has PHP hooks throughout the system that enable a developer to completely customize the behavior of the forms.
		The form designer on the back end uses a GUI system to make designing forms easy for any level of user. It has several prebuilt PHP and JavaScript functions to apply to its predefined event triggers, or you can write custom code at any of the events that are triggered throughout the form display and submission process.
		You can learn more about Breezing Forms at http://www.crosstec.de/breezingforms-15-en-mainmenu-10.html.

Other Form Creation and Management Extensions: ChronoForms (http://www.chronoengine.com/) and Fabrik (http://fabrikar.com/)

WYSIWYG Editors

As you learned in Chapter 1, a WYSIWYG (What You See Is What You Get) editor makes it possible for you to add and edit content through a GUI interface similar to popular word processing software packages. They make it easy for anyone to add or edit content without the need to be an HTML wizard. Joomla! comes with a WYSIWYG editor pre-installed, but if you are not happy with the features of that editor, other editors are available. This list contains a couple of the best WYSIWYG editors available.

Extension	License/Price	Description
JCE	GPL/Free Subscription fee for $20 to gain access to JCE add-ons.	JCE (Joomla! Content Editor) is based on the popular TinyMCE WYSIWYG editor. JCE is a pretty standard WYSIWYG editor, but it comes with several built-in features to make it stand out as a must-have WYSIWYG editor for Joomla!. With JCE, you can easily upload and manage images for embedding into your content items. It also gives you a link utility to help you link to other content items within your site. It has an optional HTML mode with syntax highlighting, making it easier to read the HTML markup of your articles. It also has a built-in spell checker, so you don't have to worry about misspelling any words. Besides having a lot of built-in functionality, JCE is can be extended with its own plugin architecture. Some of the plugins that are available include a file manager, a media manager, and an extended image manager with which you can crop, rotate, and resize images before embedding them into an article. JCE often solves problems that would have taken several extensions to solve. You can learn more about JCE at `http://www.joomlacontenteditor.net`.
JXtended WYSIWYG Editor	GPL/Free	The JXtended WYSIWYG editor is a standard editor that is based on the popular FCKeditor. It offers standards-compliant XHTML output, right-click menus, as well as many other standard features common to WYSIWYG editors. You can learn more about the JXtended WYSIWYG editor at `http://www.jxtended.com`.

Other WYSIWYG Editors: JoomlaFCK Editor (`http://www.joomlafckeditor.com/`)

E-Commerce

E-commerce is just a buzzword for selling stuff through your website. A few components are available that offer full-featured catalogs and shopping carts for the purpose of selling things online. This list contains the two most popular e-commerce components.

Extension	License/Price	Description
Virtuemart	GPL/Free	Virtuemart is the most popular e-commerce solution built specifically for Joomla!. It was originally built based on phpShop, an open source stand-alone e-commerce system built with PHP. It was originally named Mambo-phpShop because it was built for Mambo before the Joomla! project was founded.
		Virtuemart is popular for several reasons, including the fact that it was one of the first e-commerce solutions that integrated into Joomla!; it is open source and free, and it has consistently been under active development for several years. This component offers many of the features you need to run a successful online shop, including a catalog, nested categories, a shopping cart, shipping modules, and integration with popular payment gateways like Authorize.net, PayPal, 2Checkout, and many more.
		Virtuemart also has a plugin system, so you can extend the core functionality of Virtuemart. With this system, you can add custom payment gateway integrations, shipping modules, and other functionality that is not already included in the Virtuemart core.
		You can learn more about Virtuemart at http://www.virtuemart.net.
DigiStore	Commercial/ $79.95	DigiStore is a commercial component from iJoomla.com. It is not as customizable as Virtuemart, but it is a stable system for selling both digital (for download) products and physical products. It comes with integration with PayPal's standard web payments system, and other payment systems are also available for an extra fee.
		DigiStore is backed by the support of iJoomla.com, which has a reputation for selling high-quality extensions with excellent support. It offers a full-featured catalog with nested categories and customizable product lists. It also enables the addition of custom fields to give products different options, so your customers can customize the products they purchase from your shop.
		Another great feature of DigiStore is integration with Google Analytics, which helps you to measure the success of your search engine marketing campaigns.
		You can learn more about DigiStore at http://www.ijoomla.com.

Other E-Commerce Extensions: Freeway (http://www.openfreeway.org/)

Content Management

As you learned in Chapter 5, Joomla!'s core content structure offers only two levels of hierarchy: sections and categories. Also, only two basic layouts are available for displaying lists of articles: blogs and tables. Fortunately, you have several options for improving the way that content is managed by giving you greater control over categorization and presentation. This list contains a few of the best options available for improving how you are able to manage content.

Extension	License/Price	Description
JXtended Catalog	GPL/$90	JXtended Catalog can be thought of as a directory component, but its architecture lends it to being much more than just a directory component. With its system of custom categories, classes, and items, JXtended Catalog gives you the ability to create unlimited types of content items. This component can be used as a directory, a product catalog, a photo gallery, a media gallery, all of the above, or something completely different. You can think of it as the ultimate content component because with it you have unlimited options for organizing, managing, and displaying catalog items. You can learn more about JXtended Catalog at `http://www.jxtended.com`.
JXtended Magazine	GPL/$70	JXtended Magazine is a component that completely changes the way you think about how content is organized in Joomla!. It has its own articles, so it does not rely on storing articles in the core content component article table. This component organizes articles into publications, issues, sections, and categories. Articles can be cross-categorized into as many categories as you feel are necessary, which in and of itself is a major improvement over the core content structure. One of Magazine's major drawbacks, however, is the inability to submit articles via the front end of the site. However, as of this writing, the JXtended team is working on a component called Magazine Manager that will make this possible. You can learn more about JXtended Magazine at `http://www.jxtended.com`.
iJoomla Magazine	Commercial/$79.95	iJoomla Magazine is similar to JXtended Magazine in that it allows you to organize your content into magazines and issues. However, one major difference is that it uses the core content articles instead of its own proprietary articles, so it is more tightly integrated with Joomla!'s core content component. For that reason, it can leverage many of the advantages of the core content component such as the ability to submit articles from the front end of the site. This component acts primarily as a tool for displaying your content in a layout that Joomla!'s core content component does not allow without major changes. It is ideal for news or magazine sites because it gives you a professional magazine-style layout. You can learn more about iJoomla Magazine at `http://www.ijoomla.com`.
Joomla! Tags	Commercial/£29.99	Joomla! Tags is another component by the team at Blue Flame IT, Ltd. This component extends your ability to categorize content items by making it possible to add custom tags to each item. These tags are similar to meta keyword tags, but they are meant to be displayed along with the article and used to organize articles.

(continued)

(continued)

Extension	License/Price	Description
		The Tags component helps you to get past the limitations of Joomla!'s core content component categorization structure. You, or optionally your users, can add unlimited tags to an article, thereby cross-categorizing articles in a way that the core content component does not allow.
		For example, you might have an article that is about both food and travel. With the core content component, you would have to categorize the article under either food or travel, but not both. With Tags, you can simply add the tags "food" and "travel" to the article, indicating that the article is about both food and travel.
		You can learn more about Joomla! Tags at `http://www.joomla-tags.com`.
JXtended Labels	GPL/$40	JXtended Labels is similar to Joomla! Tags. It gives you the ability to add tags (or "labels") to your content items. It also works with content items generated by JXtended Catalog and JXtended Magazine.
		You can find out more about JXtended Labels at `http://www.jxtended.com`.

Other Content Management Extensions: iJoomla News Portal (`http://www.ijoomla.com`)

Real Estate

Real estate is one of the vertical markets (including automobile sales, hotel reservations, and more) supported by third-party developers of Joomla! extensions. If you are a real estate company or if you run a real estate portal, you need a way to manage agents and properties and list them on your site. Two full-featured options are available for running a real estate site, and they are listed here.

Extension	License/Price	Description
Hot Property	Commercial/ $119	Hot Property is a real estate listings component developed by the team at Mosets.com, the same team that develops Mosets Tree. Hot Property enables real estate agents to list and manage properties with standard property information and unlimited custom fields for customizing the information you store for each property.
		This component can be used for property listings from a single real estate company, or as a portal for multiple companies. Agents can add and manage properties through the front end of the site, giving them control over the information that is stored and displayed about each property.

Extension	License/Price	Description
		Hot Property also comes with an advanced search engine, so your site's visitors can easily search for properties based on multiple criteria. Mosets also offers fourteen modules that work with Hot Property, so you have several tools and options available for how you set up the system.
		A version of Hot Property that runs natively in Joomla! 1.5 is under active development, and it is available as a beta for paying customers. When the stable version of this product is released, it will be released under the GNU/GPL license.
		You can find out more about Hot Property at http://www.mosets.com/hotproperty.
EZ Realty	Commercial/ $129.95–$199.95	EZ Realty is another great option for developing a website with real estate listings. It offers many of the same features as Hot Property, although it does not offer unlimited custom fields. One feature that it offers is an MLS (Multiple Listing Service — centralized database of all properties for sale in the U.S. that is managed by the National Association of Realtors) field and the ability to search by MLS field. This is important for the real estate industry in the United States because every property for sale in the U.S. has an MLS number.
		You can learn more about EZ Realty at http://www.ezrealty.info.

Other Real Estate Extensions: Hot Property and EZ Realty are the only real estate extensions worth mentioning.

Events/Calendars

If you have events or important dates that your visitors need to know about, you need a way to manage these events. You could use a third-party calendar like Google Calendar and point your users to it, or you could use one of these extensions to manage your events right in your Joomla! administrator panel.

Extension	License/Price	Description
Event List	GPL/Free	Event List is a tool for helping your manage and display a list of events to your users. Events can be categorized for better organization. Event List also offers a way to manage a list of venues where your events will take place.
		Events can be displayed in several ways. You can display one large list of events, or you can display events by category or by venue. You can also enable users to submit events, and you can restrict user groups to specific categories.
		You can learn more about Event List at http://www.schlu.net.

(continued)

(continued)

Extension	License/Price	Description
JCal Pro	GPL/Free	JCal Pro is a calendar component based on an open source calendar application called ExtCalendar. Unlike Event List, JCal Pro displays events in a calendar format. You can display your events in a month view, a week view, a day view, by category, or as a flat list of events. JCal Pro offers a very useful calendar, but it does not handle event management like some of the other event components do. If all you need is a calendar to display some upcoming events, this is a good option for you. You can find out more about JCal Pro at http://dev.anything-digital.com.

Other Events/Calendar Extensions: JEvents (http://www.jevents.net) and redEvent (http://redcomponent.com/redevent)

SEF URLs

The core SEF URL functionality in Joomla! 1.5 is a vast improvement over how it worked in previous versions of Joomla!, and it may suffice for your site. However, it still gives you very little control over how URLs are generated, so you might want to consider using one of these components for greater control and management of your SEF URLs.

Extension	License/Price	Description
sh404SEF	GPL/Free	sh404SEF lets you create and manage custom SEF URLs in Joomla!. It extends the core SEF URL functionality by creating cleaner, more human- and search engine–friendly URLs, and giving you the ability to manage and customize these URLs. This component also goes beyond custom URLs. It also acts as your first line of defense by filtering out malicious URLs and other methods of attack. It has several plugins to help it work with many of the most popular extensions, and it gives you the ability to create custom meta tags (title, description, keywords) for each page on your site. sh404SEF also gives you the ability to create a custom 404 error page within your site for those occasions when visitors enter an incorrect URL that does not actually exist on your site. It also keeps a log of all URLs that led users to these error pages. Another feature that it offers is URL aliases, which automatically redirect visitors from an alias URL to its associated SEF URL. You can learn more and download sh404SEF at http://extensions.siliana.com/.

Extension	License/Price	Description
SEF Advance	Commercial/ €40	SEF Advance is the original SEF URL component for Joomla! and Mambo. SEF Advance has several preset algorithms for creating more human- and search engine–friendly URLs. You do not have the same level of customization features that sh404SEF offers, but this lack of customization is listed as a feature on its website because it does everything for you. It does give you some options as to how the URLs are generated, but you cannot manage your URLs and manually change them.
		SEF Advance does SEF URLs and does them very well. It is supported by the team at Sakic.net, which was founded by a Joomla! core team member.
		You can learn more about SEF Advance at http://www.sakic.net.

Other SEF URL Extensions: ARTIO JoomSEF (http://www.joomsef.net/)

Project Management

Several options are available outside of Joomla! for managing projects, but none that integrate well with your Joomla!-powered site. The project management components listed here give you this functionality, and integrate it with your site so that you can manage your projects on your site, which gives your customers a unified interface for dealing with your company.

Extension	License/Price	Description
Projectfork	GPL/Free	Projectfork is a project management component for Joomla! that makes it possible to manage your company's projects easily and effectively within your Joomla!-powered website. It offers a number of features common to project management applications such as custom projects, tasks, file sharing, calendar, forum discussions, and user access controls.
		Another feature of Projectfork that helps it to stand out is the ability for developers to completely customize the system. It comes with its own framework for building extensions specifically for Projectfork, so you can extend its functionality to do just about anything you can think of. You can also develop Projectfork themes, so you can customize the look and feel of Projectfork to suit the needs of your site.
		You can learn more about Projectfork at http://www.projectfork.net.
TeamLog	GPL/Free	TeamLog is not as full-featured as other project management systems. It is billed as a time-tracking component for Joomla!, but it also offers the ability to manage projects and to-dos. If you just need a simple solution for managing projects, to-dos, and time tracking, TeamLog is a great option.
		You can find out more about TeamLog at http://teamlog.yootheme.com.

Other Project Management Extensions: JForce Suite (http://www.extremejoomla.com)

User Management

Joomla!'s user access management is pretty basic. It offers three permission levels and seven user groups, and it does not give you the kind of granular user access control that you may need. The extensions listed here give you greater control over user access levels and offer a means to sell subscriptions for users to be able to access your site.

Extension	License/Price	Description
JUGA	Commercial/$49.99	JUGA is a component that extends Joomla!'s user access control system by making it possible to limit access to particular items to specific users or groups of users. With JUGA, you can create an unlimited number of user groups. You can learn more about JUGA at http://www.dioscouri.com/juga.
JACL Plus	Commercial/$38–$108	JACL Plus works like JUGA. It extends Joomla!'s user access control system by giving you the ability to create unlimited user groups, assign each user to multiple groups, and limit access to specific groups and users. You can learn more about JACL Plus at http://www.byostech.com.
JoomSuite Member	Commercial/€59	JoomSuite Member is also a user access management system, but it has the added feature of giving you the ability to sell subscriptions to your site. With JoomSuite Member, your users sign up for an account and purchase subscriptions to be able to access certain portions of your site. This is a good solution for building a membership and subscription-based site. You can learn more about JoomSuite Member at http://www.joomsuite.com.

Other User Management Extensions: JoomSuite User (http://www.joomsuite.com), Community Builder (http://www.joomlapolis.com)

Other Utilities

With Joomla!, you can do anything you have the time, talent, or resources to accomplish with your website. At the time of this writing, more than 4,000 extensions are currently available in dozens of categories at the Joomla! Extension Directory. Here are just a few very useful components from a variety of categories.

Extension	License/Price	Description
JoomFish	GPL/Free	JoomFish is the internationalization component for Joomla!. It enables you to manage multiple language translations for everything on your site, so you can maintain multiple versions of your site in various languages. If you have visitors from different parts of the world and you require that your content be available in more than one language, JoomFish is the component you need. You can learn more about JoomFish at `http://www.joomfish.net`. (Note: Another language translation management component called Nooku is currently under development, but will not be released to the general public until the second quarter of 2009. You can learn more about Nooku at `http://www.nooku.org`.)
JoomlaPack	GPL/Free	JoomlaPack is a backup component for Joomla!. You can use it to make a complete backup of your Joomla!-powered site and restore it on any server that supports Joomla!. Backing up your site is very important, and this is a great solution for creating backups. You can learn more about JoomlaPack at `http://www.joomlapack.net`.
AllVideos	GPL/Free	AllVideos is a content plugin that makes it easy to embed several types of media files into your articles. You can embed videos uploaded to your site in several formats including .flv, .mov, .swf, .wmv, .mp4, and more. You can also embed music files in .mp3 format. It also makes it easy to embed videos from popular video sites like YouTube, Google Video, and many more. You can learn more about AllVideos at `http://www.joomlaworks.gr`.
Jumi	GPL/Free	Jumi is a very handy utility for PHP programmers. It comes as a component, a plugin, and a module that enables you to include a custom PHP file into articles, module positions, or as a custom component. With Jumi, you can build custom PHP applications and embed them into any article or module position on your site. You can learn more about Jumi at `http://jumi.vedeme.cz`.
RokBox	GPL/Free	RokBox makes it easy to embed media into articles on your site within a JavaScript popup using the Lightbox technique. It supports several media types such as images, audio, and video. You can learn more about RokBox at `http://www.rocketwerx.com`.
SYNK	Commercial /$49.99	SYNK is a database synchronization component for Joomla! that enables you to synchronize your database across multiple Joomla!-powered sites. With SYNK, you can synchronize your user database, so users can have a single login for your multiple sites. You can synchronize any tables across your sites, so the possibilities are virtually limitless for what you can do with this component. You can learn more about SYNK at `http://www.dioscouri.com/synk`.

Other Utilities: Xmap (`http://joomla.vargas.co.cr/`), JFusion (`http://www.jfusion.org`), AcaJoom (`http://www.acajoom.com/`), **Content Item Module** (`http://diebesteallerzeiten.de/blog/`), Lazy-backup (`http://www.granholmcms.com/`)

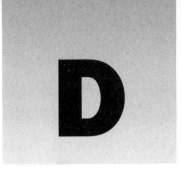

Useful Resources

This book is not a comprehensive resource for all things Joomla!. Nothing could ever be that, because the amount of information that you could possibly learn about Joomla! is so vast that no one could possibly fit it all into a single book. With that in mind, it is important that you learn some of the most valuable resources in the Joomla! community for finding information such as tips, tricks, tutorials, and help from other users, and for finding useful extensions. This appendix contains a list of useful resources, so you know where to go for help and information when you are building your Joomla!-powered site.

Help Sites

You have several places to go to find tips, tricks, tutorials, and help when you are building your website. This section contains a list of some of the most popular help sites in the community.

The Joomla! Discussion Forums

If you ever have a question about Joomla!, or if you are just looking for the solution to a problem you are having with your site, the first place you should go is the official Joomla! Discussion Forums, shown in Figure D-1. The forums are huge, with approximately 240,000 users, 320,000 topics, and 1.5 million posts. Chances are, with the Joomla! Discussion Forums, you will find that your question has already been answered, or you will find a helpful volunteer who is willing to help you find the answer to your question.

Address: http://forum.joomla.org

Joomla! Official Documentation

The Joomla! Official Documentation, shown in Figure D-2, is the central repository for information about Joomla! It contains user guides, tutorials, and general information about the Joomla! system and using Joomla!. Some sections of the documentation are incomplete and still being developed, but overall this is a great resource for finding information about Joomla!.

Address: http://docs.joomla.org/

Appendix D: Useful Resources

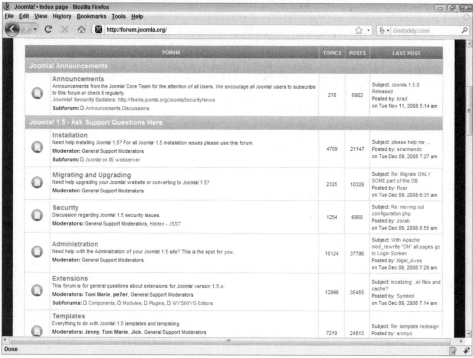

Figure D-1

Figure D-2

Joomla! Developer Site

The Joomla! Developer Site, shown in Figure D-3, is a great resource for developers working with Joomla!. It contains the latest nightly build of Joomla!, developer documentation, links to the Joomla! API (Application Programming Interface), security news, and links to developer blogs. This site is useful for experienced developers, but for novice users it might not be as useful as the forums or the documentation.

Address: http://developer.joomla.org/

Joomla! Community Portal

The Joomla! Community Portal, shown in Figure D-4, began in 2008 as an effort to centralize all community activity and information and to connect members of the community. This site contains community news, information about community events, user groups, and more. In the user groups section, you can find a local Joomla! user group near you. These groups often hold regular events where Joomla! users can share tips and tricks and get valuable help from experienced professionals.

Address: http://community.joomla.org

JoomlaTutorials.com

JoomlaTutorials.com, shown in Figure D-5, is a great resource for tutorials about Joomla!. It offers both written tutorials and video tutorials that are easy to follow and easy to understand.

Address: http://www.joomlatutorials.com

Compass Designs

Compass Designs, shown in Figure D-6, is a popular blog and source for Joomla! Tutorials. It is a great place to keep your finger on the pulse of the Joomla! community and to learn some valuable tips and tricks.

Address: http://www.compassdesigns.net

Alledia.com

Alledia.com, depicted in Figure D-7, is a great resource for search engine optimization (SEO) information about Joomla!. The Alledia blog is regularly updated with SEO information, tips, and tutorials as it relates to Joomla!. It also offers a Joomla! SEO club to help its members optimize their sites for search engine placement.

Address: http://www.alledia.com

HowToJoomla.net

HowToJoomla.net is a website that contains dozens of useful tips, tricks, and tutorials for accomplishing common tasks in Joomla!. (See Figure D-8.)

Address: http://www.howtojoomla.net

Figure D-3

Figure D-4

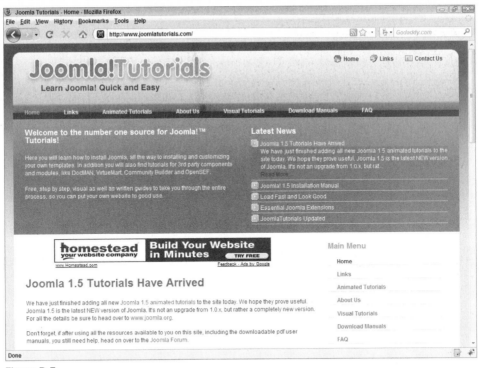

Figure D-5

Figure D-6

Figure D-7

Figure D-8

Active Third-Party Developers

The community has many active third-party developers, and their websites are usually great resources for information and useful extensions. This section lists just a few of those developers.

JoomlaTools

The JoomlaTools team consists of one of the lead developers of Joomla! and several other very talented and high-profile developers. The team is developing several useful tools and extensions including Doc-Man, LetterMan, SiteMan, and Nooku. The JoomlaTools blog is also a must read for anyone interested in learning more about Joomla!. (See Figure D-9.)

Address: `http://www.joomlatools.eu`

Figure D-9

RocketWerx

RocketWerx, shown in Figure D-10, is affiliated with the popular RocketTheme template club and is a team of developers that build several very useful components for the Joomla! community.

Address: `http://www.rocketwerx.com`

Figure D-10

JXtended

The JXtended team is made up of core team developers, and they produce some high-end extensions for Joomla! including JXtended Catalog and JXtended Magazine. (See Figure D-11.)

Address: http://www.jxtended.com

Popular Commercial Template Developers

Some of the most active sub-communities within the Joomla! community are in the forums of commercial template developers. This section lists some of these developers.

JoomlaShack

JoomlaShack, shown in Figure D-12, is one of the oldest commercial template developers in the community, and has been around since Joomla!'s inception in 2005. They offer dozens of high-quality free and commercial templates, and they have one of the most active forums in the Joomla! community with more than 120,000 members.

Address: http://www.joomlashack.com

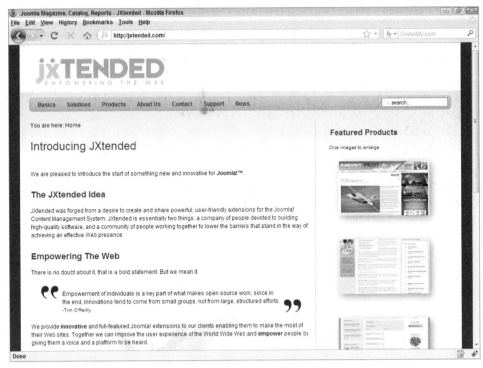

Figure D-11

Figure D-12

RocketTheme

RocketTheme, pictured in Figure D-13, is one of the oldest template clubs in the community, and has been around since before Joomla!s inception in 2005. You can purchase a subscription to the club and gain access to the dozens of high-quality templates that they offer plus a new template each month of your membership. The RocketTheme forum is another very active forum with more than 250,000 posts.

Address: http://www.rockettheme.com

Figure D-13

JoomlaPraise

JoomlaPraise, shown in Figure D-14, is relatively new to the commercial template industry. It is a template club that was started at the beginning of 2008, and has grown to become one of the more popular commercial template clubs. They also offer a number of useful extensions, such as the project management component Projectfork.

Address: http://www.joomlapraise.com

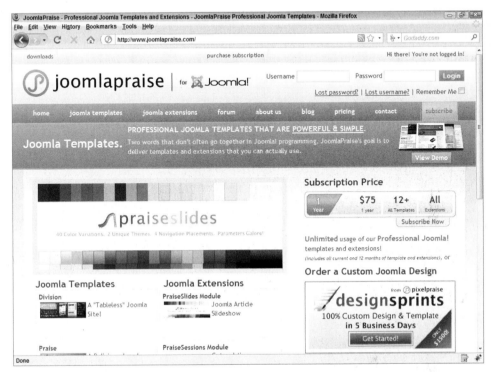

Figure D-14

Index

X

Y

Z